THE
SAN FRANCISCO
SYMPHONY

THE
SAN FRANCISCO
SYMPHONY

Music, Maestros, and Musicians

DAVID SCHNEIDER

Foreword by Edo de Waart

To Brother Mel
With best wishes for
continuing love of music

PRESIDIO PRESS

David Schneider

This book is dedicated
to all my colleagues
past and present.

Copyright © 1983 by David Schneider
All rights reserved
Published by Presidio Press, 31 Pamaron Way, Novato, CA 94947

Library of Congress Cataloging in Publication Data

Schneider, David.
    The San Francisco Symphony.

    Includes appendices and index.
    Discography: p.
    1. San Francisco Symphony Orchestra.   I. Title.
ML1211.8.S3S3   1983   785'.06'279461   83-11183
ISBN 0-89141-181-X

Jacket design by Kathleen A. Jaeger
Book design by Lyn Cordell
Composition by Helen Epperson
Production by Lynn Dwyer
Printed in the United States of America

All illustrations courtesy of the San Francisco Archives of the Performing Arts, except
as follows: 30–31, 81, 105 top, 143, private collection of Mafalda Guaraldi; 105 bottom,
private collection of Frances Houser; 8 bottom, private collection of Roy Malan; 240–41,
Gerald Ratto, courtesy of Bolt Beranek and Newman Inc.; 170, 190, 234, 237, 246, 260,
San Francisco Symphony Archives; 28, 58, 62, 69, 229, private collection of David
Schneider; 55, 64, 107, courtesy of Antonio Sotomayor.

Excerpt on page 44 from *Great Symphonies* by Sigmund Spaeth. Copyright 1936 by
Sigmund Spaeth. Reprinted by permission of Doubleday & Company, Inc.

WE ARE THE MUSIC-MAKERS
AND WE ARE THE DREAMERS OF DREAMS

—Arthur William O'Shaugnessy
1844–81

CONTENTS

	Foreword by Edo de Waart	ix
	Acknowledgments	xi
	Prologue	xii
Chapter 1	The Beginning	1
Chapter 2	Musical Chairs	21
Chapter 3	Monteux, the Musicians' Maestro	29
Chapter 4	The Facts of Life	39
Chapter 5	The Opera World	46
Chapter 6	The Turbulent Years	53
Chapter 7	Postwar Excitement	61
Chapter 8	Adieu, Monteux	71
Chapter 9	Seasons of Discovery and Decision	83
Chapter 10	Olé! Jordá	95
Chapter 11	Divisi Discordante	104
Chapter 12	Diminuendo Al-Niente	119
Chapter 13	Extracurricular Activities	130
Chapter 14	Krips, the Benevolent Despot	137
Chapter 15	The J. K. Boys	145
Chapter 16	The Eventful Years	155
Chapter 17	Auf Wiedersehen, Josef Krips	166
Chapter 18	Swinging with Seiji	175
Chapter 19	Europe in '73	192
Chapter 20	Toil and Trouble	202
Chapter 21	Ozawa and a Parade of Conductors	211
Chapter 22	Sayonara, Seiji	220
Chapter 23	Welkom, de Waart	230

Contents

Chapter 24	Our New Home	242
Chapter 25	From Carnegie to Goldmark	248
Chapter 26	The Unfinished Symphony	255
Appendix A	The First Season	262
Appendix B	Principal Conductors	264
Appendix C	Concertmasters	264
Appendix D	Members of the San Francisco Symphony Who Performed as Youth Soloists with the Orchestra	265
Appendix E	Seating Arrangements: Monteux and de Waart	265
Appendix F	Halls	267
Appendix G	Presidents of the San Francisco Symphony Association	267
Appendix H	Guest Conductors	268
Appendix I	Soloists and Chamber Music Artists Who Debuted with the San Francisco Symphony	271
Appendix J	Programs conducted by Composers	272
Appendix K	Unusual Programs	274
Appendix L	Tours	276
Appendix M	San Francisco Symphony Discography	282
Appendix N	Acoustics of Louise M. Davies Symphony Hall	311
	Index	315

FOREWORD
by Edo de Waart

My first appearance with the San Francisco Symphony was in 1974 at the age of thirty-three, when I had the opportunity to guest-conduct the orchestra. I followed closely another Dutch guest conductor, Hans Vonk, and felt a bit of competition with him. In spite of my nervousness, my first impression of the orchestra was positive: here were good musicians capable of picking up quickly whatever I wanted to convey. Apparently I made a good impression, because I was immediately offered the position of principal guest conductor. I accepted this gladly since it gave me four to six weeks each year in San Francisco, a city I love, and a chance to work with those fine musicians

Soon thereafter I was asked to succeed Seiji Ozawa as permanent conductor and music director. This was a challenge to me professionally since I could see great potential for growth in the orchestra's music-making abilities. There was also talk of a new symphony hall in the offing.

At my first meeting with the orchestra committee, however, I sensed a hostile attitude. This condition had already existed, but was further provoked by an offhand remark I made about "building the orchestra"; this was quoted in the press and started speculation that there would be numerous firings, really far from my intention. I wanted to make certain changes, of course, but only slowly and selectively. Gradually, the barrier between the orchestra and me was torn down. The musicians came to realize that I would be honest with them, and they grew to trust me. An orchestra is, after all, not merely an instrument, but a group of people making music together. So, to me, the morale of a musician is as important as his playing.

As a new conductor I came to value the opinions and advice of certain musicians who gave me the benefit of the doubt from the beginning and came to me to discuss mutual problems. Among these was David Schneider. His maturity and good judgment have been highly beneficial to the orchestra and to its conductor.

David has now written a fine book about his long tenure with the San Francisco Symphony. He handles the pen as well as the bow, writing skillfully and with great feeling about the many wonderful and peculiar things that have happened in the orchestra through the years. I learned more about the symphony by reading this book than I had previously in my six-year tenure as music director. David gives enough detail to enable the reader to trace the orchestra's development from shaky beginnings to the healthy organization it is today. While describing this road for us, he has all priorities in the proper places and shows accurately and humorously the orchestra's successes and failures.

Anyone who loves music and is interested in how an orchestra works (or sometimes doesn't) should not miss this wonderfully entertaining and enlightening book.

ACKNOWLEDGMENTS

This book has come to fruition only because of the help and encouragement of a number of individuals and institutions. The initial stimulus came from my son Bart. An author himself, he felt I had a story to tell. "You have a deep pool of memories—cast your line into it. . . ." he wrote me on my sixtieth birthday. Soon after I began, Harold Silverman, editor of the *California Living* magazine, published an embryonic chapter of the book, which gave me a strong incentive to continue.

I've had the use of the San Francisco Archives of the Performing Arts and the San Francisco Symphony Archives to aid me in my research. I am most grateful to my friend Harry Strauss for allowing me to refer to his own extensive personal program library.

As the book was nearing completion, I was fortunate to obtain the services of the fine editor Susan Weisberg. For all the work she did in bringing the book to its present state of readability, I am most appreciative. The final editing was done by Joan Griffin, who was an invaluable help.

But the one who was most instrumental in getting this book down on paper was Geri, my wife. While typing the manuscript (again and again), she pointed out discrepancies and suggested clarifications of some obscure passages. Throughout the almost three years of preparing and writing this book, she was always at my side with a kind word and a pleasant smile. This work is the result of our collaboration.

PROLOGUE

The hall was dark and silent. The contours of the magnificent
Opera House could barely be discerned. I looked around at the
empty seats in the hall and the empty chairs on stage. As the
lights came on, I began to hear the tones of the oboe filtering
through from backstage. This was soon joined by the sounds of
the other instruments of the orchestra, until there was a kalei-
doscopic montage of music emerging. We ushers had taken our
respective posts and were escorting the patrons to their seats. As
the musicians began to come on stage, I caught the eye of one of
my favorite violinists, and he answered my greeting with a wave
of his bow. A thought fleetingly crossed my mind as if in a
dream. Would I someday sit on that stage and play with all these
eminent musicians? At seventeen that possibility seemed a long
way off. The orchestra members had taken their places and the
audience was gossiping to the accompaniment of the musicians'
noodling. There was a sudden lull in the cacophony as the concertmaster walked on stage. He asked the oboe player for his A,
and the orchestra tuned. Again there was a silence. Dramati-
cally, the lights were brought up and the conductor entered. He
walked to center stage, acknowledged the applause of the audience, and ascended the podium. He turned to the orchestra,
looked around slowly and seriously to be sure he had everyone's
attention, and raised his baton for the music to begin.

Chapter 1

THE BEGINNING

"This is David Schneider. I never saw him before and I don't know anything about him." These were the words used to introduce me to Pierre Monteux, conductor of the San Francisco Symphony Orchestra. Only a few minutes before, I had met Walter Oesterreicher, personnel manager of the orchestra, and it was he who had presented me so auspiciously. I was standing in the conductor's room at the Opera House, in the presence of the musician whom I admired more than anyone else.

Monteux had come a year before to bring the orchestra back to life. The symphony had gradually deteriorated during the early 1930s to the point that in 1934–35 there was no season, and Monteux's task was to rebuild it. Monteux had already obtained fame; in forty years of conducting he had directed orchestras all over the world, premiering many modern works that have since become part of the standard symphonic literature, and had taken over the podium of the Boston Symphony in 1920. He then spent ten years as conductor for the Concertgebouw Orchestra in Amsterdam. He was ready to settle down to an easy life of guest-conducting and teaching, when he received the call to come to San Francisco.

I had seen him conduct many times in his first season in San Francisco, but this was my first personal view of him at work. He appeared shorter and stouter than he looked on stage. He seemed very tired, and no wonder; he had already auditioned forty violinists that day. No conductor would tolerate such a chore today. Now candidates are prescreened by a committee of orchestra musicians, and the conductor hears only the finalists.

1

It was past four in the afternoon and Monteux had been listening since early morning. I was to be the last. That I was there at all was a surprise to me and everyone else. I'd been practicing lackadaisically at home when Manfred Karasik, a violist in the symphony and a personal friend, came by to tell me that they were adding a few violinists and he'd heard that not all the chairs had been filled. He suggested that I audition. I wasn't keen about auditioning at such short notice, as I didn't feel sufficiently prepared. I had been a member of a professional orchestra for five months and spent nearly forty hours a week there. Chamber music took up my free nights, and, although this was good for me musically, the lack of serious practicing during this period had caused my solo playing to deteriorate. Scales and études were the only work I had been doing in that direction, in preparation for continuing my studies in New York with Mishel Piastro. But Manfred, "Monia" to his friends, would not take no for an answer. He told me to pack my violin and said he would drive me to the Opera House for the audition. "There's no time to lose!"

So there I was standing in front of Monteux, nervously awaiting what was to come. He started the proceedings by asking me a few questions.

" 'Ow old are you?" Never having heard him speak, I had no idea that his French accent was so strong.

"I'm eighteen."

"Eighteen? Well, 'av you 'ad any experience?"

"Yes. I went to the University of California in Berkeley for a couple of years, and while there I played in the U.C. Symphony under the direction of Dr. Albert Elkus. Since the beginning of July, I've been with the WPA Symphony. Ernst Bacon conducts that orchestra."

"Fine! What would you like to play for me?"

That question was a real poser. The kind of music I had been practicing lately was not suitable for an audition, but I was in a spot and had to play something. In a recital at Mills College the previous spring, I had performed the Symphonie *Espagnole*

of Lalo with some success. Perhaps I could bluff my way through
a movement of that concerto.

"Symphonie *Espagnole* of Lalo," I courageously offered. I
was suddenly taken aback by his response.

"What? Symphonie *Espagnole?* I've been listening to zat
piece all day. People (pronounced peep') think that because I'm
French I will love it. It's a bore!"

It's certainly not among the greatest pieces of violin literature, as are the Beethoven or Brahms concertos, and constant
repetition causes its triteness to become apparent. But I was
stuck. I had nothing else even remotely prepared for an audition. So I sailed right ahead, trying to ignore Monteux's antipa-
thy to the piece.

As I was playing, thoughts kept whirling around in my
head. The first thing I realized was that in the excitement of the
moment I had forgotten to tune my violin. I'd have to avoid
open strings. But how about those shifts in the beginning?
Would I hit them right? Not bad. Now let's show him I know
how to play those Spanish rhythms. Here's a nice lyrical passage. Let me give him my special Mediterranean tone. I wonder
what he's thinking now? Oh, oh! Here comes that difficult
passage and I haven't practiced it in months. Oops! I missed it.

Before my violin came off my shoulder I began apologizing.
"I'm sorry. I didn't know I was going to play an audition. I
wasn't prepared."

"Ah, but you must be prepared at all times."

That was one of my problems. A few months before I left
college, I'd auditioned to enter the Curtis Institute of Music, a
prestigious school whose top graduates almost automatically
became members of the Philadelphia Symphony. I had failed in
that audition. Now again I seemed to be doing badly. Was that
going to be my pattern of life?

After asking me to tell him again about my age and experience, Monteux suggested I read from the orchestral literature.

This phase of the audition bothered me less than playing a
solo composition. The solo I was expected to play perfectly,

while some tolerance could be allowed for mistakes of reading. Besides, I was a fairly good reader. Although I made a couple of stupid mistakes, I played the von Weber *Euryanthe* Overture competently, and I was not too displeased with how it sounded. But I was certainly not an unbiased listener.

Monteux resumed the inquisition.

"Please tell me again your age and experience." Despite the fact that the last fifteen minutes had aged me considerably, I didn't think it added much to my chronological age. I told him that I had played in both the first and second violin sections of the WPA Orchestra, a temporary organization put together during the depression as a federal project to support musicians who were too old to play in a major orchestra or too young to qualify. I elaborated a little on my advancement to principal second violin. Perhaps it would impress Monteux that another conductor considered me mature enough to assume a position of responsibility. He showed that he heard me this time by making one of his famous cutting remarks.

"Oh, zen you must show all ze uzzers 'ow to play."

With everyone laughing except me, I was dismissed summarily by the personnel manager with a "We'll call you—don't call us" remark.

I departed, saying to myself, "Well, that's that!"

Monia was waiting outside for me, eager to hear the details of the audition. When I told him all that had happened, including my mistakes, he was more upset about them than I.

"Why did you do that?" he asked.

I wished I had an answer.

My mother and father greeted my announcement about the audition with mild interest but very little hope. It was impossible for them to realize how much this meant to me. They knew I was to go to New York in a couple of weeks to continue my violin studies. I think they secretly hoped that I would not become just an orchestra musician. At any rate, they didn't see much chance that I would get this job at the present time.

I myself never seemed to have a strong desire to become a

soloist exclusively, for reasons I had never really determined. One thing I had learned in college, though, was that my work was going to be music in one form or another. Playing in an orchestra was easy and natural for me. If I became a member of a good symphony, there would be enough time to satisfy my ego with the addition of some solo playing in the area. While getting in the San Francisco Symphony at this time was not crucial for my future, it surely would resolve a lot of problems forthwith.

After hours of nail biting, when I had begun to doze off from nervous fatigue and anxiety, the shrill sound of the telephone startled me to attention. I heard the voice of Oesterreicher.

"Mr. Monteux liked your playing very much."

"Oh, boy!" My heart was pounding too hard for me to say anything else. Pictures of playing in the San Francisco Symphony flashed across my eyes as if I were already there.

"But . . ." (why must there always be a 'but"?) "he's a little worried about your youth and lack of experience." I could never have guessed. "He was wondering if you would join the orchestra on a two-week probation period, and if things work out well, as he hopes they will, you will then become a regular member of the symphony." I was delirious with joy. I had enough self-confidence to be sure that once I sat in the orchestra I could prove I deserved to be there permanently. Oesterreicher went on, "Rehearsals start tomorrow morning at ten o'clock at the Opera House. Be there a little early."

I hung up the phone and for the rest of the evening sat in a state of bliss in anticipation of the morrow. What a miracle! Just yesterday morning I was rehearsing with the WPA Symphony Orchestra. Now I was part of the San Francisco Symphony, a famous orchestra with a long history. This season, 1936–37 would mark the twenty-fifth anniversary of its founding.

The earliest record of any orchestral events in San Francisco was in 1881, when the San Francisco Philharmonic Society presented a series of concerts under the direction of Gustav Henrich. The programs were old-fashioned by modern standards. A typical concert was presented on March 3, 1882—a Cherubini overture, a Mozart symphony, an aria from Oberon, "Thou Mighty Monster" by von Weber, and a series of short concert pieces by Bruch, Berlioz, Schubert, and Meyerbeer. Except for the Mozart symphony there was nothing of substance on the entire program, and the one aria seems incongruously conspicuous between all the orchestral pieces. The year 1894 saw the beginning of a new series of several sacred concerts by the Imperial Vienna Prater Orchestra, given at the Metropolitan Temple. It is hard to determine whether the orchestra members were local or imported from Austria, since the printed programs identified the soloists and concertmaster as Herr or Fraulein. The repertoire was almost entirely of Germanic origin. The program was adorned with a picture of conductor Fritz Schell in full military uniform, complete with medals across his chest. The strong gaze from those steely eyes and the six-inch waxed mustache give the impression that his directorship was one of immense authority.

In 1896, Mr. Henrich resumed his concert series, this time adding the name of Sigmund Beel—it was now the Henrich-Beel Symphony Orchestra. (At this point I find a connection in my own life to the history of the orchestra. When I was about eight years old, my mother took me to Mr. Beel to have him teach me violin. By this time he was getting on in years and living alone, and did not relish the idea of having a young child as a student. But, at my mother's request, he listened to me play, saw some talent, and said he would try to give me lessons and see how it would work out. I had been going through a period of ill health because of a delicate stomach, and when I went to my first lesson with him, I was extremely nervous. As soon as I walked into his lovely studio with its plush Oriental rugs, I threw up. Mr. Beel kindly suggested that I seek instruction elsewhere.)

The Henrich-Beel orchestra died a natural death, but another one sprang up and played concerts in San Francisco between 1904 and 1906 under the direction of Paul Steindorf and Henry Holmes. Then came the earthquake and fire of 1906,

Henry K. Hadley, the San Francisco Symphony's first conductor and the only American to have held the position.

and not only half the city but most of its cultural life was destroyed. Not until 1911 had San Francisco sufficiently recovered from this disaster that social leaders could begin to think about starting another symphony orchestra.

This was the formal beginning of the organization known as the San Francisco Symphony Orchestra. Its first conductor was Henry Hadley, who had come to San Francisco with an excellent reputation as a conductor and composer. He also had the distinction of being the only director in its history who was an American.

On the roster of the first concert of the first season were the names of five musicians who were still in the symphony when I entered in 1936: John Patterson, violinist; Emilio Meriz first violinist; Nathan Firestone, first violinist, who later would become principal violist; Rudolf Kirs, cellist; and Walter Oester-

The San Francisco Symphony, with conductor Henry Hadley and soloist Fritz Kreisler, in its first home, the Cort Theater, February 20, 1914.

Efrem Zimbalist, soloist during the symphony's first season. In 1983, Zimbalist, age ninety-four, lived in Las Vegas.

8

reicher, flutist, who was the personnel manager of the symphony when I became a member. There were many other musicians on the 1911 roster with whom I played in the WPA Symphony or on other engagements. The soloists of the first season included the legendary pianist Vladimir De Pachman and a young Russian violinist Efrem Zimbalist. (In 1981 Zimbalist, age 94, lived in Las Vegas.)

In 1911, the orchestra consisted of sixty musicians, sixty-two by the end of the season (compared to eighty-five when Monteux took over and one hundred five at present). Sixty-one of the sixty-two were men, the one exception being a Mrs. Von Gzycki on the harp. The first violinists and the flutists, obviously the elite of the orchestra, had their full names listed on the roster; the rest were represented by their initials and last names.

Henry Hadley opened the inaugural season at the Cort Theater with a program consisting of the Prelude to *The Mastersingers of Nuremberg* by Wagner, Symphony no. 6 (*Pathetique*) of Tchaikovsky, the Theme and Variations from the *Emperor* Quartet of Haydn, and *Les Preludes* of Liszt.

That first concert was glowingly reviewed. The author, a Mr. Harvey Wickham, wrote of the difficulty—the near impossibility—of assembling on the stage of a San Francisco concert hall a group of musicians worthy enough to play a program of this kind. Yet, it was accomplished and, as he wrote, "It isn't fair to middling, or even just good—it's gilt-edged." A companion article to the review was headlined "Society Appears in Its Richest Apparel" and, underneath that, "Crowds of Limousines Bring Smart Set to the Social Event—Pleasing Spectacle."

Hadley directed and developed the orchestra from 1911 until the 1914–15 season. Then Alfred Hertz a German conductor, took over and was the symphony director until the season of 1929–30.

I had played a couple of concerts with Hertz while I was in college, but my first personal contact with him was when I was fourteen years old. My special pal, Henry Shweid, another

Alfred Hertz, conductor of the symphony from 1915 to 1930.

Basil Cameron (left) and Issay Dobrowen (right) shared conducting duties from 1931 through 1934, trying to keep the orchestra going during the difficult Depression years.

10

violinist, had the chutzpah to write Hertz on a penny post card, requesting that he and I might have the privilege of attending the Standard Oil broadcast rehearsals as music students. (These were regular one-hour concerts held at the Western Women's Club and broadcast as a public service by the Standard Oil Company. The performances were open to the public, but the rehearsals were held in private, as all symphony rehearsals were at that time.) To our surprise, Hertz answered by suggesting we make an appointment to see him to determine the seriousness of our request. Meeting him at his house, we explained that we wanted to attend these rehearsals to learn more about the profession to which we aspired. Hertz was gracious enough to let us attend.

From 1931 through 1934, the directorship was divided between Basil Cameron and Issay Dobrowen, who valiantly attempted to keep the orchestra together under the worst possible conditions of the Depression years. Despite desperate appeals to the public for financial help, the Musical Association of San Francisco could not put on a 1934–35 season. There were three people under contract for that year—Issay Dobrowen, who played the piano in addition to conducting; Naoum Blinder, concertmaster; and Horace Britt, cellist—and the symphony season consisted of three concerts performed by this trio.

At this critical time in the orchestra's history, Lenore Wood Armsby, a Bay Area social leader with a great interest in the San Francisco Symphony, persuaded Pierre Monteux to attempt to reassemble the orchestra and get a season started. Monteux had a formidable task ahead of him. There was a limited amount of money available for his salary—$10,000 was the figure mentioned by Mrs. Armsby. Not only did he, along with the association, have to bring the orchestra back to what it once was and beyond, he had to convince the people of San Francisco of the necessity of having such a cultural organization. This was not an easy undertaking, but Monteux, at the age of sixty, welcomed the challenge.

11

The first season, 1935–36, was indeed a difficult one, because he had to mold from the few remaining musicians an
orchestra that could make music inspiring both to the musicians
and to skeptical Bay Area audiences. That this was accomplished in such a short time was an augury of great things to
come.

In his second year, Monteux realized that, if his initial
success were to continue, it would be necessary to start the
rebuilding process in earnest. His first priority was to enlarge
and strengthen the string sections, which was where I fit in. But
it was difficult for me to envision myself a part of an enlarging
and strengthening group.

When I left high school, though I'd already studied violin
for eleven years with such teachers as Sigmund Anker, Camille
De Alessio, Otto Rauhut, and Jascha Veissi, I had decided I was
not good enough to make violin playing my career. I entered the
University of California in 1934 as a general music major. The
experience in Berkeley was an awakener, both musically and
socially. The head of the department, the conductor of the
orchestra, and an inspiration to me was Dr. Albert Elkus.

For the first time my mind joined my emotions in the enjoyment of music. Dr. Elkus explained the various musical forms in
all their architectural splendor. The great composers became
more than names to me as he made me aware of their styles and
the historical and social influences on their music. He and I
debated about compositions that I liked or disliked for purely
prejudicial reasons. Elkus widened my horizons so that I listened
to many works I had been previously set against. Through all
this he labored with a handicap that is the scourge of lecturers
—he stuttered! At first it seemed impossible to listen to him
when he spoke, for example, of the ba-ba-ba-bassoon. But after
a while I became oblivious to his stutter, and when someone else
remarked about it I was surprised. The lecture material was so
interesting that I had forgotten about his handicap.

At Berkeley I met other music students with whom I enjoyed communicating, both verbally and musically. But even

more exciting for me was my initiation into the adult world of social communication. It was a wonderful time in my life. I also had the opportunity to play a great deal of chamber music, which resulted in my decision to become a professional violinist.

In my last semester I began to study with Kathleen Parlow, a very fine violinist and teacher who urged me to pursue a career in music. It was she who got me to practice and take the whole process of violin playing more seriously. When she asked me what my eventual goal was, and I answered "to play in the San Francisco Symphony Orchestra," she was terribly disappointed. She thought this a very small goal and tried to explain that, if I really wanted to play the violin, I must aim higher: I should endeavor to become a soloist. To me that was unrealistic. I had neither the talent nor the physical or psychological makeup to become one of those musical supermen. If I could one day just become a member of my favorite orchestra, that would be glory enough.

And here I was, sitting in that orchestra. But I realized that my role was not merely to be a part of it but to be a "strengthener." After my shaky audition I couldn't see how that would be possible. With Monteux as my leader, mentor, exhorter, enticer, and protector, however, anything was possible. Rightly or wrongly, I felt that he treated me, perhaps because of my youth, as his special protégé, almost like a son. There was nothing specific he did or said that led me to this conclusion; that was just my instinctive reaction to our relationship. He had taken me into the orchestra against formidable odds, considering what he had heard at the audition.

Since I began on probation, I was anxious to find out if my option would be taken up. I asked our personnel manager repeatedly if he could give me any reassurance, even using the ploy of telling him it would be necessary for me to buy dress clothes—tails and grey-striped trousers—if I were to remain. "Should I or shouldn't I?" His answer was equivocal: "Buy them! Even if you don't use them now, you will later."

The climax of those two weeks of uncertainty was our first

concert in the Opera House. The most important piece, the last one on the program, was Beethoven's Fifth Symphony. Monteux had urged us during the preceding two weeks of rehearsal to give all we had in our performance of the music—especially the Beethoven. The one thing he detested was to see a musician hesitate about an entrance or show any kind of timidity in his playing. Our first concert was on a Friday afternoon and the boxes were filled with sponsors, the financial nucleus of the orchestra. Monteux warned us, "Zey must hear all ze new peep' in the orchest', so don't be afraid. If you make a mistake, make a good one!" I took him at his word.

There are some real traps for the unwary in the Fifth, one in particular toward the beginning. After a general pause, the orchestra comes in with the loudest expression of the famous *da-da-da-dah*. At this historic performance, I mistook Monteux's preparatory beat for the real one and came in, according to the prior direction of the maestro, with my "fortissimost" tone. It was like a clap of thunder in the midst of deadly silence. I thought my short, sweet career with the San Francisco Symphony had come to an abrupt end. Monteux jumped when he heard it. He was, as usual, facing the first violins, his back to us. We seconds were sitting on the right side of the stage when Monteux conducted. He made a complete about-face, as if he were stabbed in the back. I wanted to fall through the floor. But no one spoke to me officially or informally about my awful gaffe, though even members of the audience were heard to remark about it after the concert. Nothing was ever said to me about not continuing after the two-week probationary period, so I just kept on coming to rehearsals and concerts with the tacit understanding that I was now a member of the orchestra.

That first season stands out in my mind as particularly significant. It was a period when I had to find, for myself, if I fit into the organization, whether this work was what I really wanted, and if I could envision such a future as a happy one. Did the reality of playing in the orchestra match my dream? The answer was a resounding "Yes!" Granted, there were some frustrations. Other people did not live up to my expectations, and often I did not live up to my own. But that season solidified my feeling that I was in the right place and would remain there for the foreseeable future.

This season was outstanding for another reason. The soloists and guest conductors constituted one of the most prestigious groups that could have been selected at the time. Four had special significance for me: Isaac Stern, violinist; Marian Anderson, contralto; and George Gershwin and Alexander Tarsman, both composers and pianists.

Isaac Stern was the one artist I knew personally. He was raised in San Francisco and studied with Naoum Blinder. (Blinder had come to San Francisco from Russia and Europe where he had been an outstanding soloist. His post in San Francisco was his first in an orchestra.) Stern followed closely after Yehudi Menuhin in our city's history of prodigies. Stern's sponsors tried to profit from the mistakes that Menuhin's parents had made. They didn't want to rush him along too fast or exploit him at too early an age. He had to follow a strict regimen. He had so many hours a day for practicing, for school work (private tutoring), for lessons, for languages, for exercise (tennis, swimming), and time was set aside for chamber music. That is where I became acquainted with him. I often played viola in his quartet sessions. He was two years younger than I, but it was fun to be with him. He was, it goes without saying, an outstanding violinist. Even at that time he was an interesting person, and we had wide discussions on all kinds of subjects.

The times were tough, and, although the necessities were taken care of, there was not much luxury in Isaac Stern's life. He lived with his parents in a very modest flat. They were obviously living from hand to mouth, and their whole existence centered on Isaac and his future. When I became a member of the WPA Orchestra, Isaac's mother said to me, "Look, David, you're already making a living and Isaac hasn't done anything."

I didn't need supernatural foresight to say to her with conviction, "Don't worry, Mrs. Stern, your son is going to do very

15

Isaac Stern in an early appearance with the San Francisco Symphony, one of many he made throughout the years.

well, very soon!" In my first season with the symphony, my prophecy was already coming true. Although Isaac Stern has since become a superstar all over the world, in San Francisco he holds a special place of honor. He has been a soloist perhaps more than any other artist with our orchestra.

Marian Anderson, the great contralto, held a special place in my heart. It took courage for this black woman to break into the white world of classical music and carve out a place for herself. Her voice was gorgeous, the warm tone like butter. She and Monteux seemed to hit it off together very well, and in the forties, when we began to record, she was one of our soloists. A side benefit of her singing with us was that many black people came to the Opera House for the first time, a definite breakthrough. Many who came to hear her stayed to enjoy the symphony and returned time and again.

The first time I heard Gershwin's "Rhapsody in Blue" in the Opera House was in 1934, with Basil Cameron conducting. It was a Friday afternoon concert when all the society ladies wore white gloves, and the retired gentlemen, in their grey-striped

16

trousers, spats, and morning coats, were sitting and enjoying the culture that a symphony orchestra offered them. Suddenly there was an invasion from another world. From that first dirty glissando of the clarinet, there was the feeling that their raw emotions were being assailed. In the staid atmosphere of the Opera House, the rough syncopated rhythms and the raucous dissonant harmonies shocked the patrons out of their seats.

George Gershwin, a successful songwriter on Broadway, had gone on to musical comedy and then hoisted himself into the classical field. His "Rhapsody in Blue,' orchestrated by Ferde Grofe, revolutionized the whole concept of the separation of jazz and classical music. Gershwin, himself got caught up in the excitement; he wanted to learn everything he could about how to bring his own type of music into the symphonic and operatic repertoire. The story was told that, in the midst of the furor caused by "Rhapsody in Blue," he asked who the best living symphonic composer was. On being told that it was Stravinsky, he wired him in Paris: "I would like to come and study composition with you. Please inform me about the arrangements and the cost."

Stravinsky, always an astute businessman, was said to answer, "Please tell me what you do and what your annual income is." The prompt reply was, "I'm a composer and I make $100,000 a year." Swiftly Stravinsky retorted, "You stay there. I'll come and study with you."

Whether this story is true or not, Gershwin did get into the "Schoenberg circle" in Los Angeles, along with a number of movie composers, performers, and various sycophants. He had written a number of pieces to be played by symphony orchestras, most notably *An American in Paris*, Piano Concerto n F, and what is now considered the greatest American folk opera, *Porgy and Bess*. He was at the height of his powers when he came to conduct and play with us in 1937. He seemed very comfortable at the podium when he conducted the suite from *Porgy and Bess*. He was generally at ease with professional musicians, and his folklike music came out exactly that way when he con-

George Gershwin, American composer and pianist, conducted and played with the San Francisco Symphony, June 15–16, 1937. He died the same year.

ducted. Monteux conducted his Piano Concerto in F, and Gershwin was really a natural pianist. He played the piece as if he were in his own living room, and Monteux followed him perfectly. It was the ideal blending of all the elements that make up music, and I was thrilled by it.

Directly after Gershwin's departure came the appearance of Alexander Tansman, also a composer and pianist. Tansman had come with a reputation of being one of the great musicians of our time and one whose music would become part of the orchestral repertoire of the future. His approach to music was so different from Gershwin's that the contrast was startling. Tans-

18

man was a man whose entire concept of music seemed to come from his mind. He had a very solid academic background, was well versed in every aspect of music, and his compositions reflected that fact. Everything was well written, the forms were perfect, and the harmonies correct. The one element that seemed to be left out was emotion. After that electrifying week with Gershwin, Tansman's music sounded dry and stultifying. There is no doubt that Tansman knew a hundred times more about composing than Gershwin did, but what he knew Gershwin could eventually learn, whereas the elusive quality that brings music to life, which is in Gershwin's music, could never be learned. Tansman's music is not heard in the concert hall anymore, but the imperfect and elemental music of Gershwin lives on.

At the end of my first season, Monteux dropped a bombshell. He was going to audition every string player before the beginning of the next season. He knew that many of the string players were relying on the anonymity of the large sections to let their playing deteriorate. Monteux wanted to ferret out the bad ones, put them in back, or even fire a few. The good musicians he would encourage by bringing them forward to the front of the section. This was a devastating announcement to many players. At that time, some players felt that once they joined a string section they became merely members of the orchestra, almost like workers on an assembly line. There was no personal glory in sitting in a section. There was no chance for advancement, so some did a minimum of practicing and sought gratification from other phases of their lives. It was even said that certain members of the string section put their instruments away at the end of our short season and didn't take them out again until the next one began. So when Monteux made his unprecedented announcement, those who hadn't been keeping up, those who hadn't played alone for many years, those who hadn't been playing chamber music, were all thrown into a tizzy. However, Monteux did give them fair warning. They had almost six months to repair any damage that time and neglect had done to their playing, and for a good percentage of these players it was enough time to get back to where they had been.

To the young musicians this was a golden opportunity to improve their position in the orchestra. I knew that my summer was going to be taken up with study and practice with the hope that fortune and Monteux would smile upon me.

Chapter 2

MUSICAL CHAIRS

During the six months after the end of my first symphony season, I was preparing for my audition with Monteux. One of the most important things I had to do was arrange to get a better violin. The importance of having a good instrument is often underestimated; there is no way to produce a beautiful, large, and refined sound with a bad violin. Since I was still living at home, I had been able to save about $600, and a fairly decent Italian violin could be obtained for that amount of money. But there was something else I craved. Until now neither my family nor I had an automobile. There was no doubt that my professional life would be easier, and my social life would blossom, if I had a car. Which would it be? Finally, the violin dealer gave me the winning argument. If I were to buy the car, I'd spend all my spare time tooling around, enjoying myself. Gone would be the hours of practicing necessary to improve my playing and my position in the orchestra. So "right" won, and I bought a beautiful Antonio Gragnani violin.

The Gragnani gave me a new concept of violin tone. The quality in each fine instrument awakens in the performer a sense of sound that is special. This was the first good violin I had ever owned, and through it I could begin to develop a tone that would be personal and distinguishable, and, eventually, possibly beautiful. Every great violinist spends years trying to find the violin that is "his" instrument. Many of them have several great treasures, playing one for Mozart and another for Tchaikovsky. But there is always one instrument he loves best and with which he feels he can do the most.

That summer I had the opportunity to study with the first violinist of the Pro Arte String Quartet, Alphonse Onnou, my sixth teacher since I had started playing the violin at five years of age. Studying with Onnou was not violin instruction as much as a study in interpretation. Naturally, it was necessary to correct technical faults, but most of the time was spent bringing out the musical phrases, shaping the form of composition, and learning the styles of the composers so I would make my violin playing just a means to making music. The work we concentrated on more than any other was Mozart's Concerto no. 5 in A. With Onnou, I discovered in Mozart violin music that reached a refinement I had never before encountered. Mozart requires such meticulous playing that one must develop a certain technique in order to play him well. While the virtuoso pieces of Paganini and Vieuxtemps call for all kinds of acrobatic feats on the violin, the simple and pure music of Mozart necessitates greater control. Each note is important and must be produced in a clean and precise manner. The usual remark among musicians when a great instrumentalist plays a composition that requires tremendous virtuoso skill is, "Fine, but can he play Mozart?"

For my audition with Monteux in November of 1937, I played the Mozart concerto I had been studying during the summer. It brought me results beyond my wildest hopes. After sitting in the last seat, second violins, I was brought up to second stand outside that section. This was the best seat I could get, as Monteux excused the first stand of each section from the audition and had decided not to move anyone from one section to the other at this time.

The first violins were considered the elite. They were supposedly the superior players, having the finer technique and more beautiful tone. While I was in the second violins it seemed that, invariably, the first question asked was, "Do you play first or second?" With great shame I had to admit I was merely a second violinist. It was very difficult for one to move from the second to the first; in fact, Monteux was heard to remark, "Once a second, always a second!"

All the fuss about who sits where may seem silly to the outsider. After all, everyone is in the orchestra, playing the same notes in each section; so what does it matter who sits where? The business of seating has been a problem since symphony orchestras began. The feeling was, and to this day is, that a musician's prestige is inversely related to the distance he sits from the front of the orchestra. Orchestra members regard each other by the positions they hold, and the public has also learned to judge the musician in this manner. Conductors have used this feeling of pride and prestige to award or punish a player. The threat of reseating will keep a string player acquiescent to wrongs he would not otherwise allow, such as being reprimanded in front of the rest of the orchestra. The more tyrannical the conductor, the more he uses this type of procedure.

In my early years in the orchestra, it was important to sit in front of the section for another reason. It affected one's financial situation. Many engagements used just a few strings, and invariably the people chosen to play those engagements were the ones who sat in the front stands. For example, when a traveling ballet came into town, they'd augment their orchestra with eight first violins and six second violins from the symphony. The annual income of a player who sat in front of the section may have been at least twenty percent higher than of those in back. And sitting in front would also help in getting to play in the opera orchestra.

Naturally not all the musicians fared as well as I at the auditions. Many of the older players had not played an audition for years; in fact, many of them had not played a note alone for a long time. They had sat in the symphony for years, secure in the knowledge that they were doing a good job and that their positions in the orchestra would never be touched. When Monteux made his announcement about the audition at the end of the previous season, some of the musicians didn't believe him or didn't want to believe him. They went on with their lives, playing casual jobs, and did nothing to prepare themselves, hoping the audition would not take place.

One of the musicians most adversely affected by the audition was G., a veteran second violinist who was also well known as a musicologist. When I became enthusiastic about Gershwin and remarked to G. how much more creative he seemed than Tansman, he agreed with me, but only from a very narrow viewpoint: "Yes, he discovered a new chord I had not heard before."

When the audition for all the strings was announced, G. didn't take it seriously, and when the reality of the audition became undeniable, he began to panic. Finally, he prevailed upon M., one of the first violinists of the orchestra, to play the Bach Double Concerto with him. This, surely, would not give him any trouble. Technically it was not difficult, and he would have the support of another violinist to cover any deficiencies in his own playing. Unfortunately, it turned out to be a disaster for him. Monteux was heard to remark, "Even though I knew his playing would be pretty bad, I thought he was a good musician. How did it happen that he ended in the wrong key?"

At the first rehearsal of the new season, G. found himself seated in the last seat, second violin—the seat I had just vacated. Furious at this affront, he stormed after Monteux backstage and yelled at him, "Why don't you take off your coat and come outside and fight like a man, you old stuffed potato?"

Monteux, who had been sheltered from any unpleasantness all his life, backed away from him and called to our personnel manager, "Mr. Oesterreicher, Mr. Oesterreicher! This man is threatening. Take him away from me!" Oesterreicher calmed G. down, then called the orchestra on stage so that our rehearsal could begin. Monteux, now more at ease, looked around at the strings whom he had reseated after the auditions and made the unforgettable, profound remark, "Some peep' are 'appy, and some are un'appy."

Monteux lifted his baton to prepare for the first beat of the rehearsal when G. rose from his seat and walked toward the podium. Monteux instinctively took a step backward as if he expected to be attacked. But in a very mild voice G. asked if Monteux would mind taking his contract back, in other words, allow him to resign. He couldn't stand the indignity of being demoted to my former seat. Monteux gladly agreed. G. left and the season began.

This was not the last we heard of G., however. Soon after leaving the orchestra he started a lively correspondence with Madame Monteux, undoubtedly relating to her the wrongs that had been perpetrated against him by her husband. G. was an intellectual, cultured gentleman who was well able to express himself, and his personality must have fascinated Madame. The upshot of this series of letters was that G. came back into the orchestra a couple of years later for one season, which served as a vindication of his right to be there. After that he went to Hollywood and earned a very good living teaching moving picture composers some exotic harmonies and contrapuntal techniques to add spice to their music.

It is interesting that this man chose to write Madame Monteux to air his grievances. The truth was that she was an all-important member of the executive team in the symphony. Although she had no title, she carried a lot of weight, literally and figuratively. I first became aware of this while still ushering for the symphony.

There was a concert at the Civic Auditorium. The seats on the main floor of that hall are movable and numbered, and for this concert the seats were inadvertently switched so that those who were to sit on the right would be sitting on the left, and vice versa. I had the privilege of escorting Madame Monteux to her seat. When I began leading her down the right aisle, she stopped to tell me that she sat on the other side, and I explained what had occurred in the placement of the seats. She replied, "I'm sorry, but I must sit on the left side. When Pierre walks on stage he won't be able to find me. The concert will not be able to go on." With the cooperation of the gentleman in the seat she wanted to occupy, I was able to give Madame her rightful place. I was most anxious to follow Monteux's eyes when he came on stage. It was true. His glance went to the left side until he spied her. Having satisfied himself that she was there he smiled, turned around, and started the concert. After I joined the orchestra, I used to watch Monteux when he came on and offstage at the Opera House. His eyes would always dart immediately up to Box A to get the encouragement and approbation of Madame.

Madame's influence was felt in many ways by the members of the orchestra. She was most seriously interested in the attire of the musicians on stage. If one's stockings were too short, so that the skin showed between the top of the sock and the pant leg, he would hear about it the next morning. There was one season when the stage seemed to be unusually dark; the shining domes of some of our male musicians had been covered by wigs. There was no official word that these skull doilies were the result of an edict from Madame, but there was a tacit understanding that she originated the splendid idea of refoliating the bald-pated. Some of the coverings did not exactly fit the heads upon which they were placed, but the main result was accomplished. There was no visual nakedness upon the northern boundaries of those instrumentalists.

My own travels around the orchestra were not to stop at my second stand seat in the second violin section. In my first four seasons in the symphony, I was to occupy four different "permanent" seats. Before the beginning of my third season, Monteux summoned me and a young lady violinist, Mafalda Guaraldi, to compete for a seat in the first violin section. Here was my chance to get out of the doldrums of the second violins and live among the stars. Unfortunately, my playing on this occasion was not outstanding and Mafalda won the position. As a consolation prize, I was promoted to the inside seat of the first stand, second violins.

This was not an unmitigated blessing. My partner was Julius Haug, a fine musician and at that time librarian of the orchestra. Along with his musical talent, Julius had a keen sense of humor and a marvelous ability to mimic, and he kept me laughing almost continuously. The way our seats were arranged, Monteux couldn't see Julius but was always aware of my giggling presence. Almost anything could set me off on a laughing fit in my youthful days, and Monteux was aware of this. It annoyed him to see me in such a constant state of amusement. "What is so funny?" he would ask, and I couldn't answer even if I wanted to, as there was no logical reason for my laughter.

At the end of that season, I was demoted to the third stand, outside second violin. Not ever being overly shy, I went to Monteux to ask him why. He was forthright with his answers. First of all, I laughed too much. Secondly, I looked around when the woodwinds were playing, which annoyed them. (I had not been aware of this before.) And besides, I was too young for the position.

I expressed my regrets and hoped that he would forgive me. He replied, "If I didn't, you wouldn't be here at all. Anyway," he continued, "why do you worry? You're still very young. You will come up again."

"Young!" I said. "I'm already twenty-one years old."

He laughed, but, being three times my age, he may not have thought my remark very funny. Actually, I hadn't meant the remark to be facetious. I had been in the orchestra three years already, an unconscionable length of time at that age, and I had begun to feel middle age slowly creeping up on me. But despite my demotion, I was happy to be in the orchestra and especially happy to have the good fortune to work with a conductor of the caliber of Pierre Monteux.

Pierre Monteux, conductor of the San Francisco Symphony from 1936 to 1950.

Chapter 3

MONTEUX, THE MUSICIANS' MAESTRO

By my third season in the orchestra, I was comfortable enough to appreciate Monteux's conducting technique. Monteux was a person who seemed to be born for the job. When he conducted, he moved what was necessary—an arm, a finger, an eyelid, his mustache—each part of his body had its function and knew its place. Monteux was an efficiency expert in the use of motion. He had rules about conducting that he passed down to his protégés. One of the primary ones was "Know your score perfectly." If ever a conductor lived by that maxim, it was Monteux.

The score, a book about the size of a small dictionary has in it the notes, nuances, articulations, and dynamics for each player in that composition as written by the composer. To do his job well, the conductor should know every detail in the score before coming to the first rehearsal. He already has the sound of the music in his head, and he then conveys to the musicians exactly how he wants the work played. There are an infinite number of ways of interpreting what the composer wants, despite the care he takes in writing as precisely as possible. If he should put a forte sign under a passage in his music, how loud is the loud he is asking for? The forte of Mozart is not the forte of Tchaikovsky. Even the forte of early Beethoven is not the same forte as late Beethoven. Similar distinctions are made in tempo; the allegro of one composer is different from the allegro of

29

another. It is up to the interpreter to make these distinctions in performing the music, and in an orchestra, the conductor is the supreme interpreter for all. He must be completely cognizant of the various styles and periods of music to be able to really "know the score." When one realizes that Monteux conducted fifty to sixty scores a season, seldom repeating a work from one year to the next, and that he conducted each composition except for the concerti by memory, the prodigiousness of his mind becomes apparent.

Knowing the score is only the first step necessary to being a good conductor. The next thing is to convey that knowledge to the musicians, for which there are many methods. The con-

ductor can tell them with words what he desires, can sing or play it to them, or can conduct in a manner that makes clear to the musicians exactly what he wants. Musicians generally prefer to hear the least amount of verbalization. As I have often said, "If words could convey the ideas, music would not be necessary." Monteux told us a classic story. When he was a young man of seventeen, he was playing in an orchestra in Paris. During the rehearsal, the conductor stopped to explain to the oboe player how he wanted him to play a solo passage. "While you are playing this," he said, "you must think you are in the midst of a forest. Birds are singing, the white fleecy clouds are being gently wafted in the wind, and your playing must reflect this."

The San Francisco Symphony with Pierre Monteux, conductor, photographed December 1939 in the War Memorial Opera House.

The oboe player plaintively asked, "Maestro, do you want it louder or softer?"

Musicians desire to play a piece the way the conductor would like it played, but they can't if they are given imprecise directions. A good conductor can usually bring out the beauty of the music without embarrassing anybody with verbiage that can never be put into action. I've found that the ability of a conductor is in inverse ratio to the amount he talks. Monteux did the least amount of talking, but occasionally even he would talk too much. I remember a morning when we were rehearsing Debussy's *Afternoon of a Faun* for the first time. He stopped and corrected or made suggestions at every bar. One of the members began counting how many times he stopped in reading through the piece. In the intermission, he went to Monteux and said, "Maître, do you know you stopped seventy-five times before we got through the piece once?"

Monteux, never at a loss for a quick retort, responded, "If you had played better, I wouldn't have had to stop so many times."

Usually Monteux's beat was so fine that he spoke very little at rehearsals. Monteux used a baton and insisted that his students do the same. In the hands of a master, the baton can give not only the tempo but the articulation, the style, the dynamics, the phrasing—anything and everything that is inherent in the music. The baton greatly helps the musicians in the back of the orchestra to see the beat. And with a baton, much more precision can be achieved than with the hand alone. It is an extension of the hand, but brought to a very small point. With the baton, a good conductor like Monteux can draw a picture of what the music sounds like, and the audience can almost hear the music by watching the way he conducts.

All orchestra players have their own ideas of how the music should be played, and these ideas sometimes don't jibe with what the conductor wants. But even if they don't agree with him, they must do what he wants. He has to be convincing enough to make them play it his way. Bruno Walter was once asked what was the most important attribute a conductor must have, and his answer was "authority." That is what Monteux possessed and used to the nth degree. While playing under his direction, there was no doubt in anyone's mind that he knew what he wanted, that he knew how to get it, and that he was going to get it.

Watching Monteux conduct was like watching a giant puppeteer who had the strings of a hundred human puppets at his fingertips. He was in control, but he was also detached enough to disentangle any knots in the strings. At a performance of Stravinsky's *Rite of Spring*, an extremely complicated score that Monteux was, as usual, conducting by heart, and which he conducted at its first performance in Paris, a woodwind player made an incorrect entrance. It was a very important entrance and if not corrected could cause the entire piece to fall apart. Monteux tried to attract the offending player's eye with extravagant gestures in his direction. But the musician had his head buried in his music, completely unaware that there was something wrong. Monteux then began to sing his part for him until he got him back on the right track. As all this was going on, Monteux was able to keep the rest of the orchestra playing on an even keel, and the performance ended without further incident. This was a feat that I've never seen anyone else attempt—fortunately, for I can think of very few who could do it.

Such control served Monteux well in other respects. Many musicians have absolute pitch, that is, the ability to know exactly what tone is played, sung, or sounded in any manner, without reference to any other tone. Monteux had something else—absolute tempo. He could pick out of the air the exact tempo he wanted and the one he used for that piece every time it was performed.

Murray Graitzer, a former principal flutist of the orchestra, told me a story about his audition. Part of his tryout was to play the opening solo of the *Afternoon of a Faun*. Graitzer was nervous, so he took a breath at a rather unfortunate place. Later, when he was playing the piece in a rehearsal with us, Graitzer felt that Monteux's tempo was faster than usual. He went to Monteux and said, "Maître, I was nervous in New York when I auditioned for you. I can play that melody in one breath, so you don't have to conduct it faster on my account."

Monteux answered, "Oh, no, I didn't do that. The *Afternoon of a Faun* always takes nine minutes and twenty-three seconds when I conduct it."

Another incident illustrating Monteux's absolute control of time occurred when the symphony was playing a Standard Hour broadcast. At the dress rehearsal John Grover, the announcer who also timed the program, came to Monteux and said that the music was running a minute too long. Monteux answered, "Oh, that's all right. I'll conduct the overture a little faster."

"Don't you have to tell the orchestra?"

"No," replied Monteux, "why should I? It's none of their business."

It was no wonder that Monteux's ability to control every aspect of music making brought a recording contract to the San Francisco Symphony. He was the type of conductor who made the best records, because the quality of performance could be anticipated without fear of varying standards. And it was important that we begin recording, as both the Symphony Association and the musicians would benefit. The association got not only royalties but prestige—only touring is on a par with recording in getting a symphony out of the realm of being a provincial orchestra—and the musicians, of course, were paid for making the records.

We started recording very soon after Monteux came to San Francisco and continued all the time he was there. Although we made only a few discs a year, by the end of his tenure we had accumulated quite an extensive discography, ranging from Bach to Stravinsky. But considering the circumstances under which we made the records, it's a wonder that we recorded at all.

Monteux's name brought an RCA Victor contract to the San Francisco Symphony. But when the Victor engineers surveyed the Bay Area, they found no equipment adequate to record a symphony orchestra. The nearest technical facilities were in Los Angeles, 400 miles away, and it was not feasible for us to go to Los Angeles to record. The Victor people thought of an ingenious solution to the problem—we would record over the telephone. There were two trunk lines then going to Los Angeles, and Victor succeeded in leasing one of them after midnight; so that's when we recorded.

On the nights we planned to record, we would play a concert of the music we were scheduled to record, ending at approximately 10:30 P.M. Then we would change our clothes and have a cup of coffee while the engineers set up the mikes. At midnight the engineers and musicians would be ready to work.

As long-playing records had not yet been invented, everything was done at 78 rpm. The music was marked for stops at the end of each side, usually four to five minutes. First one side would be recorded. Invariably, it would end in the middle of a movement, even in the middle of a bar of music. Then the next side had to be connected with the first. Thus, a movement of a symphony would take three or four starts and stops. We had to be extremely quiet before and after every side was recorded, as there was no way of eliminating extraneous sounds. If there was any noise, that record had to be rerecorded. Needless to say, the recording sessions were charged with tension.

Monteux, who had no great love of recordings in general, tried to alleviate our nervousness. He told us to play as if we were performing in a concert. "If there is a mistake in a concert, nobody gets upset. If there should be a mistake on a record, don't worry about it. It's not any more important than in a concert." He didn't seem to realize that people play records over and over again; so if something is wrong on a record, it sticks out tremendously. An example of what Monteux's philosophy can lead to is our recording of Ravel's "La Valse." It was a popular favorite with audiences, and no one was better able to give it a definitive interpretation than Pierre Monteux so our recording of "La Valse" would undoubtedly be high on the classical hit parade.

Because our first trumpet player at the time, Benjamin

35

Klatzkin, was turned down when he asked for extra overscale pay for the recording sessions, he refused to make the recordings. Charles Bubb, an excellent trumpet player, was hired to take Klatzkin's place. The recording session was a good one, and it looked as if we had a winner except for one side in which Bubb cracked on a high note. The passage is particularly precarious for trumpet players, and Bubb had the bad luck to miss the note that one time. We made several takes of this side, but Monteux liked this one best in spite of the blooper. Bubb and the technicians pleaded with Monteux to make just one more take, but he was adamant, reiterating his maxim that since "mistakes are made in performances, mistakes may be made in recordings." There were no bad feelings after the recording session, and a few years later Bubb was engaged as our principal trumpet. In the meantime, Klatzkin returned to his position, and Monteux scheduled "La Valse" for one of the Pops concerts. When we went through the piece for the first time at the rehearsal, Klatzkin missed the same note that Bubb had missed in the recording. "Oh," said Monteux, quick-witted as usual, "you want to sound just like the record."

In spite of our cumbersome method of recording and Monteux's impatience with correcting errors, our recordings were extremely successful. Our recording of the Symphonie *Fantastique* of Berlioz was considered one of the finest ever made, and our Cesar Franck symphony was so popular that the master discs were worn down to the point that they couldn't be used anymore, and we had to rerecord it. We recorded many lesser-known works such as Chausson's Symphony in B-flat, Symphony on a Mountain Air by Vincent D'Indy, and the Protée Suite of Milhaud, as well as the Second, Fourth, and Eighth symphonies of Beethoven.

One of Monteux's great talents was his ability to accompany a soloist, as he did on our recordings of Menuhin playing the Bruch Concerto and Marian Anderson singing Brahms, "Alto Rhapsody" and the Mahler "Kindertotenlieder." But the recording I enjoyed making more than any other was Heifetz's rendition of the Gruenberg Violin Concerto. It was not a great work and quickly sank into obscurity, but the care and serious-ness with which Heifetz approached it demonstrated one of the reasons he had achieved the stature he held in the music world. Because recording is such a tense activity, it is a universal prac-tice that the musicians work only forty minutes of the hour, using the rest to relax and unwind. While we were all taking it easy, however, Heifetz continued playing, working slowly on the technical passages and doing scale passages to be sure he would not play one note out of tune. If there were any criticism of Heifetz's playing, it would be that it was too cold and perfect. When he stood on the stage, making no unnecessary motion, he looked like a mechanical violinist. He was aware of the impres-sion he made on his audience; once in an interview he men-tioned that he occasionally played a wrong note on purpose so people would realize he was human.

Jascha Heifetz, the violinists' violinist, recorded with the San Francisco Sym-phony in December 1945.

37

Another recording that was a joy to make with Monteux was Stravinsky's *Rite of Spring (Sacre du Printemps)*. His premiere of this work in Paris in 1913 caused one of the great scandals of music history, with the audience staging a battle royal to demonstrate their disapproval and the *gendarmes* arriving to quiet the theater. Now, thirty years later, this work was considered a classic in symphonic music, and who could better record it than Monteux? Our recording was given many awards and, at that period, was considered the best reproduction of the composition to be found.

All the recordings we made with Monteux are a living testament to the quality and style of our performances under his direction. They represent a good cross section of the programs we performed and reveal how a conductor of musical stature and integrity can lead an orchestra to produce first-rate music.

Chapter 4

THE FACTS OF LIFE

The late thirties and early forties were particularly difficult for musicians. The music business was going through a kind of revolution. In the twenties and early thirties, every movie house had its own orchestra, some very small and some as large as a symphony orchestra. In San Francisco, several theaters had orchestras playing shows that were practically concerts. When I was about thirteen years old, there was a violin contest for children at the Golden Gate Theater that drew hundreds of participants. This was all part of the show people came to see when they went to the movies. There were small orchestras in restaurants and cafes, every large hotel had tea dancing on Saturday afternoons as well as a regular house orchestra at night, and every big radio station had a house orchestra that played throughout the day.

Now all this was fading away. The introduction of sound to moving pictures tolled the death knell for theater orchestras, and musicians began to make records, eliminating the need for live orchestras at radio stations. On top of everything, the entire country was going through a depression and concerts were a luxury that could easily be cut out of one's budget. People would ask, on hearing that I was a member of the San Francisco Symphony Orchestra, "Fine, but what do you do for a living?" The question demanded a serious answer.

The symphony season, when I became a member, was sixteen weeks of concerts and rehearsals, after a preliminary week of rehearsals for which we received only half pay. With a weekly wage of sixty dollars, our salary for the entire season was $990 — period! No summer season, no fall season, unless one was among the forty musicians who played in the San Francisco Opera Orchestra. And in the thirties, there was no unemployment, social security, or medical benefits for symphony musicians. The association stopped paying a musician's salary when he wasn't playing. If a musician became sick, there was a collection taken of twenty-five cents a person (later raised to fifty) to help take care of his needs while he was ill. There was no pension plan, so a retired musician had to live on the meager savings he'd accumulated over his illustrious but poor-paying career.

Meanwhile, we orchestra musicians had to live, and we could not get by, especially those with families, on the salary provided by the Symphony Association. At that time, the financial base of the orchestra itself was shaky. It was supported largely by a few rich families who maintained the institution as an entertainment for the moneyed elite. The subscription season had two concerts a week, Friday afternoon and Saturday evening. The Friday audience was small and made up mainly of sponsors. It was most important that the people of wealth should be pleased with the orchestra, for if they withdrew their financial support, the orchestra would collapse, as it had in 1934. The entire budget in Monteux's first year was $265,000, a mere pittance compared to the $13½ million of the 1982–83 season. To raise this amount of money was extremely difficult, and all through those early years we existed in a crisis atmosphere.

In such a climate, it was almost impossible to ask for a raise or to extend the season. The musicians had very little power, though we all were members of the Musicians' Union. The union was our bargaining agent, and without it we would have been in an even worse financial position. However, our union was very weak, its officers so impressed by sitting at the negotiating table with the city's financial and social aristocracy that they couldn't bring themselves to demand much for us. If we finally had a chance to ask anything from our employers, we received a great deal of sympathy but not much more. "This is a nonprofit organization, you know. There is no way one can raise any more money. If you insist on more, we'll have to cease operations." We usually backed down.

Another limitation came, indirectly, from the San Francisco Art Commission. The good citizens of San Francisco had voted into the city charter an amendment that allotted a percentage of each tax dollar for the maintenance of a symphony orchestra. In order not to give too much to the Musical Association of San Francisco, the guiding force of the symphony, the San Francisco Symphony was not designated by name as the recipient. The Art Commission, which administered the fund, exercised control over the concerts it commissioned. Although the fund had always been used to purchase concerts from the association, there was always the possibility that the money could be used to put on a season with a rival orchestra. There was never a concerted effort to go directly to the music-loving public to widen the base of support. The powers that be did not want control of the orchestra to get out of their hands, which might happen if too many people became involved.

Monteux, for all his affable nature and pleasant personality, was no help in this situation. He always acted like a visiting conductor, never becoming a part of the city's musical structure. He arrived in San Francisco the day before a season started and left the day after it ended. He lived in a hotel or in a hotel/apartment. Monteux had nothing invested in the city or the orchestra. That we were out of work the major part of the year did not seem to disturb him in the least. (He could be a guest conductor the rest of the year almost anywhere in the world, especially in his beloved France.) In Europe, orchestral musicians were generally in the lowest economic stratum, and he saw no reason that American musicians should fare any better. In fact, he was surprised, perhaps unpleasantly, to learn that some musicians owned their own homes.

Monteux's lack of concern for the orchestra members cropped up from time to time. One year the Art Commission decided to put on a series of three concerts to be conducted by Sir Thomas Beecham. Instead of going to the Musical Association in order to engage the San Francisco Symphony, the commission contacted a local music contractor to get together an orchestra for the series. Many San Francisco musicians were engaged, I among them; it meant a much-needed $150 added to our income. When Monteux heard about this, he came down to the Opera House pit where we were rehearsing for the Ballet Russe and asked to speak to us. "I don't want you to play these concerts," he said. "They are in direct competition to our regular symphony season. If anyone insists on playing I will not vote for him"—implying that the offending musician would not receive Monteux's blessing for contract renewal. We knew perfectly well what he meant, and to a man we asked the contractor to release us from our obligation. He was unable to put together an adequate orchestra, so the Art Commission concerts were a fiasco. After Monteux succeeded in sabotaging the Art Commission, no further attempt to do anything like that was made. For the Musical Association and Monteux it may have been a very desirable result, but from the musicians' standpoint, it was disastrous.

Monteux again demonstrated his insensitivity when we began to make recordings. Since the recordings were made under the name of the San Francisco Symphony, the members voted that even if we played a composition calling for a small orchestra, every member would profit from it to some degree. When Monteux heard that this rule had been passed, he became irate and announced, "This will not take place. I have to wait for my money until all expenses are paid, including your wages. If you want this rule to go into effect, I will take my recordings to another orchestra. The recording company wants me, not you." It may have been true, but it was a brutal thing for a conductor to say to *his* orchestra. Nevertheless, we marched down to the union and obediently rescinded our resolution. (Today, no symphony in the country can make a recording without everyone under contract getting paid for each recording session.

Some loss of work for American musicians may have resulted from this rule, as many of the smaller works are recorded by European orchestras, but the solidarity of musicians is an important compensation.)

The attitude of Monteux was not unlike what was expected from the general run of conductors. But those of us who had great respect for his conducting and the integrity with which he approached music were disappointed to find these flaws in his personality. This was one more lesson for me to learn about the life of a musician. My natural tendency to embrace with loving abandon everything dealing with the symphonic world began to be tempered with some caution. I knew that the lot of the symphony musician was not ideal and that ways must be found to improve it, yet I never wavered from my initial desire to be part of this, my chosen profession.

A dramatic turn of events in my life occurred in the spring of 1939. At the time I had been working with a fine pianist, Kathlyn Woolf. We used to play sonatas together once a week and presented several recitals. One evening when I came to my usual Tuesday night chamber music session, I was surprised to see a young lady standing near the piano rehearsing the role of Gilda from *Rigoletto*. When the coaching lesson was over, Kathlyn introduced me to Geraldine Schwartz, or Geri as she immediately asked to be called. At once I was struck with both her beauty and her forthright manner.

I acquired her telephone number, and thus began a courtship that lasted over a year. We came from different worlds, and, in the main, it was Geri who had to get used to mine. Although she loved music and aspired to become an opera singer, Geri had never encountered the rarified atmosphere of the symphony or the narrow life of a symphony musician. My idea of a good time was playing quartets, and though Geri came along and listened, she didn't find it the most exciting thing to do on a Saturday night. To compensate somewhat, I took her to some rarely performed Mozart operas that had been translated into English by Erich Weiler, a member of the symphony. Geri

43

enjoyed these evenings, not only because she loved opera but because I introduced her to all the musicians. She could feel that she was part of the show, and I could act like a big shot, knowing the professionals.

When she began to go to symphony concerts, it seemed to Geri that she was in a foreign land, trying to understand a strange language. To prepare herself, she purchased Sigmund Spaeth's *Great Symphonies*, which presented English words as a mnemonic device to learn the main themes of the most famous symphonies. For instance, if she were to hear these notes,

she would put these words to them:

> This music has a less pathetic strain
> It sounds more sane and not so full of pain
> Sorrow is ended, Grief may be mended,
> It seems Tchaikovsky will be calm again.

She would then know it was Tchaikovsky's Symphony no. 6 (*Pathetique*) she was listening to. (We now laugh about such an unsophisticated way of learning the symphonies.) Geri also traded in all her coloratura records for symphonic recordings, a great sacrifice.

Of course, our whole courtship was not spent in playing and listening to music, and we took advantage of San Francisco's beautiful environment. That year was a fortunate one for us: the Golden Gate International Exposition opened on Treasure

Island in San Francisco Bay. We would take the ferry over and walk along the wide boulevards. Each country had an exhibit showing its native wares for export. Many United States' companies also had booths to demonstrate their products.

The American Telephone Company exhibit was one of the most popular because of a gimmick the company was using to attract people. Long-distance calls were just coming into use, and the phone company wanted to demonstrate how easy and pleasant it was to talk to someone thousands of miles away. They held a drawing every half hour, and the winner was allowed to phone anyone in the United States. One day we passed the booth and decided to try our luck—and we won. We called my Uncle Max, who lived in New York. Since that was about as far from San Francisco as you can get, we got our money's worth. We reached his number and the whole family was at home. I talked with them and then introduced my fiancée. Geri and I were not formally engaged as yet, so we actually announced our engagement over the transcontinental wires before we told our families and friends. With mazel tovs all around we ended the conversation. Only then did we realize that the calls were broadcast in the entire pavilion, so hundreds of people heard our engagement announcement! When we left the phone booth, we were greeted by a lot of raillery from our listening public.

Our marriage took place June 23, 1940. It was a religious ceremony conducted by two rabbis. We were honored to have a string quartet made up of four of my friends and colleagues in the symphony—Harry Moulin and Mafalda Guaraldi, violins; Suzanne Petty, viola; and Winston Petty, cello. They played Mozart's "Eine Kleine Nachtmusik," a favorite of Geri's. After the ceremony we stole away to our honeymoon retreat, a summer resort in Sonoma County called Lokoya, and enjoyed a three-day idyll before I had to be back for a Standard Oil broadcast. After our short but beautiful honeymoon, the real world would unmistakably return, and I couldn't miss my fourteen-dollar-a-week income, the only money I was sure to make in the summer.

Chapter 5

THE OPERA WORLD

When Geri and I started our married life, I had been in the symphony for four years. Though I played as an extra in the opera when the orchestra was expanded for German operas, there had been no openings in the violin sections for a new player. In the spring of 1941, however, when Albert White, violist of the symphony and opera, broke a bone in his arm and couldn't play the opera season, Julius Haug, the new personnel manager, asked me if I'd like to fill in. In high school I had started playing viola, as I found it helpful as a fourth in a string quartet. In college I had been so in demand for my viola playing that, for a time, I considered switching to it as my main instrument. At the same time as I was studying violin with Onnou, I also studied viola with Germain Prevost of the Pro Arte Quartet. So I was quite prepared to assume the viola seat in the opera.

There was no audition for the opera at that time. It just took a word from Julius for a musician to become a member of the orchestra. All members had to be from the symphony, however. I was delighted to be hired, for it would add $600–$700 to my annual income, an increase of twenty-five percent. This was especially fortuitous, because we had just learned that Geri was pregnant.

Up to that point, I had always felt that opera music was second-rate, not at all on a par with chamber music or the symphonic repertoire. But my attitude was mainly a matter of ignorance. Although Geri was quite knowledgeable about operatic music, outside of a couple of Wagner and Richard Strauss works, I was acquainted with only a few excerpts. That first season of music drama made me a dyed-in-the-wool opera buff. Learning the operatic literature with the San Francisco company was a quick but thorough process. I had never worked so hard and intensely in my life. Our contract called for no days off; we worked seven days a week for six weeks. We rehearsed all day every day, with rehearsals or performances every night. We were flooded with opera. If I hadn't been able to appreciate the musical excitement engendered by these stage plays, I would have gone berserk.

The San Francisco Opera Company was unique. Although the founder and general director, Gaetano Merola, might not have been as well schooled in music as some of our more famous conductors, he had a love and a flair for opera that made up for his shortcomings. He assembled a great array of singers that formed a nucleus for his company. Every year, the most famous opera stars—Ezio Pinza, Jan Peerce, Lily Pons, Jussi Björling, Robert Weede, Licia Albanese—would stay for the four-week season and sing a wide variety of roles. It was like a repertory company. Ezio Pinza, one of the greatest bassos of all time, didn't take umbrage at singing small roles such as Colline in *La Boheme*. Merola used to say that he hated to put on *La Boheme* because it cost him so much money. Casting Licia Albanese as Mimi, Jan Peerce as Rodolfo, Robert Weede or John Charles Thomas as Marcel, Baccaloni in the two comic roles, and Pinza as Colline cost an astronomical sum. But it was worth it; each singer was perfect for the part.

Pinza had an interesting background. He had once been a six-day bicycle racer. Elisabeth Rethberg, the great soprano, discovered him singing in a small cafe and took upon herself the task of educating him musically and developing his vocal powers. If rumors were correct, their relationship was not completely confined to that of teacher and student. Pinza developed into one of the most important stars in the opera galaxy. No role was too large or too small for him. One season, though he was a

47

basso, he sang the baritone role of Escamillo, the toreador in *Carmen*. It was necessary for the orchestra to transpose his arias a tone lower, as he could not possibly reach those high notes. He looked marvelous in the role, but he was obviously miscast and, to my knowledge, never sang it again. Pinza loved to play practical jokes on his fellow singers. The role of the blind king in the *Love of Three Kings* required him to strangle the princess, his daughter-in-law, who had been unfaithful to his son. After murdering her, Pinza laid her on the ground and, in his blind, fumbling way, passed his hands over her body, gently but firmly. Being dead, the princess, who happened to be Dorothy Kirsten, the beautiful, full-figured blonde, could do nothing about his anatomical exploration.

The whole opera company at that time was like a large family. The musicians in the orchestra had no fear for their jobs, because Merola appreciated each one and never entertained a thought of firing anybody. Therefore, no one took advantage of him by goofing off or doing anything unprofessional. True, the opera company had its drawbacks. We were overworked and underpaid, and there was very little possibility of expanding our tight little season. One week of post–San Francisco season opera in Los Angeles, later expanded to two weeks, was like a semivacation since we had already rehearsed the entire repertoire, and all we had to do was play evening performances and Sunday matinees. Geri usually joined me for this pleasant, Southern California sojourn.

With all this stimulus I began to love opera. Unfortunately, I couldn't keep my eyes off the stage; I was so intrigued by the action that was taking place. I often got into trouble with the personnel manager for being more involved with the stage than with the music I was playing. Julius would say, "I can arrange for you to see the stage all the time—from the audience!" but he didn't.

The experience I gained in the San Francisco Opera helped me obtain other engagements with smaller companies in the city. One such company, directed by Arturo Casiglia, was the

Pacific Opera. It used a group of local singers, and performances were put on with a minimum of expense. No matter the opera's length or difficulty, a maximum of two hours orchestral rehearsal was allowed. The Pacific Opera Company became so successful that Casiglia engaged a guest conductor, Gastone Usigli, local composer and musicologist. He was to conduct *Carmen*, and for this four-hour opera Casiglia indulged him by allowing a three-hour rehearsal. During this rehearsal a member of the orchestra asked Usigli, "Maestro, at this place is it forte or piano?"

His immediate answer was, "There is no time for such subtleties."

Small as the Pacific Opera orchestra was, it became even smaller when we went on the road for a performance or two. We did *Rigoletto* in Reno with four first violins, two seconds, and the corresponding number in other sections—one-third the usual size of the smallest opera orchestra. Casiglia also staged miniperformances of entire operas, using just two violins, a cello, and a piano. We would play off piano scores and try to cover as many lines of music as we could. No one in the audience seemed unhappy with our performances, and if we didn't know the operas before, we learned them very fast.

In later years, another opera company sprang up under the management and sponsorship of Campbell MacGregor The Cosmopolitan Opera Company, which had its seasons in the spring at the Opera House, was a little more professional, using a larger orchestra, more rehearsals, imported singers, and a well-known opera conductor, Anton Coppola. The Cosmopolitan Opera was eventually taken over by the Spring Opera, an adjunct to the San Francisco Opera Company

Meanwhile, the beloved Gaetano Merola was getting on in years and his health was beginning to fail. On August 30, 1953, a cold blustery Sunday, Merola was to conduct a potpourri of his favorite excerpts for a Stern Grove concert.

Stern Grove is an outdoor amphitheater in the midst of a beautiful wooded area presented to the city by the widow of one of San Francisco's pioneer industrialists, Sigmund Stern. (Stern was on the original board of governors of the San Francisco Symphony in 1911.) Every Sunday during the summer, concerts are given there for thousands of people who might not otherwise be able to hear good music. The rehearsal would begin at 10:00 A.M., and the audience would start to stream in soon after that, bringing with them huge picnic baskets of food. Though Stern Grove was generally very foggy during the summer months, there were always at least 10,000 people, and often upwards of 30,000, at the concerts. At some of our performances, people would be sitting or standing in every available spot of land and even climbing trees to find a perch from which to see and hear the music.

A huge crowd was on hand to enjoy the music that day, as opera has always been a favorite of San Francisco audiences. Merola had chosen Brunetta Mazzolini, soprano, as his soloist. Among the arias she was to sing was "Un Bel Di" from Puccini's *Madame Butterfly*. Merola, sentimentalist that he was, loved that opera and especially that aria. At its climax, when the soprano was to sing "Il Morire" (To Die), Merola hesitated before the downbeat—and then collapsed. The soprano stopped in midnote. A hush fell over the audience. We, in the orchestra, were shocked as never before in our lives. A drama that could have been staged by a great opera librettist was unfolding before our eyes. At first we thought that Merola had fainted, but it soon became apparent that conducting his favorite aria from his favorite opera had been his last act. There couldn't have been a more fitting close to his life.

Kurt Herbert Adler, chorus director of the San Francisco Opera Company and Merola's assistant, slipped easily and naturally into the position of general director. Adler had learned a great deal from working with Merola, but he also had an extraordinary talent for organization. Much clearer, efficient rules were instituted, and the nature of the San Francisco Opera began to change. More attention was paid to stage production than in the days of Merola. No longer could the company get

Kurt Herbert Adler, director of the San Francisco Opera Company, also conducted youth concerts with the symphony.

away with slipshod, easygoing methods of putting on productions. And there was no longer a lifetime guarantee of remaining in the orchestra. Unlike Merola, Adler fired several musicians at the end of every season, though he often rehired them the next season. He wanted his options open so that if a great instrumentalist should arrive in town, a position would be available. Adler controlled every facet of the opera company—music, staging, lighting, scenery, and publicity, even the janitorial work.

Opera began to take off in San Francisco. The season expanded, and more German and modern productions were scheduled. The fame of the San Francisco Opera was spreading, and with more rehearsals and performances playing in the opera also became more lucrative. It began to be the most sought-after musical job in the area, and, for the first time in its history, the opera company did not recruit musicians solely from the San Francisco Symphony.

Nevertheless, over the years I played with the opera, it became apparent that the orchestra musicians were least important to the production. First was everything that went on at stage level—the prima donnas and primo dons, followed by stage director, scenery, chorus, stagehands, and extras. The conductor was in the pit, but, in the main, disregarded the musicians except to keep them quiet. Often the conductors, especially of Italian operas, were more interested in correct pronunciation of the words than in correct interpretation of the music. Sitting in the pit, I felt I was a supernumerary. I took my job seriously and gave special attention to important passages. But the composer's subtle nuances held no interest to a public waiting to see how long a tenor could hold a high note. My love for opera began to diminish.

Twenty-five seasons of playing almost every well-known opera, and many modern and unusual ones, gave me a great appreciation of that art. But by 1967, the time had come to move on. High blood pressure brought on by overwork contributed to my decision. Though Adler suddenly found that he needed me very much in the orchestra and asked me to reconsider, I knew from others that his seemingly flattering request may have been simply his desire to remain in control and not have a musician quit on him. My time as an opera musician came to an end.

Chapter 6

THE TURBULENT YEARS

On December 7, 1941, we heard on the radio the news that the Japanese had treacherously attacked Pearl Harbor. From that moment on, all our lives were changed. The war even impinged on the narrow world of the symphony.

Many men in the orchestra were called up by the draft. The first contingent consisted of Manfred Karasik and Detlev Olshausen, violists; David Shapro and Ernest Michaelian, violinists; and Cesare Claudio, cellist. These were soon followed by others, including Frank Houser, Felix Khuner, and Harold Dicterow, also violinists. All these men were good friends of mine, whom I would deeply miss. Two of them, Manfred and Felix were especially influential in my life. It was Manfred who had urged me to try out for the symphony and personally brought me to the audition on that fateful day. He was someone I could lean on when I encountered problems during my first years in the orchestra.

When Felix entered the army, he was stationed in Texas and played in a military band. If one had to be in the army this was the least painful duty. However, this ideal existence wasn't fated to last very long. The colonel in charge of the post had a passionate and impatient wife who used her spare time to dally with some of the band members. Coming home one day unexpectedly, the colonel found his wife in bed with one of the musicians, exploring some of the intricacies of chromatic harmony. He was furious, and the innocent were punished along with the guilty. He disbanded the band and scattered the members far and wide over the globe.

Felix found himself on a remote island in the South Pacific, with little to do except distribute mail once a week and occasionally change a plane tire. He had a beat-up old violin with him, and he used to go up to the hills and practice. Once he was in a cool cave fiddling away, when he looked up to see a native standing in front of the opening, watching and listening. Unperturbed, Felix continued to practice for another half hour or so. He stopped, looked at the man, pointed to his violin, and said, "Good?" The native answered enthusiastically, "Good! Fuckin' good." Obviously, he had been in contact with basic GI English. Felix thought this review would be a worthy addition to his credits when he returned home.

When the world crisis began, I was not immediately called by the draft board. Eventually, however, I received one of those well-known "Greetings" letters, which left me with an awful feeling at the pit of my stomach. I've always been an ardent pacifist. Yet, if ever a war was justifiable, surely this one was. But my physical examination showed that my eyes were too weak to allow me to join the armed forces at that time. I was to be kept on standby for limited service in case of emergency. In the meantime, I was required to get a job helpful to the war effort. Playing in the symphony did not fall into that category.

There were several companies building ships in the Bay Area. I learned that IBM had an installation in each of these shipyards, and computer operators were needed. No one could doubt that I would make a much better computer operator than a welder. After taking a three-week course that qualified one to run a sorter and collator and to wire and operate a 405 computer, I immediately went to work at Marinship on the graveyard shift (from midnight to 8:00 A.M.) so that I could continue to play in the symphony.

In the midst of world turmoil, a blessed event occurred in my life, the birth of our daughter on March 14, 1942. I was jubilant when I arrived at rehearsal next morning. Unbeknownst to me, my colleagues had arranged that, when Monteux gave the downbeat for the composition we were rehearsing, the orchestra would instead play "Rock-A-Bye-Baby" in honor of little Sandra Diane. When I stood up to acknowledge the good wishes of the musicians, Monteux asked me in a serious tone, "Schneider, was it a little boy?"

Monteux Opens Another Season of Symphony

TWO-GUN MONTEUX RIDES AGAIN
He opens the San Francisco Symphony season Friday afternoon and Saturday night with the suite from Aaron Copland's "Billy the Kid"

Antonio Sotomayor, noted San Francisco artist, caricatured Monteux in the San Francisco Chronicle, November 1942.

55

"No, a girl, Maestro!"

Then with a look of mock sadness he said, "That's all right. There's just a leetle deefarance," showing a space of a half inch between his thumb and forefinger.

I am sure that at least part of this performance was staged so that Monteux could express his Gallic humor, but I appreciated his wit and the orchestra's good wishes.

My life in the symphony continued uninterrupted through the war years. During all that time, I missed only one concert, and that was a night when the orchestra played in Fresno and I had to put out a payroll in the shipyard. It was interesting having two radically different jobs, and I found pleasure in both sets of colleagues and welcomed the variety of experience they brought into my life. The one problem I encountered was getting enough sleep. After finishing my graveyard shift at 8:00 A.M., I'd get breakfast somewhere and prepare myself for the 10:00 A.M. rehearsal. Though I had gotten along frequently with little sleep, getting between four and six hours day after day for long periods of time had its effect upon me.

The symphony continued during these troubled times in more or less usual fashion. One unique concert given for the orchestra's thirty-second anniversary, was performed at the Civic Auditorium with a large array of soloists, including members of the San Francisco Ballet, John Charles Thomas, popular singer Ginny Simms and the Foursome, and comedienne Gracie Allen. Gracie performed in a clever piece written especially for her, the Piano Concerto for One Note. The orchestra played an intricate exposition, there was a sudden pause, and Gracie would play that one note. This same note was inserted into the music at various times and in different rhythms. Gracie would sit there looking pretty and dumb, as she was wont to do, and act as though she were playing that most important note, whenever it came. Actually, it was played by a pianist in the back of the orchestra. But Gracie pantomined so convincingly that it was almost impossible to discover she was only acting. The piece was a huge success.

Treasure Island, where Geri and I had announced our engagement at the exposition, was taken over by our naval forces during the war, and one Christmas the San Francisco Symphony was asked to perform for the men stationed on the island. Jascha Heifetz was to be the soloist, and the Carolers, a group of singers organized and trained by Madame Monteux, were to sing Christmas carols. At the intermission of our rehearsal, Virginia Morgan, our sweet and gentle harpist, spoke to Monteux. She said that as a child growing up in New England, she would take her little Irish harp and, with a group of other children, go from house to house to sing and play carols for the neighbors. Monteux said, "Well, I didn't," and then spying me standing nearby, "and neither did he." This was one of the few times he made reference, even indirectly, to the fact that he was Jewish. Though a member of one of the oldest Jewish families in southern France, he himself had never practiced Judaism. After marrying, he was converted to Catholicism, which Madame Monteux said was a moving and inspiring revelation to him. It was hard for me to picture Monteux being influenced by religious inspiration, because his life seemed to be ruled by reason and practicality. Nothing he had ever said to us had any religious overtones, and the inspiration he spoke of was that of the intellect and not of the divine.

In 1945 we had two great guest conductors, Leonard Bernstein and Bruno Walter, two men whose style and personality were diametrically opposed. Bernstein, a musician of enormous talent, had conducted the New York Philharmonic at a very early age, as a last-minute substitute for Bruno Walter, and was later its general director. He had been a concert pianist and a composer of both classical and popular music, and he had raised the art of musical commentating to a high level. When conducting, he combined all his talents to get the results he wanted. Never content to be merely a time-beater, he would dance, leap, yell, exhort, pray, cry, and cajole to get the musicians to respond. People flocked to his performance as much to see his histrionics as to hear his music.

Watching Bernstein conduct reminded me of an anecdote related to me by Dr. Elkus when I was an undergraduate. As part of a thesis on early American music, Elkus had visited an Indian reservation to discern the effect European music would have on the Indians. He requested that the two most musical members of the tribe accompany him to a symphony concert, to hear European music for the first time in the formal concert atmosphere. After the concert, one of the Indians was taken backstage by his host and introduced to Maestro Alfred Hertz, who was very anxious to hear what his impressions were. The Indian shook Hertz's hand enthusiastically and said, "You were wonderful. I especially liked the dance you did to the last piece of music."

Walter presented an entirely different picture of the art of conducting. His approach was that of a high priest performing a religious ceremony. In his demeanor there was a total reverence toward music. Before he entered the stage, even at rehearsals, there had to be absolute silence by the musicians. He then

Bruno Walter, one of the most respected guest conductors of the symphony.

walked to the podium through the ranks of musicians. His costume, too, looked priestly—dark trousers, black alpaca jacket buttoned up to the throat, and his baton held in his right hand as if he were about to give a blessing. His speech was very quiet, almost a whisper. When the baton came down for the first beat, the ceremony was to start. His knowledge of the music was complete, not only in the notes, rhythms, and tempos but also in the spirit. He seldom conducted anything not in the long line of Austro-Germanic greats, from Mozart to Mahler and Bruckner. Not all was perfection, however. His beat was faulty and imprecise, and we soon discovered that much of the ensemble responsibility would depend on how well we heard each other and played together—without Walter's help.

The year 1945 saw an important occasion taking place in San Francisco—the founding of the United Nations. During the ceremonial opening week of this conference, the San Francisco Symphony was asked to play a concert. Eugene Goossens conducted it, and the music performed was itself a United Nations of composers—Bach, Prokofiev, Vaughan Williams, Grieg, and others. There were enormous security precautions around the Opera House, as dignitaries from all over the world attended. But the musicians were more interested in our soloist, the lovely and talented Risë Stevens.

During these turbulent war years, my own role in the symphony was to change twice. Since I was now playing viola in the opera, I thought it would be less confusing if I joined that section in the symphony, too. And I wanted to get out of the second violin section, where I felt I'd already spent too much time. There was an opening in the viola section, so I asked Monteux if I could play viola for him. He said, "Why do you want to do that? It's for old men who hold their instrument like this," and he showed an instrument being held way down to the knees. That remark sounded strange coming from a man who played viola in the Paris Symphony at the age of seventeen. At any rate, Monteux seemed very pleased with my viola playing, so much so that he warned me not to expect to become principal violist, as the next one was waiting in the wings. (Nathan Firestone was the present principal, and, at his retirement a couple of years later, Ferenc Molnar, late of the Roth String Quartet, stepped in as planned.) Monteux did, however, give me a very good seat—second stand outside. This was not to last very long. At a ballet performance, before the next season, I committed the cardinal sin of looking at the stage and getting caught by the conductor, Franz Allers. I was summarily fired, the only time I was ever asked to leave a job. When Monteux heard about this he said, "No musician in my orchestra should do anything that could be construed wrong by another conductor." Back to the third stand!

In the middle of the next season Harold Dicterow was drafted, which left an opening in the first violin section. Yet again I asked Monteux if I could play for him. By this time he might have been tired of hearing me, but he couldn't automatically put me in the first violin section. My audition was partially successful: I did get into the "elite section," though not to the seat for which I thought I was auditioning. Monteux said he didn't want to upset other musicians of the section by putting me ahead of them. But there I was, finally, in the first violin section, where I would stay, in various seats, for the next twenty-five years.

Chapter 7

POSTWAR EXCITEMENT

Immediately following the Second World War, two exciting events occurred in my musical life: the California String Quartet was founded, I becoming its second violin; and the San Francisco Symphony went on its first transcontinental tour. These unrelated events greatly enlarged my horizons.

A great deal of pleasure can be derived from playing string quartets. The give and take of chamber ensemble combined with the opportunity to play some of the masterworks of musical literature can be extremely exhilarating. Yet I often had been left frustrated by the casual and haphazard manner with which we usually played these compositions. At last I would have the chance to work seriously on the quartets so that they would be ready for concert performance.

My three symphony colleagues who joined me in the quartet were all excellent, experienced, chamber music players. Felix Khuner, the first violin, had been a member of the illustrious Kolisch String Quartet for almost twenty-five years; Detlev Olshausen had belonged to the original University of California Quartet, a forerunner of ours; and George Barati had started playing chamber music in his native Hungary, studied music at Princeton, and, after serving in the United States Army during the war, joined the San Francisco Symphony. (Although we were all members of the symphony, the California String Quartet was not a symphony enterprise.) During the long lifetime of the quartet, we had two changes in personnel, both in the cello

The California String Quartet played to San Francisco audiences from 1946 to 1961. Left to right: David Schneider, second violin; Detlev Olshausen, viola; George Barati, cello; and Felix Khuner, first violin.

department. When Barati became the conductor of the Honolulu Symphony, he was replaced by Karl Hesse, a fine, meticulous musician. And when Karl retired from the symphony and quartet, Detlev Anders, one of my oldest friends and colleagues, became the cellist.

We planned to put on an annual series of concerts at the San Francisco Museum of Modern Art, as well as playing for the University of California and the Composers' Forum. We felt that our role in the music community was to perform modern music as well as neglected works of the past. The modern compositions included the quartets of Schoenberg, von Webern, Berg, Bartok, and Eliott Carter. We also played premieres of many composers, mostly from the Bay Area, including works by Kirchner, Erickson, Nin-Culmell, Imbrie, and Nixon. The last two, plus the quartet composed by George Barati, were recorded by us. As for works from the past, we resurrected many worthwhile and interesting compositions such as the quartets of Arriaga, Neri, Cambini, Donizetti, and our own Benjamin Franklin.

Playing in the quartet proved to be a wonderful experience. During this time, I learned more about music and violin playing than I had learned from all my formal study. There were many moments when everything jibed perfectly and I could feel an inner glow of happiness. That did not always happen, of course, but all in all this was the most musically satisfying time in my life.

The California String Quartet was an active adjunct of the San Francisco music world for fifteen years. Having insisted on not repeating any work during that entire time, we were able to perform many classical compositions as well as the new and unusual music. We had the help of a wonderful man, Hanns Floch, in promoting these concerts. After his death, there seemed to be no further impetus to continue. The California String Quartet quietly and gracefully faded from the scene.

About six months after the California String Quartet was founded, the San Francisco Symphony went out on its first major tour, one of the most ambitious, concert-packed tours ever undertaken by any symphony orchestra: eight weeks long, during which we visited fifty-three cities and played fifty-six concerts. The tour was being undertaken at the behest of RCA Victor, in order to promote the records we had been making for them. It was also felt that the orchestra had improved so much under Monteux's direction that the city of San Francisco wanted to show us off throughout the nation.

At 8:00 A.M. on Sunday, March 16, 1947, the musicians,

"Pierre Monteux, musician and globe spanner," captured by artist Antonio Sotomayor in the San Francisco Chronicle.

stagehands, librarian, and the two conductors, Pierre Monteux and assistant conductor James Sample, tramped onto the San Francisco–Oakland ferry that would take us to the train. From then on it would be one-night stands all across the nation, from Los Angeles to New York City.

Most of us looked forward to the pleasures of traveling, imagining ourselves sightseeing and generally enjoying a grand tour. It didn't occur to us that there would be any problems connected with this much traveling and playing so many concerts with so little rest. Only some of the older musicians, who already had experience in touring, spoke of the pitfalls that lay ahead.

The first problem encountered was our manner of transportation. Private train sounds very glamorous, but on seeing our accommodations we were appalled. A closet-sized cubicle was to be the living quarters of *two* musicians. To store our gear and move around without doing ourselves bodily injury seemed impossible. Here we were embarking on this wonderfully exciting tour, condemned to spend half the time in a room smaller than a prison cell. Each "roomette" contained two berths that could be folded up during the day (to allow us to sit on an upholstered bench) and a washbasin. The other plumbing facilities were at the end of each pullman car. There was no bath or shower.

We each chose a partner to share our cozy little apartment. It was natural that Felix Khuner and I would find each other, since we were friends from the California String Quartet. During the early part of our tour, we got to know each other even better. Not only did we have the love of music, quartets, bridge and chess playing in common, but we found that we both practiced the noble art of frugality. With barely adequate salaries and no additional compensation for traveling expenses, Felix and I would often eat in. Sometimes we played host in our roomette, offering juice and cookies to our guests. Felix was the most agreeable of roommates, but he was amazed that I could be so easily annoyed, since nothing ever bothered him. One of Felix's habits especially taxed my tolerance. As soon as his head hit the pillow, stentorian sounds issued from his nostrils. I'd heard snoring before, but Felix was undoubtedly the Heifetz of the snore.

Our tour through the southern states was a revelation. I had no idea that, eighty years after the Civil War had ended, the conflict between white and black had not been resolved. I should not have been so smug. Even in the 'enlightened" state of California only a few years earlier, black musicians had to join a separate union and could play only jobs with other blacks.

65

A great deal of prejudice had to be overcome to merge the parent white and subsidiary black unions. But in the South, there was not even a semblance of racial equality.

There was, however, one pleasant incident while we were in Montgomery, Alabama. Our principal bass player, Philip Karp, had read somewhere that the governor's mansion was open to anyone for a visit as long as the porch light was on. After our concert, about 10:00 P.M., a few of us passed the mansion and, seeing the light on, rang the doorbell. We were ushered into Governor Folsom's office. He was sitting on a comfortable leather chair with his large feet on the desk. When we entered, he unwound himself and rose to his six-foot-six height and greeted us with the usual Southerner's "How y'all?" Even though he hadn't been to our concerts, he wanted to know all about us. He opened some California champagne, and we spent an enjoyable half hour with him. His affability gave credence to the fact that he was one of the most popular governors of the South.

From a musical standpoint, the tour thus far had been a huge success. All the audiences we played for seemed to find the concerts exciting. The *San Antonio Express*, for example, said:

> The indelible brilliance of the San Francisco Symphony's performance left no fragment of doubt that Pierre Monteux brought to San Antonio the greatest symphonic organization which has appeared here in at least a decade. Such precision, such technical totality, and mass virtuosity as Monteux elicits from his aggregation is of such rarity that one looks upon such a performance as a precious and unparalleled musical experience.

In a more musically sophisticated city we were still praised. Ralph Lewando of the *Pittsburgh Press* wrote:

> A capacity audience listened happily last night in the Syria Mosque to the expert San Francisco Symphony Orchestra. It revealed wide powers under the superlative conducting of Pierre

Monteux. The orchestra is one of the top symphonic organizations. It has developed by Mr. Monteux into an impressive, molded group. The woodwinds are of the best in the land. The brass group is quality plus, and the percussion is handled effectively. All these are splendidly integrated. Thus San Francisco has a magnificent orchestra.

All this served as a prelude for what was to come. We were preparing for our supreme test—the performance in Carnegie Hall, home of the New York Philharmonic and the auditorium in which every great orchestra had to prove itself before the world's most knowledgeable audience. On the morning of our Carnegie Hall performance, Monteux called a light rehearsal to repair any damages done to our playing by the grueling tour. As usual, Monteux was very calm about the concert and facetiously said, "Don't worry! We'll be different from all the other orchestras. We shall play the music just as it is written." Despite outward indifference to what the newspaper critics might say, we couldn't wait to read Olin Downes' write-up in the *New York Times*. He was most complimentary to the orchestra as a whole and to the soloists, and ended by writing:

> But the summit of the concert came with the magnificent reading of Brahms' symphony, a reading which represented the thinking, feeling, doing of a great musician, self-forgeful, supremely authoritative in the performance of his task. From the orchestral standpoint this was the triumph of execution and responsive interpretation. The conception and its eloquent realization represented the achievement of one of the great Brahms interpreters of this period.

Such superlatives are hard to believe, especially from a person who had seen and heard all the great orchestras. Although the French are not supposed to be great Brahmsians, it was true that Monteux did interpret his music marvelously. It was a wise choice for the orchestra to perform Brahms in New York. (On the other hand, Virgil Thomson's review was quite negative.)

There was a capacity audience in New York, and among the listeners were some famous names in music, including Louis Persinger and Mishel Piastro, both former concertmasters of the San Francisco Symphony, Isaac Stern, and Horace Britt, who had been principal cellist of the orchestra in pre-Monteux days. Among the conductors in the audience were Efrem Kurtz, William Steinberg, and Andre Kostelanetz. And seen standing and cheering in one of the boxes was a little Italian man, also well known as a conductor—Arturo Toscanini.

From a musical standpoint, New York had to be the climax of the tour, but Monteux did not save himself just for the big spots. It didn't matter if he conducted in Boston or Ottumwa, he gave his same honest, straightforward musical performance. Over seventy years old, he didn't spare his energy at any time. James Sample, our associate conductor, had precious little to conduct.

One aspect of the tour was publicized more than all others combined. It was the presence in our orchestra of an authentic "sex goddess"—one of our violinists, Marcia Van Dyke. She was an excellent musician who did some "pop" singing in San Francisco nightspots and hoped to go into show business and the movies (she eventually did get into pictures). If Marcia's individual features were judged, she was not exceptionally good-looking, but her personality exuded sex appeal. She was outgoing and drew men to her in droves. When newspaper reporters and photographers came to meet us at a train stop, the first question they asked was, "Where's Marcia?" There were so many pictures taken of her coming down the steps of a train, she could have been running for president. In fact, Marcia received so much publicity that the question was raised whether the whole tour had been arranged to further her career. This situation was accepted by most of the orchestra with either amusement or indifference, but some of the women musicians showed signs of the green-eyed monster. Marcia reacted with complete nonchalance.

There was one "extra" that the California String Quartet

First violin section in 1947. Standing left to right: Frank Houser, Louis W. Ford, Artur Argiewicz, David Schneider, Mafalda Guaraldi, William Wolski (assistant concertmaster), Ferdinand Claudio, Cicely Edmunds, Henry Shweid, Thorstein Jensen Holm, David Sheinfeld, Felix Khuner, Peter Heyes. Seated: Naoum Blinder (concertmaster), Marcia Van Dyke. Not shown: Mischa Meyers.

got out of this tour—the opportunity to play away from our home base. We played two concerts, one in Washington, D.C., and the other at Harvard University, both under the auspices of the patron saint of chamber music, Elizabeth Sprague Coolidge. We also performed at the home of Arnold Schoenberg. It was exciting to play for this grand old master of music, especially since we did a work for him which he had never heard—the Barati String Quartet. George was anxious to get Schoenberg's opinion of his composition, as there was no one's judgment he more highly valued. Schoenberg was in a genial mood that day (not always, so I was told), and he was most gracious in his comments about George's writing and our playing. There was a special feeling about that afternoon that I look back upon with joy.

From an artistic and publicity standpoint, the tour was a tremendous success. Financially, however, it was a disaster.

Even though we played so many concerts, mostly well attended, the costs were not accurately projected. Starting with a fund of $20,000, the association ended up $50,000 in the red. The deficit was carried on the books for years, which put a damper on any further adventures for the orchestra. The debt was also used as an argument against raises or lengthening the season in contract negotiations. One year, the association even came to the musicians to borrow $50,000 from our embryonic pension fund.

Still, overall feeling about the tour was positive. The orchestra emerged from obscurity and showed the country that culture could come out of the Far West, that we were to be reckoned with when fine orchestras were mentioned. We had broken ground and moved into the upper echelon of symphony orchestras.

Chapter 8

ADIEU, MONTEUX

After the excitement of our grand tour, the orchestra settled down to its usual routine. Monteux continued to conduct the bulk of the subscription concerts. Even though we only had a couple of guest conductors each season, over the years we had the opportunity to play under the direction of some of the greatest musical personalities of that era. Leonard Bernstein, Bruno Walter, Artur Rodzinski, Dimitri Mitropoulos, Guido Cantelli, and Igor Stravinsky are among the illustrious stars of the music world who conducted the San Francisco Symphony during these posttour years. The soloists, too, were all top-notch artists whose fame has not faded during these last four decades—pianists Rudolf Serkin, William Kapell, Arturo Benedetti Michelangeli, Yaltah Menuhin, Clifford Curzon, Robert Casadesus, Arthur Rubinstein, and Aldo Ciccolini; violinists Tossy Spivakovsky, Jascha Heifetz, Zino Francescatti, and Ossy Renardy; vocalists Kathleen Ferrier, Jennie Tourel, and Marian Anderson. All these names evoke memories of past glories, tempting one to think of those days as the golden era of music. But each generation has its greats, and we cannot allow ourselves to fall into the trap of saying "those were the days and we'll never see or hear the likes of them again."

One of Monteux's ongoing projects was the furtherance of local musical talent. San Francisco is known for the many violinists whose careers were "hatched" here—Yehudi Menuhin, Isaac Stern, Ruggiero Ricci, and Anshel Brusilow among them. Monteux had not been the first to promote some of them, but he saw to it that they were heard again and again. So it was for pianists Leon Fleisher, Stephen Bishop, and Ruth Slenczynska. Even more valuable to the music world was the interest Monteux showed in presenting works of local composers such as David Sheinfeld, Emanuel Leplin, Gastone Usigli, William Denny, Ellis Kohs (from Southern California), William Bergsma, and Isidor Freed, many of whom later became nationally known. If Monteux hadn't given them their first opportunity, their works might have never been played. This is one function of a metropolitan orchestra—not only to entertain audiences with the "Top 100" symphonies but to present contemporary music. The audience can gradually absorb the modern genre, and the composers can tell if what they write makes musical sense.

Monteux usually allowed the composers to conduct their own compositions. This gave them a chance to become more intimately acquainted with how the orchestra functions and to see if what they wrote worked. It also provided Monteux a brief respite from his continuous conducting chores. He would sit in on the rehearsals, however, to help the composers technically in what they were trying to achieve. When an important work required skillful conducting, he would conduct it himself. Such a piece was the Second Symphony of Roger Sessions.

Although he respected Sessions for his musical erudition, Monteux was not sympathetic to his music, especially the Second Symphony. It was the kind of music Monteux neither understood nor cared to understand. While rehearsing it, he made snide remarks about the piece, much to the delight of those musicians who hated modern music in general. Added to the problems was the poor manuscript we had to read from. Trying to understand difficult music that is also illegible causes irritability and noncooperation in performers. But despite these obstacles, the Sessions Second Symphony attained a great deal of critical success. When it was repeated on the university campus in Berkeley, the students stood and cheered. Monteux was heard to remark, "Zey, of course, understand zis music!"

For all his greatness, Monteux often showed signs of petti-
ness not expected from men of his stature. His cutting remarks
about other conductors implied that their reputations far out-
distanced their abilities, and in other ways he showed an unwillingness to subordinate his own aims to another's needs. Anshel
Brusilow, a student of Naoum Blinder with a great talent, was
ready to begin his career. Monteux and his wife Doris took
Brusilow under their wings and helped launch him. He was presented as soloist in many of our concerts and seemed well on the
way to a brilliant future. As he grew older, however, he did the
unthinkable—he fell in love! Doris and Pierre decided that there
was no time in his life for such nonessentials, especially with
someone they felt not of a social status to help him on his way,
and they asked him to break off his romance. Brusilow refused,
and, forthwith, Monteux stopped helping him and would not
allow him to solo with the orchestra again except for one already
scheduled concert in Richmond, California. Richmond was not
known for its musically sophisticated audiences, and the concert
was attended by a mere few hundred people, evoking one of
Monteux's cutting remarks: "Brusilow really draws a big audience." He conveniently ignored the fact that Pierre Monteux
also had been unable to attract many people to the concert.

Many musicians in the orchestra were presented as soloists,
usually the first chairs, but once Monteux decided to give a
section violinist the opportunity to play a solo with the orchestra.

In 1950, Monteux conducted a series of chamber orchestra
concerts, called Classic Interludes, which featured music of the
baroque and classical periods. In order to heighten interest both
in the public and in the orchestra, he announced a contest. All
the orchestra violinists were invited to play a Mozart concerto.
Their playing would be judged by Monteux in the preliminaries
and by critics from the local papers in the finals, and the winner
would have the privilege of playing his Mozart concerto with
the orchestra at one of the Classic Interlude concerts. Although
no one was required to play, almost all the first violinists and a

few from the second section did. I prepared the Concerto in A that had proven so successful for me in the audition before my second year in the orchestra.

About half a dozen of us survived the preliminaries and went into the finals. This part of the contest was a particularly harrowing experience, because we had to come back again and again to play different sections of the concerto. Finally, the list of contestants was narrowed down to three: Cicely Edmunds, Ervin Mautner, and me. The eventual winner, one of our most virtuosic instrumentalists, was Ervin Mautner. Ervin's playing was not that of a classical-type violinist; being of Hungarian descent, he brought a little gypsy interpretation into whatever he played. At first I felt, as did some others, that the critics had made a mistake. Cicely and I both played Mozart more traditionally. It took me a while to realize that it is better to hear a piece played with some imagination, flair, and brilliance than a more precise, academic, and (let's face it) dull performance. It was a hard lesson for me to learn but an important one. Mautner went on from this solo appearance to play with Arthur Fiedler and the Boston "Pops" Orchestra, presenting the premiere in Boston of the Kabalevsky Violin Concerto.

In 1951, I had an opportunity to see another side of the symphony from a personal perspective. James Sample, who had been the orchestra's associate conductor on our tour, was the new conductor of the Portland Symphony Orchestra in Oregon. He wanted to get a concertmaster for this orchestra, preferably from the San Francisco Symphony, and I was recommended for the position by Monteux and possibly by Blinder as well. One consideration was remuneration. I couldn't expect to uproot my family and go to an unfamiliar place and lose money in the process. So when Sample asked me what I needed to take the job, I mentally added up what I made from the symphony, opera, teaching, and odd jobs and came up with the figure of $10,000. This staggered Sample; I doubt he was making more than that himself. For him to justify that kind of salary for me to his board, I suggested that I could be not only concertmaster but assistant conductor.

Sample took my idea seriously, because soon afterward Monteux said he wanted to see me conduct. He didn't say it was at the behest of Sample but rather that he was often asked to recommend someone as a conductor, and he wanted to evaluate how I would do. It was arranged that I would conduct part of a rehearsal of the San Francisco Symphony, and he would observe how I handled the situation. I chose to rehearse the First Symphony of Beethoven. Technically it is one of the least difficult pieces to conduct, and I thought I knew it well enough to do a creditable job. I had about a week to prepare the score, but I had very little training in that art. The actual conducting technique would not present many difficulties, I thought, but learning the score well enough to give a decent performance was another story.

The morning of my "tryout," Monteux announced what would happen after he finished his portion of the rehearsal. My reception wasn't too cordial, because if there is anything musicians dislike more than rehearsing, it is rehearsing unnecessarily. I conducted part of each movement of the symphony, thanked the musicians, and descended from the podium. Monteux politely complimented me but suggested that I should not be ashamed of my height. "Stand tall and command their respect. Don't bend over and act apologetic." What had happened was that I had not raised the music stand to the proper height, because I wanted to give the impression that I knew the score better than I did. But I had outfoxed myself. Within a few bars, it was clear that my knowledge was superficial, and if I wanted to do anything besides beat time I had to lean over to see the score better.

Most orchestra musicians who have been playing for a number of years believe that they could conduct if the opportunity presented itself. It's often been said, "It's not hard to conduct, it's hard to get the job." If that were true, there would be a lot more capable conductors around. But the apparently simple technique of conducting is deceptively difficult. Nevertheless, it is a big thrill to stand on the podium, bring down one's baton, and hear an enormous sound emerge seemingly right out of the

75

end of the baton. The power one feels in controlling all those people parallels what a general must feel in directing his forces in battle. Conducting has other rewards, too: a much higher salary than that of performing musicians and the independence of presenting one's own interpretation of the music, with strength and authority. All these things gave me, along with my fellow musicians, a strong urge to become a conductor. But it is necessary to follow up that urge with the appropriate groundwork and a deep study of the scores.

None of my colleagues said a word about my conducting that morning, but I couldn't let it go without comment. So I asked my quartet colleagues for their opinion. George Barati answered, "David, you followed the orchestra very well." Monteux, however, seemed pleased with what I had done, and he always implied that conducting would be my eventual career. On the picture of himself that he gave me before leaving the orchestra, he wrote, "To David Schneider, with best wishes for a brilliant conducting career. Sincerely yours, Pierre Monteux."

In fact, I didn't become concertmaster or assistant conductor of the Portland Symphony. But my life did change in 1951, for that was the year my son Bart was born. He brought an entirely different dynamic into our lives after our quiet first child, Sandra.

In 1952, the San Francisco Symphony saw yet another style of conducting when it played under the direction of one of England's most famous citizens, Sir Thomas Beecham. His style seemed the simplest of all. He would set the tempo at the beginning of a movement and let the orchestra take over. Occasionally, he gave a little indication of a ritardando, an accelerando, a crescendo, or a diminuendo. The music he chose for his concerts was almost all standard repertoire, which he could rely on a professional orchestra to perform with little or no effort on his part. Unlike most conductors, Beecham did not relish rehearsing. Once when he was guest conductor with the Chicago Symphony, a Brahms symphony was scheduled to be performed. After rehearsing everything else on the program, he said, "We

76

The appearances of guest conductor Sir Thomas Beecham are remembered as enjoyable experiences by San Francisco audiences and musicians.

are also going to play the Brahms symphony. You know it and I know it, so let's just enjoy it when we play it tonight."

The third horn player, a very young man, said, "Maestro, I've never played the Brahms before."

"Oh, you haven't?" replied Sir Thomas. "Well, you're going to love it!"

When Beecham came to us that year, he was suffering from sciatica, an illness that causes severe pain in the back and thighs. He was able to get through the Thursday and Friday concerts, but by Saturday night the pain was so intense he could no longer go on. He kept hoping he could conduct, so he didn't contact the management until two hours before the start of the concert. There was nothing to do but cancel it, one of the only scheduled concerts that has ever been canceled since I've been in the orchestra. By the next week, his health had improved sufficiently to permit him to conduct all three concerts. His appearance on stage at the end of the first one brought forth a standing ovation. Always comfortable with an audience, Beecham turned to them and acknowledged the applause with this little speech.

"I'm reminded of a concert I conducted long ago in London.

77

There was a gentleman of military bearing—indeed, he may have been a military man—sitting near the stage, and when I turned around to bow to the audience, he turned to his companion and said in a loud plangent voice, 'My dear, what's the conductor mean by bowing? It's the orchestra doing all the work.' As I have grown older, year by year, I have realized the force of this whole thrust, and this evening when my old friend, Concertmaster Naoum Blinder, said to me, 'You relax, and let us do the work,' I said, 'I will.' And as you have seen, they have been doing a devil of a lot of work."

The musicians enjoyed working with Beecham and showed their appreciation of his trust in them by doing a bang-up job every time he conducted. He was very careful to choose music that would present no technical problems—he had natural good taste and feeling for tempo—and he left the rest up to us.

Basically, Beecham was a glorified amateur conductor. Born into a wealthy family (Beecham's Little Liver Pills), he was drawn to music at an early age. His wealth made it unnecessary for him to do all the usual menial jobs before reaching a position in the front ranks of conductors in Great Britain. He was very musical and had a great deal of innate intelligence. He never conducted anything in poor taste, but he also never conducted anything requiring more than the most basic conducting technique and musical analysis. He correctly understood the general musical public's desire to hear the 100 famous classic and romantic symphonic works. He featured those along with a sprinkling of English composers such as Delius, and his repertoire was sealed. He didn't venture from this formula and conducted successfully for several decades, pleasing the public, himself, and even, in most cases, the musicians.

The last concert of the 1952 season was also Monteux's last concert as our permanent conductor. It featured, as did every last concert of the seasons that Monteux conducted, the Ninth Symphony of Beethoven. It also included the "Good Friday Spell" from *Parsifal* and the Cesar Franck Symphonic Variations, with Agnes Albert as piano soloist. (Agnes Albert, a vital force in the symphony for many years, was largely responsible for many youth projects of the San Francisco Symphony.)

When Monteux first came to San Francisco in 1935 as general director, he said in an interview, "We are going to rebuild the San Francisco Symphony." These or similar words have been used by every permanent conductor who has taken over the podium, and it was time, now that Monteux was leaving, to evaluate what he had done. There was no doubt that the orchestra had achieved a much higher level of recognition from the music world through his reputation, the recordings, and the transcontinental tour. Monteux had widened the musical awareness of the Bay Area public by his presentation of modern and unusual compositions and by his definitive interpretations of French music.

One estimation of Monteux was the following anonymous statement that was printed on the frontispiece of the final program of the season:

To Pierre Monteux

A Man Who Belongs to the World, But Who Lives in The Hearts of San Franciscans.

The day you came to San Francisco you gave us hope.

In the days that followed you translated that hope into promise.

With the passing years, you have brought the promise to magnificent fulfillment in the greatness of our San Francisco Symphony Orchestra.

Now you are moving on.

The challenge of art, you say, is elsewhere.

You leave behind not only a great musical instrument, but also an example, which will stay fresh always, of the sincere artist's approach to music.

And you leave warm memories in the hearts of thousands.

Go, with gratitude and our blessing.

For the most part, this glowing tribute could be subscribed to by the orchestra. But the musicians had some reservations about Monteux's contribution to the lives of members in the San Francisco Symphony. It was true that our lot had improved because of the success that had come to the orchestra. But it was also true that Monteux was detached from musicians' problems, except when they touched his own life. The orchestra members felt that Monteux could have done much more to better the financial condition of the musicians. Our salaries had gone up from the starvation level when he arrived to poverty level when he left. There was a feeling of sadness in the orchestra that such a great man could have failings that clouded the ideal image we would have preferred.

A final example of Monteux's all-too-human qualities occurred in 1951, when the Israel Philharmonic played in the Opera House as part of their worldwide tour. This was a fantastic organization of musicians culled from the greatest orchestras in Europe—musicians whose lives had been disrupted by the Fascist regimes and then resurrected in Israel. The string sections were especially fine, as they were recruited by the Polish violinist, Bronislaw Huberman, who lured them with promises of good positions in the embryonic orchestra. Conducting this orchestra for the concert in San Francisco was Serge Koussevitzky.

Monteux resented the success of Koussevitzky, especially since he had gained most of his fame in Boston, where Monteux had formerly conducted and had not fared so well. Monteux sat in Box A and saw and heard the orchestra play marvelously under the exhortation of Koussevitzky. Knowing Monteux was in the box and wanting to impress him, the conductor put out a superhuman effort. In fact, it was an effort of such energetic excess that soon after this Koussevitzky suffered a heart attack, and he never conducted again.

Monteux came to our rehearsal the next morning livid with rage and vindictiveness. "I was told that strings cannot sound good in this building, as the hall is too dead. Last night I heard strings of another orchestra, and they sounded tremendously alive—brilliant. I've been watching you string players lately.

Doris and Pierre Monteux at their farewell party, 1952, responding to musicians' good wishes.

The women musicians of the symphony, entertaining at the farewell gala.

Some of you can play and aren't trying. Some of you used to be able to play but can't anymore, and some of you never could play. I'm going to hear each one of you before the end of the season, and we'll see what happens." This time the orchestra members decided they would not take the threat lying down. A meeting was held at the Musicians' Union Hall, and a resolution was passed that said such an audition would not be allowed. The audition was not held. But at the end of the season, members of the committee and other orchestra musicians who spoke out at that meeting were fired. Such a vindictive act did not become a man of Monteux's stature and certainly did not add to his popularity with the musicians.

Nevertheless, a gala farewell party for Monteux was given at the Fairmont Hotel with food and drink and entertainment, which included a performance of the famous cancan by the women of the orchestra. Monteux was absolutely ebullient, making only one statement of regret. "Why did zey wait till I go to do zis for me?" The Monteux era ended in grand style.

We could look back on the Monteux years with happiness and sadness. The mere length of his tenure, from 1935 to 1952, assured a close family feeling between the musicians and their conductor. He was a solid conductor who left behind him an orchestra well schooled in many styles of music. He helped the orchestra develop a special talent that continues even to this day—reading and learning new works well and quickly. The unhappiness was that opportunities were lost. Too often Monteux would settle for "good enough." Occasionally there was a Franck, a Berlioz, a Ravel, or a Brahms piece that gave us a glimpse of those heights we were capable of scaling. But Monteux did not have the drive necessary to insist on that type of performance at all times. He was, perhaps, too civilized to make those difficult demands on us. The San Francisco Symphony was an orchestra well prepared to do the very best, but it was not yet one of the country's great orchestras.

Chapter 9

SEASONS OF DISCOVERY
AND DECISION

As soon as the announcement was made that Monteux was retiring as conductor of the San Francisco Symphony, speculation arose about his successor. Many conductors were mentioned as possible candidates. Would it be another established personality like Monteux, someone just emerging into the upper echelons of the conductor corps, or possibly an unknown whose career would shape and be shaped by our orchestra? There was strong sentiment not to have a conductor who had already established his reputation and would spend his declining years in San Francisco. But there was an equally strong argument that the successor should not be so green that he would have to learn his trade at the expense of the San Francisco Symphony and its public.

The orchestra management tried to circumvent both these arguments by having a two-year buffer between Monteux's departure and the naming of the next conductor. These two seasons were called the "season of discovery" and the "season of decision." It was a clever ploy to convince the public that there would be an elimination contest among a number of conductors, out of which, after the second season the winner would emerge triumphant, wreathed in laurels. What actually occurred was not so clear-cut.

In those two years—1952 and 1953—eleven conductors

took over the podium, but of these, only three or four could seriously be thought of as the next conductor of the San Francisco Symphony.

Georg Solti had just become known in this country. He had conducted in the San Francisco Opera the year before and, at the time, was considered more suited for opera than for symphony. Ferenc Fricsay, a Hungarian conductor who was the director of the Berlin Radio-Orchestra, was considered a promising star of the future. Massimo Freccia, who had guest-conducted in Monteux's final season, came back in the season of discovery, but he was thought by most to be too lightweight for such a prestigious position. One candidate was a complete unknown to both the orchestra musicians and the general public—Enrique Jordá, a Spaniard who was then the conductor of the Cape Town Symphony in South Africa.

It was Jordá who was to open the season of discovery. No greater contrast to Monteux in style, appearance, age, and method of conducting could be found. Jordá was forty years old, Monteux well over seventy; Jordá was flamboyant, Monteux conservative; Jordá was emotional, Monteux, detached. If the management wanted to make a dramatic departure from the past, this was an ideal choice to demonstrate it.

Jordá was born in San Sebastian, Spain, studied in France, and had conducted in many European countries and South America. He was known in the United States only through his records, mostly of the Spanish repertoire. Because of the ebullience of his conducting, Alfred Frankenstein, the critic at the *San Francisco Chronicle*, dubbed him "The Bounding Basque of the Baton." From the very beginning, Jordá received the admiration of the San Francisco critics for his versatility, brilliant interpretation, and musical skill. Dorothy Walker wrote, "After last night's symphony concert, San Franciscans will not soon forget Enrique Jordá, the tall, graceful Spanish conductor, who for the past three weekends has delighted audiences with his spirited conducting."

And, indeed, Jordá did evoke a great deal of enthusiasm from the audience. Just to see a man get on the podium and show such joy in the music he was conducting, to be so obviously involved with all he was doing, brought out a very positive response from a public jaded from the near-perfect, controlled performances of Monteux. Something else seemed to capture the fancy of the audience—Jordá's frequent tumblings. It was a rare concert that his baton didn't fly out into the audience in his excitement. By the time a concert was over, his collar had become detached from his shirt and his tie had found itself hanging under one of his ears. He was covered with perspiration from the moment he lifted his baton for the downbeat, and his feet were often in midair in the midst of a climactic passage. All this endeared him to the public, as a gifted child would be cherished for his awkwardness along with his prodigiousness.

As for the orchestra, the reaction was mixed. True, Jordá's enthusiasm and love of music carried over to the musicians and made it possible to ignore many of his handicaps. He was young, and many of us wanted to give him the benefit of any doubts, in the hope that age and experience would rectify his errors. The older and more cynical musicians, however, saw no possibility that he would eventually emerge as a first-rate conductor. After conducting for three weeks in the season of discovery, Jordá was still an unknown factor. There remained a feeling among us that it was no mere accident of fate that he was the first conductor of the season of discovery.

Coming directly after Jordá was one of the "old masters," Leopold Stokowski, former music director of the Philadelphia Orchestra, who had conducted us in some Art Commission concerts and would now make his debut in our subscription season. His role, at least at this point of his career, was to break down traditions he thought detrimental to good music making. He said, "We are not professors sitting in our attic reading scores for our enjoyment; we are making 'music.' " This breaking away from the expected customs of orchestra playing was manifested in many ways. One of the most obvious was in bowing. There are reasons why string sections arrange the bowings so that all players go up or down at the same time, use the same part of the bow, and articulate exactly alike. This is the only way that phrasing, precision, note emphasis, and type of sound can make each string section sound like one glorious instrument. But precision was not Stokowski's ultimate goal. He wanted to achieve an orchestral sound that would be overwhelmingly lush. He felt that if each string player had more liberty in bowing and phras-

Leopold Stokowski, an iconoclast among conductors, scorned use of a baton. Musician and writer Oscar Levant once commented: "It was a great moment in musical history when Leopold Stokowski discovered his hands."

ing, though the music might lose its rhythmic exactness, he would get the most out of each player. He would, in addition, have blurred all the sharp corners, so that the music, be t Bach or Debussy, would sound like a Monet painting—impression-istic.

Stokowski was not too interested in sticking to the text of the great composers' scores. He would do anything to get the effect he wanted, whether it was what the composer wrote or not, with no apologies. For example, during the rehearsal of Brahms' Second Symphony, he stopped and said, "That cre-scendo and accelerando before the letter B—I'd like you to make more of it." When our concertmaster said, "We haven't any-thing like that in our parts," Stokowski answered in mock dis-may, "Oh, you don't have it marked? Well, I'll take home your parts tonight and mark them. Then you'll be able to play what I ask!"

Stokowski also made changes in our seating arrangement, constantly experimenting to get the best acoustical effect from the orchestra. Since he felt it unnecessary to follow established custom, he did some radical things. During one set of concerts, Stokowski sat all the winds on one side of the orchestra and the strings on the other. Another time, he distributed the strings around the back of the stage, with the winds in front.

In spite of Stokowski's idiosyncracies, the critics recognized his talent, even genius, in conducting a symphony orchestra. Alfred Frankenstein wrote:

> Blindfold tests for music critics will, no doubt, be applied among the tortures of the posthumous hereafter, but one suspects that even a music critic might have been able to tell without looking that Leopold Stokowski was in charge of the San Francisco Sym-phony concert Thursday night at the Opera House. The aural signals of Stokowski's generalship were numerous and unmis-takable, and those that resulted from his unusual seating of the instrumentalists were perhaps least important. Most character-istic of all was the fantastic Stokowskian gamut of shading and its consistently surprising, exceptional, and iconoclastic use.

Although Stokowski was one of the three conductors who appeared in both seasons of guest conductors, I feel he was not given serious consideration as the permanent conductor of our orchestra. His age may have been a factor. There was also a belief that Stokowski would not accept a position with a relatively unknown orchestra in an out-of-the-way place such as San Francisco, after the prestigious posts he had occupied.

It is interesting to contemplate the fate of the San Francisco Symphony if Stokowski had taken over its reins. Certainly it would have been more exciting and more inviting to the public than it had been. Whether, in the long haul, the general level of our music would have been enhanced is a question that can never be answered.

Erich Leinsdorf had come to San Francisco for the first time as a conductor of Wagner for our opera company. He was just twenty-seven years old at the time, and he was already famous for his experience as assistant conductor to Bruno Walter and Arturo Toscanini at the Salzburg Festival. He was subsequently engaged as conductor of German operas with the Metropolitan Opera Company. It looked then as if his career, which had just been launched, would reach great heights. Unfortunately, he had one, almost fatal flaw in his personality. He would get so involved with the music that his judgment would be impaired. This would manifest itself in an uncontrollable temper, both in rehearsal and in performances. He would yell and scream and kick (once getting into trouble with our orchestra by kicking the stand of a clarinet player). This type of unreasonable behavior was the biggest deterrent to what could have been a meteoric career, and he later took steps to overcome it.

When Leinsdorf next guest-conducted for us, in 1952, he was director of the Rochester Philharmonic Orchestra. He gave an interview when he arrived in San Francisco, intelligently outlining the steps to take in finding a conductor for an orchestra. In our case, he felt the geographical remoteness was a handicap. He said that many different orchestras should be heard in a city each year so that audiences will be better able to judge their own. It was rare for an orchestra touring the United States to come to California, and if it did it would most likely play only in Los Angeles. Leinsdorf conducted three weeks of very fine concerts, climaxing with a magnificent performance of Bach's *St. Matthew's Passion*. Many of us felt that Leinsdorf would take the position in San Francisco if all the factors were to his liking, but that our management was not serious about Leinsdorf as our permanent conductor and did not make him an offer.

Leinsdorf was followed by the one-week engagement of Alfred Wallenstein. Wallenstein, who began his musical career as cellist in the San Francisco Symphony, had been the conductor of the Los Angeles Philharmonic and was then a guest conductor with many orchestras. He was very polished and put on first-rate performances whenever or wherever he conducted, but he had a quirk in his rehearsal technique—he cried a lot. He'd stop the orchestra and say in a tearful voice, "My God men, don't you see a piano there? Jesus Christ, you're playing forte," meanwhile holding his head in his hand in a gesture of utter pain. I was sitting with Khuner in the opera on one of these occasions, and Felix said to me, "If he hates music so much, why doesn't he get out of the business?"

Karl Munchinger came to the orchestra preceded by the fame of many fine recordings he made with his Stuttgart Chamber Orchestra. Alas, the man in the flesh did not equal his reputation on wax. When he began conducting at the first rehearsal, we realized that a symphony orchestra would be an awkward instrument for Munchinger to handle. A chamber orchestra, made up of very few select musicians, can, with a little guidance from the conductor, almost play the music itself. But a symphony orchestra, with its vast proportions, must have a strong hand to keep all its diverse forces together. It was abundantly clear that Munchinger was not the man to make this transition.

Most appalling was Munchinger's lack of knowledge of the scores and what to listen for in them. For example, at Tossy Spivakoysky's first performance as a guest soloist in the Brahms Violin Concerto, he went over to Munchinger before starting the third movement and whispered something. It appeared that there was no tympanist on stage. In Munchinger's chamber orchestra there was no need for a tympanist. But in a symphony orchestra, no one is more important than the person who plays the kettledrums. Not only does he establish the rhythmic basis for the composition, his tuned instruments give the harmonic base to the orchestra. That Karl Munchinger neither saw nor heard that the tympanist was missing was proof of his amateur standing in symphony conducting.

The most professional guest conductor that season was George Szell, conductor of the Cleveland Orchestra. It was he who brought that orchestra on a par with the New York, Philadelphia, Chicago, and Boston orchestras, to make it one of the finest in America. There was never a glimmer of hope that Szell would be enticed away from Cleveland to come to San Francisco. If he had come, the history of the orchestra would have taken an entirely different turn. He was a strict disciplinarian; everything he conducted had to be done perfectly—the way he wanted it. There was no room for any vagary by individual players. The string parts were all marked as to bowing and even fingering. Our orchestra, especially after the last years of Monteux, could have used some of that discipline and precision. Szell's programs for his two weeks with us were typical. The first was an all-Beethoven program, consisting of the *Coriolanus* Overture and the Fifth and Sixth symphonies. In his second week, the repertoire was more varied and unusual. Along with the Overture to the Meistersinger and Schubert's Symphony in C was Szell's own orchestration of the string quartet "From My Life" by Bedrich Smetana, his compatriot from Czechoslovakia. This provocative treatment of an already famous chamber work allowed us to play what seemed like a newly discovered Romantic symphony.

The season of discovery ended with two weeks under the direction of Bruno Walter, another noncandidate for the position. The season that started with the youthful exuberance of Enrique Jordá ended with the mature profundity of Walter. Of

90

Georg Solti (left) and William Steinberg (right) both directed the symphony during the "Season of Decision"—the search for a new conductor after Monteux's tenure. Solti later went to the Chicago Symphony, Steinberg to the Pittsburgh Symphony.

the nine conductors on the roster for that season, only three returned for the season of decision—Jordá, Walter, and Stokowski—and of these only Jordá was seriously considered as our future conductor. Along with him, three more conductors were added to that second season: Ferenc Fricsay, Georg Solti, and William Steinberg. All these conductors were warmly received by the public, critics, and orchestra. Fricsay presented two interesting programs, including a local premiere of Frank Martin's Petite Symphonic Concertante. He also demonstrated his outstanding accompanying ability when Arthur Rubinstein played Brahms' Second Concerto with our orchestra.

William Steinberg, who like Leinsdorf directed the opera, was engaged for two weeks. His wit and vivacity set him apart from the intellectual Leinsdorf, despite similar backgrounds. His rehearsals were always pleasurable, too, because of his ability to lighten the seriousness of our work. I remember his insistence on a change of note in the part of a clarinet player who had been playing the wrong note for years. After telling the musician what the note should be, Steinberg said, "I may be wrong, but I don't think so." This quality of not taking himself too seriously endeared him to the musicians and made the tediousness of our rehearsals more bearable. I believe that if a truly concerted effort had been made to get Steinberg as our permanent conductor, he might have come.

With all these conductors shuttling in and out of San Francisco during the years of discovery and decision, the public was supposed to have been kept in a state of excitement and suspense. There were even suggestions from the association that audience members write in the name of their favorite for the post. But rumors began very early, even during the first season, that Jordá was going to get the post. Everything was pointing to him. The newspapers downplayed the other conductors but gave Jordá prominent mention at each of his appearances. The critics, who should have been detached from what was going on in the Opera House, wrote as if they were privy to a secret. All were inordinately kind to Jordá in whatever he did, not mentioning any shortcomings he might have in assuming such a prominent position in the music world. The only fault they found was with his programming, which they hoped would improve if he became the permanent conductor.

In truth, I, like many others, was not averse to having Jordá become our regular conductor. My romantic side imagined this almost completely unknown personality coming out of obscurity and raising himself and the San Francisco Symphony to great heights. Though my reason suggested that a solid, established conductor would do more for the orchestra, my emotional side took over and wanted the charming, gracious, music-loving Spaniard.

J. D. Zellerbach had assumed the post of association president from Leonore Armsby when Monteux left. It was his responsibility to discover and decide on the new general director of the orchestra. Enrique Jordá had come to his attention through some recordings, and when he met Jordá he was fascinated by him and the music he conducted. Zellerbach was certain that this man would be ideal for San Francisco. Being an extremely successful industrialist, he was not used to having his decisions questioned; so when he had finally focused on Jordá, it would have been almost impossible to change his mind Using all his public relations techniques, Zellerbach waited until all possible candidates had been heard to make his announcement that Jordá would be the next conductor of the San Francisco Symphony. The orchestra members looked forward to the next season and the new conductor with a combination of hope, apprehension, and skepticism.

Enrique Jordá, conductor of the San Francisco Symphony from 1954 to 1963.

Chapter 10

OLÉ! JORDÁ

Before the beginning of his first season as permanent conductor of the San Francisco Symphony, 1954–55, Enrique Jordá was interviewed by critics from the major newspapers. He spoke of plans that promised Bay Area music lovers programs they had not heard in the last seventeen years—Spanish music, modern music not suited to Monteux's style, large choral works and certain classical and baroque compositions that had been neglected. As he spoke, the forty-two-year-old Spaniard conveyed a confidence and vitality that his listeners felt would help him bring fresh, new ideas to enliven the city's musical life.

From his first concert, the critics began a campaign of praise for Jordá. For example, Alfred Frankenstein wrote:

> The Beethoven (*Pastoral*) came out under Jordá's baton like a session with a particularly knowing and enthusiastic collector of paintings, embroideries, or old coins. Each modulation, each subtlety of rhythmic transformation and instrumental effect was brought forth as if it were the most remarkable thing that ever happened, and as if the hearer was equal to his guide in the fineness of his connoisseurship.

Such words made it hard to doubt the exciting future that lay ahead.

There were many beautiful concerts under Jordá's direction. His musicality and boundless energy covered up many of his shortcomings, and the musicians, sometimes despite themselves, were inspired by his deep love of the music. Spanish music, which had little exposure in the previous two decades, was brought to the audiences of San Francisco in all its glory. Jordá also conducted large choral works very well. He had been an organist and must have had a great deal of experience with large vocal forces. The compositions, usually religious in nature, were the type he understood both musically and spiritually. In his first season he conducted Handel's *Messiah* with great success, using an excellent group of soloists. Many interesting soloists joined the symphony during Jordá's reign. San Francisco has always had a predilection for pianists, and Jordá indulged the public. In the 1956-57 season, besides Gary Graffman and Arthur Rubinstein, who recorded with us, there was Geza Anda, a Hungarian pianist who played his countryman Bartok's Second Concerto. There was also a concert with Leon Fleisher and Eugene Istomin in which three Mozart concertos were performed—a solo concerto by each of them and a double concerto by both. It might have been too much of a good thing. As my grandson Michael once commented when I was practicing, "Grandpa, I love your violin playing, but even Disneyland you can get tired of." From Italy we were sent the virtuoso pianist Pietro Scarpini, another of the burgeoning number of virtuosos who came to play and then leave without a trace.

One pianist deserving special mention is Glenn Gould, the most eccentric and unusual of all those who played with us. The word genius is bandied about too freely, but it could rightly apply to Glenn Gould, who started playing the piano at the age of three, learning to read notes before words. He was a hypochondriac who indulged in all kinds of rituals: soaking his hands and taking pills before performing, wearing two pair of gloves when not performing, taking his shoes off at times while playing. He arrived at the Opera House with a rolled-up piece of carpet that he put under his feet when performing so the banging of his feet on the stage would not drown out his piano playing. He brought his own very low stool with him and had the piano put on stilts so that he was reaching up to the keys. Despite these idiosyncracies, the beauty and purity of Gould's playing were unmistakable. Bach was his specialty, and if anyone ever thought there was a lack of emotion in the number one "B," he had only to hear Gould to find out the contrary. With us he played Bach's Concerto in F Minor and then, for contrast, the flamboyant *Burleske* of Richard Strauss.

At the end of the 1955-56 season, we had a surprise soloist —Mstislav Rostropovich, the Soviet cellist, playing Prokofiev's Cello Concerto in the first of many appearances with our orchestra. Certain soloists seem to do well with an orchestra and have a special affinity to its members. Rostropovich was one of these. On this occasion he presented each woman of the orchestra with a long-stemmed rose, which has been a traditional symbol of his gallantry. Rounding out the roster that season were two guest conductors, Bruno Walter and Sandor Salgo.

In 1956, the Symphony Foundation was launched. This fund-raising organization offered a number of enticements for people to join. For ten dollars, a member and his family could go to a free concert and also to a contest for young instrumentalists. The contest would have a number of winners, and one or two would have an opportunity to play a solo with the symphony. The first year's winners were Rosalyn Frantz, Robert Mueller, and David Del Tredici, pianists, and George Nagata, violinist. Each of these young people went on to a successful musical career.

Earl Bernard Murray, another local talent, had joined the orchestra as a second trumpet player and later became assistant conductor. A student of Monteux who had won the prestigious "Disciple de Pierre Monteux" award, he was a guest conductor in Jordá's first season. An unfortunate series of events kept this talented man from fulfilling his true potential.

The most interesting novelty that Jordá introduced was Master Peter's Puppet Show of De Falla, a large undertaking that used many different artistic media—singers, mimes, puppets, and oversized scenery. It was well received, as well it might be; for when can one get that much entertainment from a simple, often dull, symphony concert? This was a chance for the San Francisco public to hear and see works of an unusual nature that were denied it during the Monteux years. And so the popularity of the lively, dramatic Jordá continued for most of our audience.

It is axiomatic that every new conductor must rebuild an orchestra according to his image. New, young players must be brought in to replace the "dead wood" that seems to be a blight suffered by all orchestras. Jordá made his first replacement during his second year as permanent conductor—the principal French horn player, Ross Taylor, a local boy who had made good in New York and Cleveland before being considered for this orchestra. In that year, Jordá also brought in a couple of violinists, a violist, and a bass clarinet player. This was just the beginning. In his third season, he brought in new principals in the clarinet, bassoon, and tympani positions, replacing the incumbents with Philip Fath, Walter Green, and Roland Kohloff. He was able to make so many changes so quickly because a pension fund had at last been established, and older people could be retired without too much trauma for either the Symphony Association or the retirees. The initial pension amounts were just a token, but they helped justify important "improvements" to the orchestra.

Along with the replacements came the inevitable reseating of the strings. Each conductor rewarded the string players he liked with good seats, and those he didn't like he shoved to the rear. As for Jordá, he had his own explanation for seating changes. He would say, "Your tone sounds best from that special seat." We were amazed that his knowledge and control of acoustics could place each tone at the exact right spot on stage. He answered those who asked why they were put in the back of the section: "We need strong players, both in back and in front." Fortunately for me, my tone was best suited for the third stand outside the first violin section, the best seat I had ever

had. Because concertmaster Naoum Blinder was troubled with
eye problems and couldn't play most concerts, I spent a good
part of that season in the second stand, inside, which my tone
seemed to accommodate equally well.

Because I was sitting in the second stand, I had the opportunity to play a solo with the orchestra. Maestro Jorcá had
scheduled the Four-Violin Concerto of Antonio Vivaldi and I
played the fourth violin. Frank Houser, my old friend from college days, who was acting concertmaster, played first; Henry
Shweid, my boyhood chum, played second and Ferdinand
Claudio, my partner of many years, played third. We enjoyed
working out the solo ensemble problems at Frank's house. Most
orchestra musicians act very blasé about newspaper criticisms,
but, when it comes to a performance in which they have a personal stake, they suddenly take the reviews very seriously. We
were quite pleased to read, the day after our first performance,
Alfred Frankenstein's commentary in the *San Francisco
Chronicle*:

> In recent years members of the San Francisco Symphony have
> all too seldom been brought forward as soloists with their own
> organization, but four of its first violinists were delightfully displayed Thursday night at the Opera House when they played
> the Vivaldi Concerto in B Minor. . . . The concerto is a bit of
> hot jazz, baroque style. . . . The whole point is to underline the
> individuality of each player in the combo, and in this respect it
> demands precisely the opposite psychology from that ordinarily
> required of symphony violinists. . . . It was given with immense
> gusto, drive, and pleasure in its soloistic give-and-take. The stars
> were Frank Houser, Henry Shweid, Ferdinand Claudio, and
> David Schneider, and a more highly skilled, adept quartet would
> be difficult to assemble.

Despite the various interesting and successful programs,
skepticism about our new maestro's capabilities grew among the
musicians. The optimists among us hoped that, with his
immense knowledge of music, his enthusiasm, his devotion and

99

vitality, Jordá would emerge as a fine conductor. But there were many more who could see no future for the man. His ineptness was becoming more evident to me day by day. All his knowledge served no purpose when he tried to use it in his conducting chores. He had a beautifully lithe body, but his matadorlike poses were not helpful in conveying musical ideas.

Furthermore, Jordá's knowledge of the scores was sketchy. Occasionally, he would conduct a score by heart in a concert, a perilous act on his part. Though he knew the score well enough to conduct it by memory if all went well, one mishap could throw the performance into confusion. He could not right the wrong and still keep the music rolling along; so there would be bars of chaos until we musicians were able to pull it back together again. The modern scores, which Jordá professed to know and wanted to present to the San Francisco audiences, were usually a complete mystery to him. He had an interesting way of preparing these difficult compositions at rehearsal: he avoided working on them until the last possible moment, as if hoping that some divine intermediary would save him from his difficult task.

Rehearsing was the worst facet of Jordá's technique. As we had only eleven hours of working rehearsal time each week, it was imperative to use them in the most advantageous way. The conductor must know how much time should be allotted for each composition on the program. Usually, technical problems should be solved in the first three rehearsals so that the "dress" would be just a run-through with a few touch-ups of trouble spots.

Jordá, however, approached the first rehearsal of the week as though he had all the time in the world. He would start with a standard piece we had played scores of times and play it through with seemingly no problems. Then he would put down his baton and say, "Now, we work!" He would start talking about each bar of music, which instrument should come out and which remain in the background, and the kind of tone he expected in each part—all in a monotonous, steady drone.

Gradually, the musicians would begin talking among themselves, get up and walk around, or clean their instruments, undisturbed by what was going on at the podium. Suddenly, Jordá would stop speaking with the statement, "Now, we play!"

The reaction from the musicians was astonishment: "Where?"

"Where?" replied Jordá. "Where I've been talking. After all, logic is logic." Interspersed in every sentence Jordá uttered was the polite phrase, "Please, thank you." One musician, trying to stay awake, counted one hundred twenty "Please, thank yous" in an hour.

Going into what should have been our dress rehearsal, we might have only played through one or two of the compositions on the program. Again the rehearsal began with the standard pieces we knew so well. By the second hour, we would frantically begin working on the hard pieces, but it was apparent we weren't going to make it. Jordá jumped from one place in the music to another. "Two bars before F, please, thank you; six bars after M, please, thank you." And so it went. During the final fifteen minutes, Jordá kept one eye on the music and the other on the clock. At precisely one o'clock, no matter where we were in the music or what we had not accomplished, he put down his baton and said, "Thank you, ladies and gentlemen. Good luck, tonight!" We needed it. That we got through each concert, sometimes very well, sometimes in a shaky fashion but never completely disastrously, can be attributed not only to Jordá, who put out such a great effort during the concert, but to the professionalism of the orchestra members.

Another problem with Jordá was his poetic rather than practical directions to the musicians. "This must not sound sad; it must sound nostalgic." Even if we agreed with him, there was no way we could translate those directions into action. When we played the *Eroica* Symphony, he said, "This is national grief, not personal grief"—a true statement if ever there was one but what were we supposed to do about it? Musicians, too, feel the emotions in the music, but we must play notes on time, in rhythm, with the right dynamics, and in perfect ensemble—in this way much that we feel is brought out. The rest can be left to the inspiration of the moment and the expressive conducting technique of the maestro. Telling us to play "with all the joy in the world" doesn't help.

In the first week of 1956, our guest conductor was Eduard van Beinum, then conductor in chief of the Concertgebouw Orchestra in Amsterdam. His presence with our orchestra brought us face to face with the difference between our regular conductor and a mature, profound, and capable musician. Though Jordá showed in a dual news conference with van Beinum that he could hold his own intellectually with anyone, the execution of his knowledge had not yet reached the degree of control we wanted so much for him to have.

At the same time, the first stirrings of discontent were beginning to emerge from the heretofore ecstatic audience. Chastised for praising Jordá uncritically, *San Francisco Examiner* critic Alexander Fried commented: "Of Señor Jordá I often write enthusiastically because I find he has most remarkable rare gifts as a creative, imaginative, and passionate interpreter of music. At his best he is inspired." He went on to write that too much importance is given to mere technique. "If a conductor has a limited imagination, he does not need a lot of technique to get what he wants from the orchestra—for he doesn't want much. Whereas a conductor who hears nuances and subtleties in the music that go unobserved by others requires a great deal of technique to bring out from the musicians what his imagination has perceived." (Unfortunately, Jordá did not have that necessary technique.)

What Fried has said is perfectly true. I have played with "hack" conductors who just beat time and do an adequate job but bring nothing of themselves into the performance. However, it is not too much to ask that a conductor who wants certain results should learn how to achieve them. The basic technique of conducting is rather simple; the necessary motions can be not only learned but perfected by a small child. What is difficult is to keep these elementary motions controlled even while trying to be expressive. If the excitement of the music overwhelms the conductor's ability to conduct the piece, then, no matter how vivid the imagination, the results are doomed to failure. One would not condone a violinist who uniquely interpreted a famous piece but played badly out of tune or messed up every technical passage. Nor would one take kindly to a pianist who kept his foot on the pedal during the difficult parts of the music to cover up his lack of finger control. Why should we say a conductor is great despite the fact that he has inadequate technique?

In the middle of Jordá's second season as regular conductor, the orchestra learned through the newspapers that, although his contract had another year to go, Jordá had already been awarded a three-year extension. We had played under his directions for four seasons, and the improvement in his conducting ability and mastery of the scores had not matched our expectations. The general mood in the Opera House was not good, for if we were to spend another three and a half years with this man, and his conducting did not improve, there would certainly be difficult times ahead. Though the eternal optimists among us pointed out his many good qualities, a growing seed of skepticism made us all wonder if Jordá was just a flash in the pan. Was all this jumping and shouting and exhorting just a cover-up for his incapacity to approach music and the act of conducting in a serious, mature manner? We would, willy-nilly, have several years to find the answer to this question.

Chapter 11

DIVISI DISCORDANTE

When Enrique Jordá returned from a triumphant tour of Australia to open our 1957-58 season, the love affair between him and the music critics continued unabated. Meanwhile, the life of the symphony went on.

That year marked the formal retirement of Naoum Blinder as concertmaster. His eyes were giving him more and more trouble, and it was impossible for him to see the music anymore. I received this news with great sadness because I had always admired Blinder, both as a musician and as a warm human being. His violin playing of the Russian school was sometimes a bit wild for my taste, but Naoum was a fine concertmaster, with real leadership qualities. Blinder's students were among the flower of the violinists who emerged from San Francisco, the foremost being Isaac Stern. I was one of the few young violinists to join the orchestra during his time who had not studied with him, but he treated me with equal respect and courtesy. I remember being invited to join him and his brother Boris for afternoons of pinochle. (Blinder always enjoyed a card game, and we occasionally played during intermissions at the Opera House and during runouts on the bus.) Naoum would sit under a lamp with a strong light and for a few hours forget his troubles. There is an old cliché that no one is irreplaceable, but Naoum Blinder was one whose influence would be felt in the orchestra for many a year and whose absence left a noticeable gap.

Naoum Blinder, shown here with guitarist André Segovia, was concert-master from 1932 to 1957. On his retirement, Frank Houser (below) took over and served in the position until 1964.

At his opening press interview of the season, Jordá announced that Frank Houser had been appointed to the post of concertmaster, in which he had substituted with great success the previous year. Frank was a talented, mature, and serious musician, though he did not possess much virtuosic flair. He filled the position exactly the way Jordá wanted it filled, and at no time can I recall any problem between them.

A concert in this forty-sixth season raised an important question in the minds of many: Was the symphony orchestra the important element in the concert, or should it act mainly as an accommodation for soloists? In this concert, Isaac Stern played the Bach Concerto in A Minor. Leonard Rose played the Rococo Variations of Tchaikovsky, and together they performed the Brahms Double Concerto. The orchestra played only one short work, the William Schuman Credendum. It is true that any Brahms concerto allows the orchestra a large stake in the proceedings. But in a concert such as this, with inordinate stress placed on the stars, one begins to wonder if the orchestra is just a necessary addendum—the background against which they can shine. That year a similar problem arose when Yehudi Menuhin appeared as soloist with the New York Philharmonic and, over management's protest, insisted on playing an encore.

There are many reasons why encores are considered poor practice and are virtually never done. The obvious one is that the symphony concert deteriorates into a solo recital with orchestral accompaniment. Another is that a good conductor plans a program very carefully so that each piece fits into a perfectly balanced pattern; throwing in an encore can change the whole scheme of things. Lastly, an encore or two can cause the program to be overly long.

At any rate, Yehudi did play an encore, a movement from a Bach solo sonata, and the symphony management told him not to do it again. In his second performance, Yehudi stubbornly insisted on playing an encore, and the management asked his personal manager to tell Yehudi to cease and desist! The third

Yehudi's Mr. Menuhin Now

The violinist puts away the costume of the child prodigy and dons the uniform of maturity as he prepares to open his season with concerts Thursday evening and next Sunday afternoon at the Memorial Opera House.

Yehudi Menuhin, the first San Francisco prodigy, portrayed by Antonio Sotomayor in the San Francisco Chronicle.

night Yehudi did not play an encore; he made a speech instead. He told the audience he was not allowed to play an encore and continued with a sarcastic remark quite unusual for him: "I am not sure you are allowed to applaud either. I am sure that if Bach could realize what damage two or three minutes of his music could do to the tradition and the budget of this great orchestra, he would be very sorry." This performance recalled a story (which may or may not be true) that I heard when we were both young. Playing for the first time with the San Francisco Symphony Orchestra, Yehudi, a preteenager, asked Alfred

Hertz, the conductor, how much he would be paid. When Hertz said all the soloists received $1,000, Yehudi responded, "I think I should get more than anyone else." Hertz took a dollar bill out of his pocket and gave it to Yehudi so he would be paid more than any other artist. From a young boy this was considered cute, but setting oneself apart from one's fellows is poor taste in a mature artist. (To Menuhin's credit, he did donate his services for a benefit concert when the San Francisco Symphony Orchestra was in financial trouble in the early thirties.)

Another, related, question was brought up at this time: What makes a good listener? This was put to Igor Stravinsky, who was in San Francisco as part of a tour to celebrate his seventy-fifth birthday. Stravinsky commented:

> To be a good listener, you must acquire a musical culture, as in literature. You must be familiar with the history and development of music. To receive music you have to open the ears and wait, not for Godot, but for the music, and to feel that it is something you need. Others let the ears be present and they don't make an effort to understand. To listen is an effort, and just to hear is no merit. A duck hears also.

Also visiting us in 1958 was Alexander Brailowsky, the famous Russian pianist, as soloist in the Rachmaninoff Second Concerto. He was considered perhaps the greatest exponent of this work, a new-Romantic composition that had captured the imagination of audiences almost from its first performance. As in much Russian music, the heart was not only on the sleeve, it was on the fingertips, ready to present to every passerby. We felt fortunate that Brailowsky would record the Rachmaninoff with us. Although this is one of the most popular concertos, it is not easy to accompany. We had played three performances of it, but recording is a different story, as any slight discrepancy in ensemble can easily be detected on a record. At the beginning of every recording session, there are problems of balance and acoustics which must be worked out, and in this case there were further complications. Not approving any Steinway we had in the Bay

108

Alexander Brailowsky, the famous Russian pianist, recorded the Rachmanin-off Second Concerto with the orchestra, the last recording made in San Francisco by Jordá.

Area, Brailowsky had his own piano freighted out from New York for the occasion, at RCA Victor's expense. Jordá's ineptness in accompanying was magnified on the recordings, and we had to do it over several times. All the repetitions began to show on Brailowsky. He began to tire, and mistakes cropped up in his usually infallible performance. After five hours, we finally finished the recording, a mediocre one at best. It was the last record we made with Jordá.

Because of problems like this and many others, we were astonished to learn, again through the media, that the symphony's board of governors had awarded Jordá another five-year contract while the last one still had a year to go. The press, as usual, was ecstatic about the news. Though Alexander Fried acknowledged the controversy concerning this announcement, he said that he, along with a large number of concertgoers, was delighted at the news. Fried praised Jordá for his maintenance of high standards in musical performance and repertoire, for his modesty, for his courtesy, for almost everything. That other concertgoers were outraged to the point of canceling subscriptions, Fried ascribed to their having a more Germanic feeling for music. Actually, the overwhelming majority of the audience as well as the patrons supported the decision, but that, to me, simply denoted the conservative nature of patrons and music lovers. It has not been my experience to see many revolutions started by patrons of the arts.

Fried talked about the orchestra musicians not in favor of Jordá, calling them "grumblers." "No one denies," he wrote, "that Jordá's imagination and subtlety in tone color are supreme. And I have heard no one deny that he has lately brought the orchestra, with a gradual one-third change of personnel, to the best turn of its long career." Mr. Fried should have taken Stravinsky's words about listening more seriously, because many people in and out of the orchestra were denying just these things and more. Fried concluded his article by writing of Jordá, "Until a couple of years ago, critics and public in a number of places gave him the same sort of mixed response he has had in San Francisco. Lately, the tide of favorable recognition of him has become definitely and consistently high. My firm feeling is that he has a destiny as a truly great conductor, here and throughout the world." We in the orchestra had heard completely opposite reports.

The orchestra was in worse shape than I had seen it since I became a member. The rehearsals were getting so ridiculous that no one was paying any attention to them. One strange habit Jordá had was to beat ahead of the music. We would try to catch up to his beat and he would again be ahead of us. It took years after Jordá left for the orchestra to learn to play exactly with the beat.

In spite of these troubles, however, the 1958–59 season had its share of interesting, unusual personalities. In 1957, Van Cliburn had won the Tchaikovsky Competition in Moscow, the most prestigious honor in the world of piano. This precipitated a barrage of media coverage that far exceeded any hitherto afforded classical musicians. Long articles were written about his personality, his reading habits, his religious beliefs, and even occasionally about his piano playing. Less than twenty-two months after his triumph in Russia, Cliburn appeared on the Opera House stage as soloist with our orchestra, playing Mozart's Concerto no. 25 in C, K.503, and Prokofiev's Concerto no. 3.

Everything about Cliburn's appearance was dramatic; even the fact that he could afford to play only one performance with us was dramatic. The audience went wild over him—and why not? Wasn't he an authentic folk hero? He in turn rewarded them with a brilliant performance of Liszt's Hungarian Rhapsody no. 12. It would be good to be able to say that Van Cliburn's piano playing was as marvelous as his publicity led one to believe. But in truth he was simply a very good pianist who happened to be in the right place at the right time. For the sake of political détente, an American had to win that year in Moscow. Had circumstances been different, any number of other competitors might have won. If only his musicanship and piano playing were as great as his personality, he would still be concertizing as much as many of his contemporaries.

During the same week as the Van Cliburn concert, there was a "Pops" program commemorating the 150th anniversary of Abraham Lincoln's birth. For this occasion, Andre Kostelanetz conducted a program that included Aaron Copland's *A Lincoln Portrait*, narrated by Carl Sandburg, the greatest of Lincoln historians. Perhaps Lincoln's words could have been more eloquently spoken by an actor but never more deeply felt or more profoundly understood.

In contrast to the serious nature of these two events, a pension fund concert featured Jack Benny on the violin. No one could epitomize so well the violinist's struggle to negotiate the problems this instrument presents. I've often been asked if Benny really played well but simulated bad playing for comedic reasons. No, he tried as hard as he could, and that was the best he was able to do. When he ran into technical problems, he could turn what to others would be an embarrassment into an immense joke. He once said he would gladly have given up all he'd achieved through comedy to play the violin like a Heifetz or a Milstein. In his program with us, he did bits of "Gypsy Airs" of Sarasate and the Mendelssohn Concerto. At one point in the proceedings, a stagehand wandered onto the stage in his overalls, and Benny handed him the violin while he fixed the stand; to Benny's amazement and consternation, the stagehand whipped off a virtuoso cadenza. The "stagehand" was our old friend Ervin Mautner, who also has a fine flair for comedy. In spite of his cultivated reputation for stinginess, Benny, as had Rudolf Serkin earlier in the season, donated his services to our pension fund. This is not always so; most artists are paid for such concerts, though they may ask for less than their usual fee.

Just two days after the Benny performance, a violinist of a different stature came to play the Brahms Concerto with us. Nathan Milstein has everything it takes to make beautiful music on the violin—a gorgeous tone, an electrifying technique, a deep feeling for the composer's style, and a personality that reaches the audience. At these concerts, however, he felt himself hampered by a clumsy and inflexible accompaniment from the orchestra. He felt that Jordá had given him very poor support for his performances, and he avoided San Francisco for many years after this unfortunate week.

Josef Tal, an Israeli composer experimenting with electronic instruments, came to town about this time. Visiting at the same time was French composer Pierre Boulez, who also was involved

A SPECIAL CONCERT

with the

San Francisco Symphony Orchestra

Enrique Jordá

Conductor and Musical Director

Featuring Guest Soloist

JACK BENNY

to benefit the

San Francisco Symphony Pension Fund

Monday Evening, March 2, 1959, at 8:30

War Memorial Opera House

with these modern devices. Hans Popper, an amateur violinist and successful industrialist with a deep cultural interest, invited Tal and Boulez to an informal debate with Andrew Imbrie and Robert Erickson, composers of music for conventional instruments, on the subject of electronic versus conventional music. The crux of the issue was the role of the performer vis-à-vis the composer, and the main protagonists were Boulez and Imbrie, two of the most knowledgeable musicians extant. Both had a thorough classical music background and a wide education in art and literature.

Boulez spoke of writing music that he wanted played exactly the way he'd conceived it. To perform one of his compositions, he trained the individual instrumentalists personally—musicians who had not already been spoiled by having played music carelessly and thoughtlessly. Despite working with these musicians for months and reaching the point where he felt the music could be taped, the end result was far below his expectations. The human factor was too great a barrier. With electronic instruments, there was no problem in getting the exactness the composer envisioned. He could play four quarter notes and then double the speed and double it again ad infinitum, and they would always be in perfect relationship, one note to another. The same could be done with dynamics, pitch, or any other factor that makes up music. Why deal with a medium so imperfect as a human being?

Imbrie's approach to music was quite different. Although he wrote down his music as clearly and precisely as possible, he welcomed the added element of the performer. He felt that music was incomplete without being filtered through the mind and heart of the performer. Music needed two personalities for its performance, the composer and the interpreter; without the latter, it was just a dry piece of paper with some squiggles on it.

The natural response to this debate by a performer, such as myself, is that Imbrie is right all the way. To me, music doesn't consist only of an orderly arrangement of notes, rhythms, and dynamics. There is a three-way line in communication of music, from the composer through the performer to the listener. And it is not one-directional; there is feedback from performer to composer, information that the aware composer uses to revise that piece or do something different in his next composition. There is even some feedback from the listener to the performer and composer. Music is not static; it is in a constant state of flux through these three essential elements of music making. The experience of the last twenty years indicates that the classical approach has persevered, and electronic music, except as an added factor, has fallen by the wayside.

In 1960, Monteux came "home" again, to conduct the symphony for two weeks. We also made two recordings with Monteux that season, Wagner's *Siegfried Idyll* and Strauss's *Death and Transfiguration*. He was approaching his eighty-fifth birthday, and it was amazing how much of his old power he still retained, conducting by memory with perfect technique. For those of us who had been in his orchestra, time and distance made Monteux even greater than he had been. The new people wondered what all the glorification was about. Still, it was a wonder that he functioned so well at that age.

Until recently, it was taken for granted that upon reaching the age of sixty-five, a person would retire and live out his life in quiet relaxation. But here was living proof that a man can use his brain and talent long past this arbitrary milepost. What is it about conducting that allows a man such a long and productive life? For not only Monteux but Toscanini, Fiedler, Stokowski, and hosts of others were professionally active in their seventies and eighties, some even into their nineties. A lot of thought has been given to the answer. All in all, the work is strenuous enough to keep you healthy, fulfilling enough to give you satisfaction, important enough to give you a sense of power, and admirable enough to give you a sense of pride. And most of all, you are a musician making music in the best possible fashion.

Having Jordá as our leader did bring us some extra bonuses. Because he was a Spaniard through and through, we performed the whole gamut of Spanish music. Additionally, we were visited by several Spanish soloists. Two of the most famous were part of our roster in the 1959–60 season.

Andre Segovia, the first name that comes to mind when the classical guitar is mentioned, made one of his many appearances with us that year, playing the Concerto in D by Castelnuovo-Tedesco and the Sonatina by Frederic Moreno Torroba. There is no disputing that Segovia was a remarkable and innovative guitar player. Unfortunately, performing with a symphony orchestra at the Opera House, he couldn't be heard. The only advantage to appearing there was that a great number of people could come to see him and pay him honor.

The other world-famous Spanish dignitary who appeared with us that year was Pablo Casals, who had done for the cello what Segovia had done for the classical guitar. Casals had come, however, not as a cellist but as a conductor and composer. On the program were two of his latest compositions, "The Three Magic Kings" from his *Christmas Oratorio* and "Sardena," performed by sixty-four cellists.

A former member of the orchestra was honored by the San Francisco Symphony toward the end of the 1959–60 season by having two of his compositions performed while an exhibition of his paintings was shown at the Opera House. The composer and artist was Emanuel Leplin, who had been stricken six years before by bulbar polio. Hospitalized for eight months, he emerged able to move only his head and two fingers and the thumb of his right hand. This would have been a terrible blow to anyone, but for Emanuel, it was devastating. I had known Emanuel since our early teens, and he was one of the most vital persons I've ever known. He had won the prestigious Prix de Paris for composition, and while in France he had met Monteux and Darius Milhaud and studied with them. Upon his return he became a member of the viola section in the symphony. He conducted the symphony in many of his compositions, and his *Comedy* was part of our 1947 tour repertoire. After his polio attack he could not leave an iron lung, but Emanuel had a strong will. He began to paint holding a brush between his teeth. Soon he started writing music, holding his pen between his thumb and fingers and moving the paper with a rubber tip he wore on his middle finger. The compositions we played that week, and the paintings on exhibit, had all been done after he had contracted polio.

The beginning of the 1959–60 season had found the orchestra in deep financial trouble. For the first time in several years the season was expanded, from twenty-two to twenty-four weeks, and the basic musician's salary was raised to $3,000 a year. This, along with the accumulated deficit of $71,000, brought out a cry for help to raise $225,000—or there would not be another season! This threat had been used in almost all of our contract negotiations with the association. Now the Bay Area public was threatened with the loss of its symphony unless every citizen came through with some kind of donation. In the orchestra's early days, the budget was so small that a few wealthy families could make up the deficit, but now we were getting into higher finance. The bigger the deficit, the more difficult the task of management to meet it. There is no doubt that the financial problems of a symphony orchestra are extremely complex. The ticket sales cover, at best, no more than half the expenses incurred in presenting concerts to the public. The rest must be made up from donations, grants, subsidies, and so on. At any rate, the public responded sufficiently, and the musicians continued to exist on minimal rations; so the orchestra season did go on.

It didn't go on in peace, however. For the first time, a public acknowledgment of the bitter war between the proponents and opponents of Jordá was brought out in an article by Alexander Fried. The question was how the problem could be handled without permanently damaging the music scene in San Francisco. The association's extension of Jordá's contract for an additional five years had made the mood of part of the public ugly. Some people were actually withdrawing or threatening to withdraw their patronage from the symphony. Others said they would attend only when there was a guest conductor. Fried proposed a novel solution: an opposition committee on the board of governors could take up ideas contrary to the establishment's and try to have them openly and fully discussed. The public, instead of fighting from the sidelines, would have an avenue for expression through established channels. Needless to say, that idea was never tried.

In spite of all these problems, the newspaper critics' wrap-up at the end of the season had more pluses than minuses. The emphasis was put on *what* music had been played rather than *how* it had been played. Suggestions were made to add more modern music from the Bay Area and have more local soloists (perennial suggestions by the critics). There were references to the need for improved personnel within the orchestra but absolutely no mention of the need to change or improve the conducting situation. We in the orchestra, however, could not avoid hearing public rumblings that indicated all was not well with our symphony and its leadership.

Chapter 12

DIMINUENDO AL-NIENTE

An article written by Alexander Fried before the opening of the 1960–61 season gave the first indication of a break in the solid pro-Jordá front of the San Francisco reviewers. To be sure, he did not come out and say that Jordá had proven himself unworthy of the job, but he did imply that the symphony's problems may have started with its leadership. Response to this article ranged from praise of Fried for airing the problems to criticism for his not being more specific about Jordá's role in the situation. There was no doubt that the music-listening public was aroused by this issue. Many patrons had canceled their subscriptions and others wouldn't attend the concerts Jordá conducted, further clouding the frequently dim financial picture. The musicians, themselves, were terribly frustrated. As we started the first of four more seasons of the same problems, we couldn't see the light at the end of the tunnel.

The forty-ninth season had its share of violin soloists. The first was Soviet violinist Leonid Kogan, who made his debut with the symphony that season. Christian Ferras was another newcomer to our city. This Frenchman was a marvelous instrumentalist, but his claim to fame, as far as we were concerned, was the introduction of the Alban Berg Violin Concerto to San Francisco audiences. The third violinist who was not a regular on our program was Erica Morini. There was more than the usual local interest in her appearance, because she was the sister of the well-known San Francisco pianist and teacher, Alice

Morini, the wife of our former assistant concertmaster, William Wolski.

Jordá and the association did some other unusual programming in order to feature some of our symphony members as soloists. The first of these was Frank Houser, our concertmaster. He was playing solo for the first time, and the vehicle he chose for his debut was the *Four Seasons* of Vivaldi. This interesting work tends to be neglected by traveling artists since it is not very flashy. It is up to the local violinist, usually the concertmaster, to give the audience an opportunity to hear such works. Frank did a fine job, bringing out all the effects called for by Vivaldi, but he was happy when his stint was over. He felt much more comfortable sitting in the orchestra than standing in front of it.

Paul Renzi, our principal flute player, and Ross Taylor, Jeremy Merrill, Herman Dorfman, and James Callahan from the horn section were also featured players.

The 1960–61 season again brought us several guest conductors. Monteux conducted for two weeks, once again amazing his audiences with some of the music he had all but patented—the Symphonie *Fantastique* of Berlioz, *Jeux* of Debussy, and *Til Eulenspiegel's Merry Pranks* of Richard Strauss.

That season marked the local debut of Josef Krips, who came for only one week. Nearing his sixtieth year, Krips was at the top of his career. At that time he was conductor of the Buffalo Philharmonic, but the feeling was that he was waiting for a post with one of the big orchestras to open up. His whole background was based on the Austro-Germanic tradition, of which we had not had too much since the Alfred Hertz era. At that point, we had no idea we would become much more intimately acquainted with Krips in the not too distant future.

Also conducting that season, but only his own work, was Leon Kirchner. This was his Concerto for Piano and Orchestra, with Eugene Istomin as soloist. The circumstances of Kirchner's performance were unusual in two respects. First, Kirchner was not noted for his conducting, and second, unlike Monteux, Jordá conducted almost all the modern works. Kirchner, however, felt that Jordá had so distorted a work of his in the past that he wanted to conduct this one himself. Kirchner's concerto was a huge success, despite its modern nature. It was a piece that would bear repeating in a subsequent season so that it could become familiar to the orchestra and especially to the public. But a modern work, no matter how fine it is, is almost invariably heard only once. Alfred Frankenstein once started a fund to have second performances of worthwhile modern pieces presented by the symphony. I don't recall anything coming from his idea.

In the middle of the season, Frankenstein again took on the role of defender of the royal throne or its occupant, Enrique Jordá. With the increasing brouhaha about the worthiness of the maestro to remain in his post, Frankenstein wrote a learned treatise on the role of the permanent conductor compared to that of a guest conductor. The latter had it easier, Frankenstein contended, because he was in each city for just one or two weeks, could pick the repertoire he knew best, and could usually get out of town before his weaknesses showed up. The permanent conductor, on the other hand, had to appear week after week conducting a varied repertoire, not all of which he could be expected to master. Yet, with all that, wrote Frankenstein, Jordá was able to introduce many works, both old and new, never heard before by our audiences. And his improvements in the orchestra's personnel (more than half the members of the present ensemble had been brought in by Jordá) were all to the good. Frankenstein predicted that "if a new conductor were to come in tomorrow, very few of Jordá's appointments would be changed." This statement alone cast doubts on Frankenstein's knowledge of the nature of conductors.

The season ended with open verbal warfare between the critics from the two leading San Francisco newspapers. Fried fired the first shot by pointing out that the symphony was seeing a lot of empty seats, and many patrons were withdrawing their usual donations because of disenchantment with Jordá and the realization that he would be with the orchestra for another three years. He noted that George Szell, an excellent maestro, would be coming for two weeks the next season, and, for the good of the orchestra as well as the audience, it might have been wise to engage him for at least half the season.

Frankenstein took umbrage at almost everything Fried had written and replied in an extremely unfriendly manner. He cited some very inventive programs of Jordá's and wrote, "Programs like that ought to arouse the interest of a musically cultivated public. If they fail to arouse interest, one can only conclude that the public to which they are offered is not very cultivated." He suggested that it was not Jordá's fault that the houses were bad but a combination of an unknowledgeable audience and a vindictiveness on the part of some elements of the press. Frankenstein said he felt reluctant to enter this territory because

> we like to encourage a wide latitude of opinion in San Francisco's musical criticism—but this is way out of bounds. I become alarmed, not only for what such criticism may do to the orchestra, but also for the integrity of my own profession in San Francisco. What is involved here is not at all a matter of opinion, but a matter of fact. And when I read similar distortions of fact over and over, I can only conclude that a campaign of vilification is being directed against Jordá similar in method and identical in aim to that with which a newspaper of the same chain drove the late Sir Thomas Beecham from Seattle.

Thus, with a few sentences in defense of Jordá, Frankenstein questioned the culture of the San Francisco audience, the knowledge and integrity of his fellow reviewer, and the motives of an entire chain of newspapers.

Fried's reply to this diatribe contained a few sentences that could be used as criteria for critics:

> Now as for the integrity of critics, let each man answer for himself, in his work day by day and year by year, covering the local scene. Let the answer be measured by the patient attention the critic pays to everything in that music that is laid before him. Let

it be measured by his will to hear the qualities of music clearly and objectively, regardless of whether the music may be produced by friends and professional associates. Let it be measured by his resolute independence from the institutions he is writing about.

(This last sentence was a reference to Frankenstein's assignment for twenty-five years as annotator of the symphony programs.)

The general tone of these remarks could well serve to test the sincerity of critics' commentaries. Is the critic too involved in the proceedings to offer a detached judgment? Has he come to the concert with preconceived ideas and expectations? Can he treat each performance independent of any other he has heard and judge it by itself? These questions must be resolved positively if criticism is to be taken seriously. There is nothing wrong with a difference of opinion between two critics. After all, each has his own background, his own set of musical values, and his own ears to judge with, and it would be curious if critics agreed on everything. The problem lies in what the critic is listening to, the actual concert or his preconception of that concert.

One unfortunate by-product of this explosive situation was that two fine gentlemen, tops in their profession, allowed their differences of opinion to become so acerbic that they ruined a beautiful friendship. For years they would not talk to each other, and hostesses were very careful not to invite them both to the same party.

Such animosity was a far cry from the unanimous praise with which critics had greeted the symphony's inaugural concert in 1911. The exact program—the Prelude to *The Mastersingers of Nuremberg* by Wagner, the Symphony no. 6 *Pathetique)* of Tchaikovsky, the Theme and Variations from the *Emperor* Quartet of Haydn, and *Les Preludes* of Liszt—was played again in a special Gala Concert opening the Golden Jubilee season of 1961–62. This program might be considered "old hat" and Pops to a modern audience, but it was quite a different experience for an audience in 1911. In fact, the Tchaikov-

sky was written only eighteen years before the first San Francisco performance. Though we may be satiated with records of
these classics, the populace of the early part of the twentieth
century did not have that privilege. Nor were concerts as preva-
lent then as they are now. The entire first season of the San
Francisco Symphony consisted of thirteen concerts; by 1961,
the symphony performed over ninety concerts a season.

The Jubilee performance of this concert, conducted by
Jordá, was again reviewed by the two chief critics, who as usual
heard what seemed to be two different concerts at the same time
and place.

The Symphony Association used the occasion of the Jubilee
season to bring back many of the child prodigies who had
launched their careers in San Francisco—violinists Yehudi
Menuhin, Isaac Stern, and Ruggiero Ricci; pianists Samuel Lipman and Ruth Slenczynska—and some newcomers from the
Bay Area, including violinists David Abel, Jeanne Marvin, and
Austin Reller. Pierre Monteux was brought back for another
two-week engagement, and an aspiring young conductor,
Thomas Schippers, was brought to San Francisco for a second
time. Aram Khachaturian was scheduled to conduct the program on which Ruth Slenczynska was to perform his concerto.
He bowed out, however, which was not unusual for Soviet
artists, and an extremely young genius from Japan was engaged
to substitute. His name was Seiji Ozawa, and he had recently
been assistant conductor to Leonard Bernstein in New York.
Underneath Ozawa's terpsichorean splendor, it was clear that
this was a solid musician who would have to be reckoned with
in the future.

Another guest conductor that season was one of Jordá's
favorite compatriots, Pablo Casals. The first time he conducted
with us, a year earlier, Casals was doing only works for a large
body of cellos; so this was the first time the rest of us had an
opportunity to work with him. He had been a legendary cellist
who late in life began to conduct. A clique of idol worshippers
surrounded him, and he began to believe what they were saying

—that he was the all-knowing guru of music—and issued categorical proclamations that were never challenged. He seemed to be a nice old gentleman of eighty-six or so, but I was bothered by the people who hung on his every word.

The guest conductor who carried the greatest impact that season was George Szell, the man whose name had aroused such hostility between Fried and Frankenstein. Szell was known for the strict discipline he imposed on his orchestra. Before we were through a half hour of rehearsal, we realized that the nonchalant, frivolous attitude we developed over the Jordá years would have to go immediately! We were expected to play the right notes at the right time with the correct dynamics—before we even started rehearsing. We were expected to take our parts home to study and bring them back with all the technical problems solved. There was a story that at home in Cleveland Szell would peek out of his office window in the auditorium to see which musicians were taking the music home—and vice to those who didn't. It might have been a bit exasperating at first

Cleveland conductor George Szell caused a scandal when he disapproved of the "state of musical affairs" in San Francisco.

125

to work under a martinet like that, but, as the week worked down to the concerts, we began to find pleasure in the realization that we were capable of performing some decent, clear, and polished concerts after all.

When we arrived for the first rehearsal of Szell's second week of concerts, whom should we see on the podium but our old friend Enrique Jordá. We were told that Szell had become ill and fatigued and would not be able to conduct the second week of his engagement. We looked at each other in amazement. Within moments after the rehearsal started, we realized that all we'd accomplished in the last week had been lost. We were back in kindergarten. Discipline was abandoned, and as Jordá was patiently explaining the music of Beethoven's Sixth and Brahms' Second symphonies, the musicians were paying as little attention to him as senators to a filibuster.

The word was out about the defection of Maestro Szell, and suspicions circulated about the real reason for his premature departure. Szell himself would grant no interviews, and the official explanation stated categorically that he was badly in need of a rest.

Frankenstein was not satisfied. He wrote Szell asking for certain clarifications along with explicit suggestions for Szell to follow in order not to leave any doubt in people's minds about his withdrawal. Szell was furious at Frankenstein's presumption and not only answered him but sent copies of the entire correspondence to his rival paper. The correspondence follows:

March 24, 1962

Dear Mr. Szell:

Many thanks for your extremely kind and thoughtful letter. We were very much distressed, of course, to learn that you could not conduct here this week, and hope you had a good refreshing rest. We are all very sorry that we could not hear you this week, and I personally also regret very much that we could not lunch together.

As the enclosed telegram [an internewspaper message seeking further information about Szell's unexpected departure] indicates, there has been a grand crop of rumors all over the country about your withdrawal from the local scene, and this has not been at all good for the San Francisco Symphony. It would, therefore, be a just, proper and pleasant gesture if Mr. Jordá could be invited to serve as guest conductor in Cleveland next season. I hastily add that I propose this entirely on my own and that Jordá would be furious at me if he knew I was doing it.

In a letter of March 26, Szell replied:

Dear Mr. Frankenstein:

Up until this moment I have tried to be as polite and discreet as possible about my early departure from San Francisco. Your letter of March 24th, however, contains a tactless provocation which compels me to step out of my reserve.

Since your pressure to tell me what would be a "just, proper and pleasant" thing to do, I feel forced to say that your delicate dual position as Music Critic of the *Chronicle* and Program Annotator for the San Francisco Symphony, which in itself is liable to cast grave doubts upon your objectivity, should have prompted you to exercise particular restraint in this matter. It is entirely out of order for you to suggest my taking a step designed to be interpreted as implicit approval of what I found to be the saddest state of musical affairs I have encountered in any American or European city during the almost fifty years of my active conducting career.

Since you have reopened this question which I thought had closed, and because it is a matter of public interest, I reserve the right to make our correspondence accessible to other persons.

J. D. Zellerbach, president of the Symphony Association as well as founder of the paper company bearing his name, took exception to Szell's statements. Among other things, he said, "He sounds a little bilious to me. . . . I think the man is immature." Zellerbach was extremely sensitive to criticism of "his" symphony and "his" conductor. I had heard one story about his

127

reaction to the vitriolic criticism of Jordá by Alan Rich on the public-owned radio station KPFA. When the station refused to bow to his demands that Rich be silenced, Zellerbach threatened to withdraw his company's contributions to KPFA.

"We'll be very sorry if that happens," the station manager replied, "but we must maintain the integrity of the station."

"Well, that's that!" remarked Zellerbach.

The station manager called his entire staff together and said, "I have an important announcement to make."

Everyone waited breathlessly for what was to come. The manager said, "Mr. Zellerbach, the paper magnate, called. There will be *no more toilet paper.*"

Many orchestra members were hurt by what Szell had said. They thought we'd played very well for him by the time the concerts came and that he hadn't rewarded them for their extra effort to make his performances successful. But some of us had entirely different views of what had transpired. We thought that something as strong as dynamite was needed to effect a change in the symphony leadership, and Szell provided that dynamite. Despite Zellerbach's protests to the contrary, it was now clear that Jordá would have to go. The pressure from all sides was too much for even his staunchest defenders to withstand. It was Zellerbach's unhappy duty to inform Jordá that his contract was to be prematurely terminated. He would stay one more year as conductor of the San Francisco Symphony; the rest of his contract was bought back from him.

Everyone seemed relieved that this period of chaos in our orchestral history was soon to end. Even Jordá might have secretly welcomed the end of all this strife and conflict. He had come into his tenure with the orchestra the most urbane of men. His every statement was a sign of the civilized gentleman he was. But the pressure and the criticism that had been leveled against him, and his own realization of what a difficult task he had before him every week, had levied its toll. His veneer of politeness began to wear off, and he would snap at us and scream whenever things didn't go his way. It must have been apparent, even to him, that he had undertaken too big a job when he accepted the position as conductor of the San Francisco Symphony.

This time there would be no buffer years of discovery and decision. The Symphony Association made a quick search for a conductor who could bring a degree of order and stability to the affairs of the orchestra, and it was fortunate to obtain the services of Maestro Josef Krips, the most conservative, conventional, and classically based conductor available. With him we would leave the rough seas with the Spanish Armada and reach calm and gentle waters where no more disasters could overtake us.

Chapter 13

EXTRACURRICULAR ACTIVITIES

Though being a member of the symphony may have satisfied the soul, it certainly could not supply all the necessities of life. Each musician had to find some other way to fill his pocketbook and round out his life. Because of the symphony's erratic hours (morning rehearsals and evening concerts), it was not possible to take another full-time job. I tried both selling and stockbroking part time and was a stunning failure at each.

There is one field that most symphony musicians get into sooner or later—teaching. I gave my first lesson when I was in the fourth grade in grammar school. I had been playing the violin for about four or five years, so I considered myself well versed. My student was a most unlikely prospect, one of the tough kids in school who was involved in daily fights. But having heard me play the violin, Butch decided he would like to also. He asked how much I would charge, and I gave him the first number that came to mind—one dollar. He had no violin, so he used mine. In that first lesson, I taught him how to hold the violin and bow and how to play all the notes on all the strings in the first position. Convinced he had learned everything there was to learn on the violin, Butch paid me forty cents toward the lesson price and left, never to return. (I believe that after fifty years, the remaining sixty cents is an uncollectable debt.)

The next time I ventured into the field of pedagogy was during my college days. I was living at my grandparents' house in Oakland, and I put a handsome sign reading Violin Teacher in the front window. No students came to me, but I was offered a playing engagement. A pianist saw the sign, rang our bell, and told me that some violin and piano music was needed at the German Consulate. This was in 1935, when Nazism was just beginning to be heard about in the United States, but the pianist assured me that it was just a club of German Americans with no connection to their European compatriots. When I arrived at the building, however, a Nazi flag was flying in front of it, and no amount of persuasion could make me enter.

Though it was easier getting students after I became a member of the symphony, it was still very slow going. My initial price for lessons was that same dollar, but now I received the entire payment. It was difficult at that stage to determine who was being cheated, the teacher or the student, for I was learning as much as I was teaching. The process of teaching requires a great deal of patience from both parties. Teaching music can be a very personal matter, a musical instrument even more so, and the violin the most personal. When I see a young student start to learn the violin, I shudder to think of the formidable task ahead of him. I often say to my students, "Learning to play the violin is very difficult at the start. But with each step you take upward it becomes more difficult, until you get to the stage where I am, when it becomes impossible."

Over the years I taught at both the San Francisco Conservatory of Music and San Francisco State College (later San Francisco State University). I was also on the staff of the University of California at Berkeley and at Lone Mountain College in San Francisco; in both these cases, students would study with me at home and get credit at their respective schools. My private student class was growing also, so some years I had no free afternoons. In 1967, I took a leave of absence from the opera to teach and play chamber music under the direction of Darius Milhaud at Mills College.

One of the courses I most enjoyed teaching at San Francisco State was violin playing for non-violin-playing music majors.

There were no specific goals for this course, but my students were talented in music and open to any ideas I could give them about playing the violin. For students who eventually hope to become proficient on the violin, each step must be very slowly undertaken so they don't get into bad habits. In this case, I had no such restraints. In fifteen weeks, I would try to instill as much about the art of playing the violin as I could, without regard to their ability to perform each technique, and they learned much more about violin playing than they might have expected.

At one time I had a student who was sent from the government of Saudi Arabia to study at San Francisco State for the summer. Among his courses was one I was giving, a group of six lessons on the violin. He was a very musical young man but had never played the violin before, so too much could not be expected from this experience. At the end of the course, I asked him what he was going to do with the violin, now that he had gotten started. He answered, "I'm going back to Saudi Arabia to teach others how to play the violin." I'm not anxious to hear the premiere of the Saudi-Arabian Philharmonic, if those grand-students of mine constitute the violin section.

During the years I have been teaching, hundreds of students have studied with me. There has often been frustration when we were unable to get past a certain level of playing, but there were also many happy times when a student reached the point where good music was coming from the violin. The pleasure a teacher has in seeing a student do well compares to a parent's feeling for his child. And many of my "children" are now holding down positions in various symphony orchestras around the country. My former student, Amy Lozano, is now sharing the fourth stand, first violin, with me. I derived almost as much satisfaction when a not so talented student, by our mutual perseverance, would raise his playing to the level where he could enjoy performing with amateur chamber music groups or small, local orchestras.

Along with teaching and performing in the symphony, it was necessary for me to do some serious violin work to keep up my own playing skill. When I entered the orchestra at the tender age of eighteen, some well-meaning friends said to me, "That's the end of your growth as a violinist. An orchestra is the cemetery where talent is buried." The smaller the group one plays in, the greater the personal responsibility of each player, and it is true that one can be submerged in a large string section, where technique and tone can deteriorate very rapidly. To avoid that, I engaged in a number of activities that were not financially remunerative but afforded me great personal satisfaction. One of these was the California String Quartet, which helped my playing immensely. I was also a member of the Little Symphony of San Francisco, a group of musicians, mainly from the San Francisco Symphony, who played chamber orchestra music under the direction of Gregory Millar. We played many interesting concerts and even did some recording.

Another chamber orchestra I played in was organized by the first cellist in our quartet, George Barati. We had a series of concerts every year which he planned and conducted and for which he was able to get sufficient backing. After lengthy consultations about grandiose, fanciful, and imaginative names for the new group, George found the perfect name for his ensemble —the Barati Chamber Orchestra. We started the concerts on a very high plane and kept up the standards throughout the ensemble's existence. The Barati Chamber Orchestra might still be going if George hadn't received the "call" to go to Hawaii and conduct the Honolulu Symphony.

Succeeding this group was the San Francisco Chamber Orchestra under the direction of Edgar Braun, a lawyer and accountant as well as a conductor. We played interesting music with him, but the standards were not quite as high as with the Barati ensemble. There was one memorable occasion when the concertmaster suddenly became catatonic and couldn't leave his car. I was pressed into playing concertmaster in the *Verklaerte Nacht* of Schoenberg, with only two hours rehearsal for the entire program.

I also belonged to the San Francisco String Ensemble, an

organization of thirteen players from the symphony, molded after the Zagreb String Ensemble of Antonio Janigro. This group had no official leader, but the organizer and first, first violin (I hesitate to say concertmaster of such a small group) was Zaven Melikian, an Armenian born in Yugoslavia who had lived in Beirut and Paris before coming to the United States. Getting thirteen musicians to play together without a conductor, especially when all are supposed to be equal, is an arduous task and requires a great many rehearsals. Tempers flare, as each person has his own idea about musical style, tempo, articulation, and all the other problems that must be solved in order to make good music. Many of our rehearsals were held at Zaven's house, and I remember not only the arguments but the marvelous Armenian food his mother cooked. One of the sponsors of the ensemble was George Mardikian, a well-known restaurateur and self-styled diplomat. Our dress rehearsal was held at his restaurant, Omar Khayam, where we were again regaled with succulent viands, so that this enterprise fed our bodies as well as our souls. We gave a number of critically successful concerts, but the String Ensemble was a time-consuming and thus expensive operation and unfortunately did not have a broad enough base to support it; so it existed only two seasons.

In addition to all this, I gave a violin recital or a series of recitals at least once a year. In 1960, Reina Schivo, the symphony pianist, and I played a series of four concerts in Monterey, performing eighteen Mozart sonatas. I repeated this in 1961 at the San Francisco Conservatory of Music, this time with William Corbett Jones at the piano. At San Francisco State my recitals were intended to be educational as well as entertaining. One year, a group of the wind and keyboard faculty joined me in a series of trios. Paul Renzi, flute, Bruce Franklin, harpsichord, and I played a sonata from the *Musical Offering* of Bach; Don Carroll, clarinetist, and Carlo Bussotti, pianist, played *Contrasts* of Bartok with me; and James Callahan, horn, Bussotti, and I did the Brahms Horn Trio. The Frank De Bellis Library of the college presented an all-Busoni program in which

Bussotti and I played the *Grand Sonata*. This virtuoso work is seldom played, and I was happy to add it to my repertoire. On another program, Karen Rosenak and I did two great twentieth-century sonatas, the Bartok Second and the Duo Concertante of Stravinsky. With Deborah Cohen I did an all-Israeli program, playing music I had found during one of my trips to Israel. None of these were great box-office programs, but a college is a place where unusual ideas and experimental programs should be presented.

From those early days of attempting to be a salesman, I reached the point where I spent most of my spare time with the violin, teaching and playing recitals. When I became a member of the symphony, I had just barely qualified, and to keep up with the progress the symphony was making I had to improve my own work. All these extracurricular activities in small ensembles, solo playing, and even teaching contributed toward making me a better violinist and a more well-rounded musician.

Josef Krips, conductor of the San Francisco Symphony from 1963 to 1970.

Chapter 14

KRIPS, THE BENEVOLENT DESPOT

The 1963–64 season started a new era in the history of the symphony in San Francisco. Josef Krips came to our orchestra with excellent credentials. The word we generally heard was "Krips is a thorough professional. He knows his business. He is a fine conductor." Alan Rich of the *New York Herald Tribune* wrote: "The particular kind of musicianship that Josef Krips brings to the podium is something to cherish. Treasure it, there aren't many like him these days."

Krips himself, in speaking about his aspirations for the orchestra, said:

> I hope to create a situation in which every individual in the orchestra feels he is singing with his instrument. . . . I do not allow the musicians to just play notes they see in the score. They may do that very well but if that is all, it is nothing. I teach them the singing approach. The method, properly applied, can change the tone of an orchestra in one minute.

Alexander Fried outlined what he thought the aims of the Krips regime should be: to increase concert attendance to inspire loyalty and enthusiasm so as to bring new support from patrons, bequests, and foundations; and to steadily improve the quality of the orchestra.

Krips certainly had a great background from which to

accomplish these aims. At nineteen years of age, he was a choir-master of the Vienna Volksoper. That same year he conducted his first opera, Verdi's *Masked Ball*, and his first full-fledged concert. His star kept rising in the musical heavens. He had done a great deal of recording, and we hoped he would revive our flagging recording experience. Over the last few years, he had raised the Buffalo orchestra to a higher level than it ever had been. Krips was known as the "builder of orchestras," and he was brought in to rebuild ours.

I believe that Josef Krips was promised a great deal in order to attract him to the San Francisco Symphony—not only a high salary but the freedom to do what he wanted with the orchestra. To help him make changes, management instituted, for the first time in the orchestra's history, a mandatory retirement age of sixty-five. Thus, before Krips even started his first season, there were five openings to be filled. Needless to say, the musicians felt this was unfair, and a protest meeting was held to forestall the new policy. We knew that our new conductor was almost sixty-two years old but would not be forced to retire at sixty-five. We felt that as long as a musician fulfilled his job and his playing did not deteriorate, he should be allowed to remain. It was incongruous that a man could be good enough to play in the orchestra at the age of sixty-four years but incompetent the day he became sixty-five. Management argued that this arbitrary retirement was successful in industry, so why shouldn't it be used in symphony orchestras? Furthermore, they contended, most musicians would want to continue forever, and it would be difficult to say one could stay because he still played well while the next couldn't stay because he didn't play well. All our arguments came to naught, and we lost our case.

Before his first season, Krips held auditions for openings created by the retirements. Among these was the principal viola position, and I decided to take a stab at it. Some of the violists opposed anyone local trying out for the spot, because they believed Krips had already chosen musicians from the East for the "important" positions and he shouldn't be given the satisfaction of this feeble gesture. But I was naive, as usual, and thought that if I played well enough it would change Krips' mind. My playing seemed to please him, but the naysayers' prediction was correct. It was later revealed to us that Krips had already chosen his first violist, as well as several other important positions.

The replacements in personnel were not the only changes in the symphony. J. D. Zellerbach had died and his place as president of the Symphony Association was filled by Philip Boone. Joseph Biskind had replaced Alfred Frankenstein as program annotator. The most dramatic change, however, was a new acoustic shell designed for the Opera House stage by Heinrich Keilholz. This $76,000 structure was intended to alleviate unfortunate conditions that made the hall sound uneven and dull, even dead in some spots. The new backdrop of strange-looking geometric angles was very cumbersome, and changing the set required a few hours and several stagehands. But the sound was improved. Everything was now set for the beginning of Krips' first season.

The first programs scheduled by Krips set the tone for what San Franciscans could expect during his tenure. Every composer came from the Austro-Germanic school: Mozart, Beethoven, Mendelssohn, Schumann, Brahms, Handel, and Strauss. After seventeen years of Monteux and nine years of Jordá, we were getting back to the "meat and potatoes" music that is the strength of the standard repertoire. This was also the kind of music best suited to bring the fundamentals to an orchestra that had been having trouble in the last few years. The public welcomed this music—music they knew and loved—and Krips became an instant hero.

We of the orchestra had greeted Krips' arrival with both hope and fear. Hope, in the possibility that he would bring normality to the symphony scene; that we could play our music without wondering if it would fall apart at any moment; and that we could again find some pleasure in what we were doing. Fear, because Krips was one of the last conductorial despots—

benevolent at times but despotic always. He had been given full
reign to do what he wanted when he took the position, and, by
God, he was going to do it. In the process, he might trample
over a few musicians, but they were an expendable commodity.
The woodwind players, each a soloist in his own right, were
treated especially roughly. There was one who, after being brow-
beaten at each rehearsal, used to go home and throw up almost
daily. When a person in authority uses his power to cause someone else to question his own ability, it can create havoc in his
life. And that is what Krips did constantly. He wondered why
musicians were upset by this; he thought them overly sensitive.
He said, "An orchestral musician just has to wake up in the
morning and he is already offended."

Krips had a good command of the English language but
with a very heavy German accent. He was determined to make
a distinction between what he was—Austrian, specifically Viennese—and Germans. He used to say, "I hate those 'Cherman'
boots," snapping his heels together. We, who couldn't tell the
nuances of these Germanic types, thought he was the epitome
of a Prussian.

Sometimes Krips' diatribes against individual players back-
fired. Once we were playing a composition in which the contrabassoon player had an important part, and something he did
disturbed Krips. After the passage was repeated a number of
times, never to his satisfaction, Krips called over Al White, our
personnel manager, and said, "You must get me another contra-
bassoonist. I don't care if you go to the moon to get one, but get
me one!" The contrabassoon player, Frank Hibschle, was naturally offended and immediately resigned. Al White began to
search for other contrabassoon players—I don't think he tried
the moon—but the end result was unsuccessful. Krips had to
woo Hibschle back to the orchestra. He brought him into his
room, patted him on the back, told him he was great, promised
he wouldn't look at him during the performance (it is an unwrit-
ten rule that the conductor will not look at a player during his
solo, as it makes him nervous), and then offered him one of his

famous cigars. The cigar offer was a big gesture on the maestro's part, because cigars were one of his greatest pleasures. He even used the smoking of cigars to illustrate his points in rehearsals. When describing a phrase he would say, "It should go up to heaven like the smoke of a good cigar." Frank was won over and rejoined the orchestra, and he was not bothered again by Krips. But he never quite recovered from this experience, and one of his happiest moments was when he became eligible for retirement and left the orchestra, and Krips.

My own situation, at first, was an enviable one. My playing seemed to please Krips. Robin Laufer, director of the San Francisco Conservatory of Music and also on the symphony board, told me that Krips said, "Ferdinand Claudio and Schneider combine to comprise the best second stand, first violins of any symphony orchestra in the United States." He was given to high-flown praises like that, and we didn't take it too seriously. However, when rumors circulated that a big-name concertmaster would be brought in at the beginning of the second season, Krips assured me that no matter what happened on the first stand, I would not be moved. He wanted to keep the team of Claudio and Schneider intact.

At about 1:00 P.M. on the day of our first rehearsal of Krips' second season (the rehearsal was to take place that evening at seven o'clock), I received a phone call from Al White. He reminded me that Mr. Krips had been quite impressed by my audition for principal viola, and he would like to switch me to the viola section. I answered in the negative. Al urged me again, saying, "It will do you a lot of good with Krips." I asked where I would sit. "Third stand, outside."

Another emphatic "No!"

Al White said I had better think it over because Krips wanted me there and my position in the first violin section had been already filled. He hung up.

Two hours later he called again. He explained that not only had Jacob Krachmalnick (formerly associate concertmaster of the Cleveland Symphony and concertmaster of the Philadelphia

141

Orchestra and the Concertgebouw Orchestra of Amsterdam) been hired as concertmaster, but three other violinists had also been hired, and there was no room for them unless I moved over to the viola section. "Have you changed your mind?"

"No, I haven't, and if Mr. Krips is insistent on my moving to the viola section, I will tender my resignation as of this moment." There was a period of almost three hours in which I didn't know if my resignation had been accepted. At last, at about 6:00 P.M., Al called to tell me to come to rehearsal in an hour and sit in the seat in which I'd sat for the last nine years.

A few days after the season opening, Krips called me into his room and apologized for trying to move me. "But," he said, "if I'm offered three priceless pearls, I can't throw them in the street." The three "pearls" he spoke of were the new women violinists he had hired for the first violin section.

At this time, the symphony contract still covered only half the year. During the fall, half the orchestra played the opera, and in the summer we played the Pops concerts. Arthur Fiedler, the Pops conductor, was always popular in San Francisco, as he was almost everywhere. His personality accounted for much of his popularity. Fiedler was never shy about publicity—he had his picture taken at fires, wearing his honorary fire chief's hat, or at a restaurant, describing the most expensive meal he could find in San Francisco. His every action was known to the public.

Fiedler brought to symphony audiences music that they would not ordinarily hear—Broadway show music, jazz and popular tunes, older music that had been forgotten—a wide array of offbeat repertoire. All these he conducted capably if unimaginatively. It amazed me that such a man could make his reputation in performing light music and still be so heavy-handed. The squareness of his approach was unbelievable; his head buried in the score, he would beat a one-two, one-two, that would do credit to a German band. If he accompanied a soloist, Fiedler was the one to be followed, not the other way around. However, he had become so popular, so famous, that he could do no wrong. He had a quick and violent temper and a witty, sarcastic tongue. Once, when particularly displeased with the brass section, Fiedler screamed so loudly and unexpectedly that I literally jumped out of my seat. Seeing me jump Fiedler turned and said, "You're very sensitive, aren't you?" Well, perhaps I was, perhaps I was.

One summer I had an opportunity to play concertmaster with the New York Ballet, which was performing at the Opera House at the same time as the Pops concerts were going on in the Civic Auditorium. I received permission to take two weeks off from the summer concerts to play the ballet. I had a great time, because a section player rarely has the chance to play some of those lovely solos, such as the ones in *Swan Lake.* When I came back to the Pops concerts, Fiedler inquired about the conductor of the ballet, Leon Barzin. He had a reputation as an outstanding conductor, and Fiedler wanted to know my

Arthur Fiedler, Pops conductor par excellence, attracted large audiences in San Francisco.

143

opinion. I said, "He's very good. Of course, he's not as good as he thinks he is, but who is?"

Fiedler's answer was, "I think I'm better than I think I am."

By the end of his first season, Krips was already hailed as our new musical hero. He had brought the orchestra out of the doldrums and near disaster of the Jordá era, and audiences were beginning to hear music with which they were familiar. Krips was nothing if not traditional. At the same time, the new concertmaster, Jacob Krachmalnick, was the strongest, most exacting and opinionated violinist to sit in that all-important seat since I became a member of the orchestra.

Many of the musicians were apprehensive about their future under the careful scrutiny of these two men. Demotion or even separation from their job could result from an unfavorable evaluation of their playing, and rumor had it that either man was capable of bringing this about. I, too, had a strange foreboding of things to come.

Chapter 15

THE J. K. BOYS

Jacob Krachmalnick's reputation preceded him into the orchestra. He was known to be a fine concertmaster but also to have had a lot of trouble wherever he had been—mainly with his fellow musicians.

The role of concertmaster is unique. Though a member of the orchestra, he is also a member of management. He has all the privileges of an orchestra member except one—he does not have tenure; the concertmaster holds his position at the whim of the conductor. Thus, when the conductor is changed, a new concertmaster usually appears soon after. He must work very closely with the conductor, understanding all that makes up his individual style. Each conductor-concertmaster relationship is different. With a man like Szell, the conductor was dominant; he dictated how a passage was to be played, even the bowing and fingering. Krips was much more reliant on Krachmalnick, deferring to him in all string problems. For his part, Jake would not listen to a word critical of Krips. In any dispute between conductor and musicians, he would always take the conductor's side. He used to say to us, "If you are going to be difficult, you'll lose Krips, and if you lose Krips, that is your last hope of getting yourselves out of the mire you've been in. Krips goes, and the orchestra will sink down to the nothingness it was before he got here. No one any good will ever come here again."

Jake was extremely autocratic. He would look around the orchestra, making disagreeable faces whenever a musician had a solo, not only in the strings but also in the winds. He held most of the orchestra in great contempt. In my case, he was particularly critical, because, from where he was sitting, I was the violinist he heard most clearly. Both Ferdinand Claudio and I were always on the firing line; nothing we did was right. Jake's head was constantly swiveling around in protest at what he'd heard. That is characteristic of concertmasters, but the constant turning around disturbed me. At rehearsals I didn't object, but at concerts I began to get angry. It was as if he were advertising to the audience that the musicians behind him were doing something wrong. Nothing I did pleased Jake—he didn't like my rhythm, vibrato, tone, or intonation. Had I been the only one he found fault with, I'd have felt even worse than I did, but he acted as though no one deserved to be in that orchestra with him except Marc Lifschey, our new first oboe, who was Jake's colleague in Cleveland. I remarked that if Jake felt so superior, he should go to an orchestra where his talents would be appreciated and his colleagues would deserve him. I knew I was not long for that second stand.

Jacob Krachmalnick was known as an excellent concert-master but a hard taskmaster. He held the position from 1964 to 1970.

146

Before the 1965–66 season, Jake took it upon himself to reseat the violins. Though Krips had moved a few violinists in his first season, Jake's realignment left very few of us sitting in the same seat as the year before. All kinds of crazy reasons were given for these changes, my favorite being that I was moved to the outside fifth stand of the first violins because I was tall and could see better. Sitting with me was Ezequiel Amador, the shortest man in the section. At that first rehearsal there was almost a revolt. Though a strike to protest the high-handed and arbitrary manner in which these changes were made was narrowly voted down, this was a forewarning of things to come. There was no contractual clause restricting the concertmaster or conductor from doing any reseating they wanted, and we knew something would have to be done about it.

I'd sat in the first violin section very close to the front for the last ten years, and in front in one section or another for most of my symphonic career. When I began the season in that fifth stand, I realized how difficult it was to sit back there. It was the worst place to hear, I couldn't see the conductor well in spite of my height, and it was almost impossible to hear any verbal messages to the front stands. My sympathy went out to those who had long sat in these distant outposts. No wonder they felt isolated and seemed disinterested at times in the ritual proceedings taking place in front. The audience's attention was riveted on the inner circle surrounding the conductor. It seemed to me that the rest of us could have been sitting in the nude and nobody would have noticed.

Personally, I was humiliated to receive that demotion. For the last twenty years, everything had gone so well for me in the orchestra. The conductors, including Krips, all seemed to like my playing, complimenting me by their actions and words. To have endured the first season with Jake and then get this obvious token of my inferiority was a difficult blow to absorb. And it was so obvious! When a person is demoted in an office or another place of business, it is unpleasant, but the whole world doesn't hear about it. But here, in front of the entire music public of San Francisco, my humiliation was demonstrated. At the same time, no matter how hard I tried to avoid it, I also lost self-esteem. I had great respect for Jacob Krachmalnick (despite his nastiness), and if he thought I played badly, it was hard to disagree. Egos are easily bruised, at least mine is, and I had to fight to maintain confidence in my own ability.

After an early rehearsal, Maestro Krips met me in the hall and told me how marvelous it was to have me sitting in back of the first violins at that particular corner. He had never heard the section back there sound so big and fine. Although I thanked him for the compliment, I hardly appreciated it. I asked Krips if we might talk for a few minutes one day, and he replied with his usual magnanimity, "Of course! Anytime." So we met in his room after rehearsal.

Krips took out a cigar, lit it, and offered me one. Since I had never smoked, I didn't think this was the time to start. He again told me how much he enjoyed me in the orchestra.

I thanked him and then said, "I'm sorry, I won't be able to play the Mozart concert with you at the Legion of Honor."

"No? Why not?"

My answer was ready, "Because you are using four stands and I'm sitting on the fifth."

"I'm sorry," he said, "but it just works out that way. In the long run, though, it is better for the orchestra if you sit back there."

"That's all very well," I replied, "but I'm losing money not playing these kinds of concerts."

Again he apologized, reached into his pocket and said, "How much is it? I will pay you."

"No, it isn't the money. It's that this is an important concert, and I've been part of everything that has been going on in this orchestra for the last twenty-five years. I don't like the feeling of being left out." He mumbled some words of sympathy and I left.

At this time the principal second violin, Charles Meachem, disenchanted with all the machinations going on in the string sections, had made plans to disengage himself from the orchestra. I replaced him at the Mozart concert, after which was informally approached about becoming the orchestra's regular principal second violin. Although playing second violn again didn't fill my heart with exultation, I felt that this would get me out of exile and back into the thick of things. I mentioned to Krachmalnick that I had been approached for that position, and he scoffed. To him, playing second violin was a degradation not to be borne, and he felt I was selling my self-respect for a few extra dollars. To me this was not true. Being a principal, even second violin, carried a certain responsibility with it. Besides that, I'd hear and see better and would be cognizant of things going on that get lost by the time they filter to the back of the orchestra. So, at the beginning of the 1966–67 season, I assumed the position of principal second violin.

When Josef Krips came to the orchestra, his reputation was that of a solid old guard conductor who would pull the orchestra out of the morass it had sunken into. With those opening programs of Beethoven, Brahms, and Richard Strauss, we went along with this idea: one starts with the fundamentals; frills could be added later. However, some of Krips' idiosyncrasies were hard to live with.

One of these was a cliché he used over and over again, a verbal phrase for every musical phrase. If we played a piece ten times during the week's rehearsals, he would repeat the same admonitions: "Don't rush." "No crescendo." "Don't move." One reason he did this, I felt, was to help him memorize the works. During the concert, he'd just remember the words that went with each musical phrase. During the entire rehearsal, he did not stop talking, even when the music was going on. Still, we did play more music in rehearsal than with Jordá. Some musicians, in fact, felt we played too much. After rehearsing a piece until we had done everything we could to improve it, Krips would say, "Let's play it one more time." We felt that nothing could be gained by another reading of the work, but Krips, who had an unlimited allowance for overtime, believed that the more times a piece was rehearsed, the better it became.

Rehearsals with Krips were very noisy because of his constant chatter. He never said anything in a quiet voice, and my eardrums ached after a three-hour session. He was merciless with anyone he thought made a mistake in rhythm or, especially, intonation. He'd shout, "Go home and play this passage with the piano, and you will hear that every note is out of tune!" He would correct some phrasing of a woodwind player, saying, "Have you not heard this on the gramophone?" The rehearsals were constant battles, with Krips attacking the players while they tried to defend themselves. After a concert went especially well, he would talk to us and say, "Now, if we can start at this point and build from here, we will begin to make music." He was never, or at least he never admitted to being, satisfied with what we had played. It was only the beginning of something that someday would be great. I don't know if he really believed this or if he was just unable to simply say, "The concert was very good last night."

Meanwhile, Krachmalnick oversaw the strings—correcting, chastising, and punishing those whom he thought needed it. This was done in as fine a variety of sarcasm as I'd ever encountered. Now that I was principal second violin, I had to work very closely with him. I did everything I could to play each passage as he wanted it played, keeping my eyes glued to him even more than to Krips. But there was nothing I could do that didn't exact some form of criticism from Jake.

My one consolation was that, despite what went on between Jake and me under his nose, Krips continued to want me as his principal second violin. After each harrowing season with Jake, I received another raise in my overscale, so that my salary went up with my blood pressure.

Krips believed that "there are many fine violinists but only a few great concertmasters." He appreciated Jake in the capacity, liked his take-charge attitude, and had confidence that whatever he did as far as bowing and phrasing would be right and workable. As for Jake, he used the knowledge gained from his years with George Szell in his decisions about how a passage should be handled. He had standard solutions for every bowing problem; often they were good, but I sometimes felt that he tried to fit a phrase into the standard bowing, even though a better solution was available.

During Krips' tenure, Krachmalnick soloed with the orchestra more often than any soloist during my years in the symphony. As a whole his solo playing was very fine. He had a big, robust tone, and he could also play in a pure, almost ethereal style. With his well-developed technique, nothing in the violin literature was beyond his capacity. I encouraged my students to attend concerts in which he was featured, because I felt they could learn much from him. I was sometimes surprised that they didn't enjoy his playing as much as I did. What happened on the stage did not fully project outward, and though his solo playing was well accepted by the audience, it never made the sensation that I felt it usually deserved.

During Krips' tenure, more musicians from the orchestra were featured than in any other period in its history. Besides Jake, Krips presented the other two string principals, Rolf Persinger on viola and Robert Sayre on cello, on a yearly basis. In 1967, he presented another orchestra member, Ernestine Riedel, violinist (one of the "pearls" he brought in during his second year). Krips liked her playing of the Walton Concerto, but he felt she should display a little more fervor. He said he regretted that he was married because otherwise, "I would show you what passion is." His offer was enough to frighten Ernestine into a good simulation of passionate playing.

Though he had a reputation as a solid, classical conductor, Krips did some strange things technically. In performance, his right arm (the beating arm) would begin to swing back and forth in an arhythmic manner, as if it were detached from his body and his will. He would put the top of his little finger in his mouth, hum, and let that right arm swing, somewhat like a daydreaming little boy. The orchestra continued on its way, because nothing he did really interfered with the music, and when crucial moments arose, he would snap back to life and everything would come together. He displayed one endearing quality when something went wrong during a performance — he'd continue conducting with his right arm and hit his shining forehead with his left hand, holding it there in an attitude of astonished horror. This served two purposes. It let the audience know that something had gone awry, and it provided the offending musician enough self-doubt that he would never again play that passage without fear.

Despite these histrionics, there is no doubt that a great love of music motivated Krips in all his actions. He was a romantic, unrealistic in his expectations and extravagant in expression of his love. The great shining star on his horizon was Mozart. Playing Mozart, to him, was reaching the highest pinnacle of cultural achievement.

Once, when discussing with him the possibility of my playing a solo with the orchestra, I said, "It doesn't have to be a big work; I'd be satisfied to play a little Mozart concerto."

"Just a little Mozart concerto? Mozart is the most difficult to play!" he exclaimed.

Whatever work we played, even a cacophonous modern piece, he would say, "It must sound like Mozart. If it isn't Mozart, it isn't music." This sounds ridiculous if taken literally, but what he wanted to emphasize was that all music should sound as pure and clear as Mozart. Another of his phrases was "You must play with your heart. Leave your fingers at home. It's your heart I want."

It was easy to laugh at Krips' high-flown expressions, but without emotion we would just be playing a mechanical game instead of communicating the essence of music. Jordá, too, had spoken of music in emotional terms, but, as I saw it, there was something different about the language he used and that used by Krips. Jordá used words to cover up what he was unable to do with his baton, whereas Krips used hyperbolic phrases to draw musicians away from mundane, mechanical playing and into emotional involvement in the composition. And he sometimes succeeded, though in the process he would exasperate, humiliate, and generally trample upon the sensitive souls of his orchestra members.

Unfortunately, Krips' harsh words and actions lost him the trust of the symphony members. The musician exists on the good will of his conductor. If he begins to feel the maestro is out to get him, there are a few measures he can use to counteract the hopelessness he feels. He can try to prove the conductor's opinion erroneous (difficult); he can resign and go somewhere else (drastic and desperate); or he can remain and hope to outlast the conductor. Once a director starts to zero in on one person, it is almost impossible to get away from his attacks. Krips had a special talent for making players feel insecure, and his influence carried over to succeeding conductors who have asked, "Why are the musicians so suspicious?" The answer is simply that, after being burnt by a flame a number of times, one is reluctant to stretch out one's hand.

Three important events took place in regard to the 1967–68 season. The first was the negotiation of a crucial contract between the association and the orchestra; the second, a tour of Japan. The third affected me personally, and circumstances leading to this event began in the fall of 1966. The American composer Roger Sessions was spending a year in residence at U.C., Berkeley, and all the musical organizations and academic institutions in the area were paying tribute to him by playing some of his works. Laszlo Varga, conductor of the San Francisco State University Orchestra, asked me if I knew the Sessions Violin Concerto. I did not know it, nor had I ever heard it played, but I immediately went to a music store, purchased it, and started to learn it. Within a month, I made an appointment with Laszlo to play the first movement for him. From what he heard and with the confidence he had in my learning the rest, we scheduled the concerto for a performance on the university orchestra's spring program. It was to be the Bay Area premiere of the Sessions, and, therefore, it was important for both me and the orchestra.

When the Sessions Concerto was first published, it was said to be too hard to play. However, the instrumentalist must solve the problems a composer poses. In this case, it was quite a task to project the essence of the piece, through all the technical foliage surrounding it, to a public hearing it for the first time.

I worked very hard to accomplish this, fitting in practicing time at odd hours. When the time came, I asked some of my symphony colleagues to come to the performance, but only a very dedicated musician gives up a Sunday in springtime for another symphony concert. I even asked Krachmalnick to attend (I thought his ideas about me might change), but he not only didn't want to listen to me, he had no interest in hearing the Sessions Concerto. "Why do you play a piece like that?" he asked. "You must get the same thrill playing the Sessions Concerto as you get from kissing your mother-in-law."

Though Krachmalnick did not deem it worthwhile to hear me play the Sessions, two others did—Roger Sessions and Josef Krips. There can be no greater thrill for a performer than to play a composition in the presence of its composer. Roger Sessions was an old acquaintance from my early California String Quartet days. He had been on the U.C. faculty while we were preparing some of his chamber music works and had sat in on some rehearsals. He was very diffident about making performance suggestions unless we pressed him to. Then he was very explicit and direct about what he wanted. His quiet dignity did not reveal to the casual observer his immense knowledge about everything dealing with music. Here was my chance to show my respect and devotion to Sessions' music and to new music in general, and every ounce of concentration and energy I could muster went into this performance. When Roger Sessions shook my hand afterward, and I saw the warm smile on his face, I received all the reward I could ever hope for.

When I realized that Josef Krips had driven alone out to the campus to hear me play the Sessions, which he had never heard before, I was amazed. After the concert, Krips grasped my hand and said, "This Sessions Concerto we must put on next year's symphony series." The season had been mapped out already, and he just squeezed the Sessions into an already overcrowded program, with Andre Watts as the "other" soloist. For the next six months I used every spare minute to work on the Sessions so I could do it and myself justice.

Chapter 16

AN EVENTFUL YEAR

Before the exciting 1967–68 season could get under way, it was necessary to negotiate a contract satisfactory to both the musicians and the association. Negotiations for a symphony contract had always been difficult, but this year they threatened to be especially formidable. After all our problems with Krips, we wanted more control of our destiny and that of the orchestra. We wanted a say in who was to be hired, tighter control of the firing procedure and reseating—in fact, the whole gamut of orchestral policies. Across the country there had been steadily increasing unrest among the members of symphony orchestras. Strikes were breaking out all over. After long being treated like second-class citizens, musicians wanted some of the gains achieved by workers in industry, such as medical benefits, adequate pensions, and job stability—benefits taken for granted in almost any other line of work but never enjoyed by symphony musicians. Management and the public had always acted as if musicians were a breed apart (we may be) who didn't require all of those routine things to make us happy; we wanted management to realize that we are subject to the same needs and desires as everyone else, even though we have the added pleasure of making music.

In preparing for negotiations, the orchestra committee and the Musicians' Union studied the contracts of other orchestras to get ideas on how to reach our goals. Only three orchestras so far had reached our primary goal of full-time employment: New

155

York, Boston, and Philadelphia. Our present contract called for thirty weeks of work. Half the orchestra was playing the opera, which gave another eight or nine weeks' employment. If it were possible to get the cooperation of the Opera and Symphony associations in combining those two orchestras, we would be near our goal. But we knew this was unrealistic at the time; so we needed to find some alternative to use the services of the non-opera-playing personnel during the fall months.

Though the Symphony Association was willing to negotiate certain material provisions, they wouldn't even discuss anything that impinged on the "artistic" prerogative of the conductor. Traditionally, a conductor has had the right to decide who was in his orchestra and who was not, and no one could take away that right, least of all the orchestra. This situation had been exacerbated for us by Krips, whose autocratic and arbitrary manner had caused much pain to a large percentage of the orchestra members.

Taking charge of the negotiations for the association was their attorney, George Bahrs. Since he was getting nowhere with the committee from the orchestra, he sent out individual contracts to each member two weeks before the season opening. These contracts were the "last offer" from the association; we were told to sign and return them if we expected the season to start on time. In this test of strength, Bahrs had incorporated enough unpleasant provisions to offend every musician. If his aim were to precipitate a strike, there could have been no better way. The five-day week, which we worked for years to attain, was taken away; the principals' overscale (the amount paid over the minimum in the contract) was reduced; the retirement age was lowered to fifty-five at the conductor's discretion; and the weak tenure provision in our previous contract was taken out completely. Nothing we asked for was being offered except a small raise in wages. It was a giant step backward, and the orchestra rejected it overwhelmingly.

The symphony season didn't start on time. The association called it a strike. We called it a lockout so we could collect unemployment insurance, but the courts did not allow this. So we were officially on strike, the first in our history. The public expressed some amazement, because musicians are not thought of as workers with problems that lead to strikes; they are considered artists who should be above those mundane problems. It was difficult to get our message through to the public, because attention was focused on limiting the powers of the conductor. The public, especially in America, is greatly influenced by the media, and often the conductor is idolized, glamorized, and given God-like powers; it is inconceivable for people to imagine that a mere musician or group of musicians should be allowed to stand in his way. People who had no idea of our problem with Krips, or with any conductor, offered opinions about what we should or should not do. I, myself, feel that a conductor is by nature of his job an all-powerful person—powerful enough to use a body of professional musicians as his instrument! When things don't go his way, the first and easiest thought that comes to the conductor's mind is change the personnel. We wanted to make it a little harder for him to take out his frustrations on the musicians and encourage him to find other ways of improving the situation.

The president of the Symphony Association, Philip Boone, was an intelligent and reasonable man who tried to understand our point of view. He talked not only with the committee but with individual members of the orchestra. However, he was only one man on the association board, and we needed to turn around the thinking of many dedicated and sincere people who were sure they were doing the right thing when they denied us what we asked for. On our side, the unanimity of the musicians was surprising. The old and the young, the first-chairmen to the last-seat string players, stuck together in their desire to see our working conditions improve. When the strike started, we were not sure when it would end. There were threats that if we did not back down from our demands, the entire season would be canceled, and yet, despite the hardship many musicians suffered, there was no panic. Mayor Joseph Alioto intervened to try to settle the strike, but, in the final analysis, it was the understanding and good will on both sides of the table that broke the deadlock. This may have been one of the least acrimonious labor struggles ever fought.

I believe it was also one of the most successful strikes ever achieved by a labor union, not just in the obvious gains we reaped from the new contract but in the philosophical turnabout—the status of musicians was elevated to one of dignity and honor.

Of course, there were important specific gains: a completely new and complicated hiring policy that included a ten-member committee as well as the conductor; nonrenewal of a tenured player's contract was possible, but it could entail a difficult and lengthy process; the pension plan was improved; two weeks' paid vacation and medical insurance were provided; and starting with the contract's second year, the season would be thirty-six weeks long. It was also understood that the association was committed to reaching a full-year employment status; how long it would take to achieve this was not specified, but, for the first time in our history, this goal was expressed. Also for the first time, there would be a fall in-school concert program for orchestra musicians not employed by the San Francisco Opera Company; though the compensation was minimal, it got our toe in the door. Reseating was strongly restricted. And last, but not least, the salary was considerably improved.

This contract was a step forward, not only for the musicians but for the association. It forced the governing board to deal with a major orchestra and all that implies. The method of fund raising had to change, and the association was aided in this regard by recent grants from the federal government and private foundations. Additionally, the orchestra was now comparable to the top ten in the nation. It suddenly became possible to attract the finest musicians from all over the country, for now we had not only our fair city to boast about but one of the best orchestra contracts anywhere. (In this contract the association was allowed to hire from anywhere in the country, whereas previously they were required to use only local musicians, except in unusual circumstances.) Businessmen on the board would soon realize what a boon such an orchestra could be in attracting tourists and new city residents, and knowledgeable music lovers would understand that an orchestra not idle for half the year would have a better chance to become a great one. I think it no exaggeration to say that this contract was a turning point in both the symphony's history and the classical music scene in the Bay Area. From then on there was a thrust forward to make this part of the world a major music center.

The next important event in the 1967–68 season was one that would give joy and satisfaction to everyone involved in the symphony. We were going to concertize in Japan. This first extended tour in over twenty years was made possible by the fame of Josef Krips and the prestige he brought to the orchestra. The contrast between this tour and our transcontinental tour of 1947 was striking: this was a seventeen-day trip of twelve concerts, compared with eight weeks of almost nightly concerts; we had first-class hotel rooms instead of bunk beds on a train; and spouses could now go on a companion trip with the Symphony Foundation. Everything was done on a much grander scale, down to individual wardrobe trunks and specially made boxes for the instruments, with insulation to protect them from rough handling.

We left early Tuesday morning, April 9, 1968, on Japan Airlines. We finally arrived in Japan after a rather harrowing trip and the usual interminable customs procedures.

Our first personal contact with a Japanese person was on the bus that took us to Osaka. Mark Takeda, a charming young man who was to be our guide, introduced himself and explained his function on the trip—to help us, to guide us, to translate for us, everything that we would want from a guide. He said if we ever needed him, we should just call "Mark! Mark!" and he would come immediately. His name to us became Mark Mark.

After a seemingly endless midnight ride to Osaka, we finally met our spouses and got a much-needed rest. A rehearsal was scheduled for the next afternoon. Krips was not a lazy man and he did believe in rehearsing. Besides twelve concerts, six rehearsals were included in our schedule, a formidable task considering our six traveling days during the seventeen-day tour. This would be a model for what not to do in planning future tours. The maestro was forthright in reacting to our bitching: "We're here to play concerts, not to go sightseeing." But it was the first time most of us had been in the Orient; so we drank in everything we could of that exotic land. Since I would play the Sessions Concerto with the orchestra as soon as we returned to San Francisco, I had to fill some of my precious free time with practicing. Nevertheless, Geri and I were able to spend the first few days sightseeing in Osaka, which was gorgeous at that time of year. Spring could not be better expressed than in the cherry blossoms of Japan.

Truly, though, we were in Japan to play concerts, and that we did very well. This was not an unsophisticated audience for which we were playing. In the previous ten years, they had heard symphonies from Berlin, Amsterdam, London, Leningrad, Boston, and Philadelphia, and the finest chamber music groups in the world. They had their own symphony orchestras and soloists. So when we read rave notices about us, we could take them seriously. Fuzo Stotyama, a noted conductor, wrote in the newspaper *Asahi:* "Our ears have been accustomed to the best, but what we heard was even better." Music critic Klaus Pringsheim said, "The most striking is the warmth and rich sonority of the orchestra's large string section which is moreover marvelously disciplined." He went on speaking of Krips' interpretation of the Brahms' First: "Great dramatic and emotional tensions were brought out in a truly gripping performance to which the enthusiastic audience responded with a tempestuous ovation." Our own critics who came along on the tour—Alexander Fried and Robert Commanday—were also most complimentary in their reviews of the Osaka concerts. Commanday of the *Chronicle* wrote: "The orchestra has never been heard in the San Francisco Opera House playing with such a uniformly excellent, occasionally ravishing tonal display."

As ever, the two San Francisco critics found something to disagree about, Krips' reading of Wagner's *Siegfried Idyll*. This was a piece we had played innumerable times with both Monteux and Jordá, but Krips put his own stamp upon the work. Commanday wrote of our Osaka performance of the *Idyll*: "Krips' by now long-breathed view of the *Siegfried Idyll* makes Wagner's home serenade for wife and new infant into a major tone poem." Whereas Fried of the *Examiner* wrote: "The slow-motion note to note plod of Wagner's *Siegfried Idyll* (which really should be sunny-natured and affectionate, not lugubrious) was incomprehensible, unaccountable." In general, though, both San Francisco critics were healthily detached in their reviews of Krips' concerts. They did not feel it incumbent on them to either defend or attack him; so each concert was a fresh experience they could listen to and evaluate without preconceptions. Krips had an already established reputation; so they were not called upon to make a hero of him. He was a professional conductor whose work with the orchestra could be judged for itself.

After Osaka we went to Hiroshima, site of the first atomic bombing. In the afternoon we visited the Hiroshima Memorial, where Krips and Philip Boone laid a wreath in memory of the tens of thousands who had died there, and a short ceremony took place. The actual sight of the destruction wreaked by the atomic bomb had a most sobering effect on all of us. That evening there was a concert in which the real memorial to the dead was given—the symphony's performance of Beethoven's *Eroica*. It was a masterly reading by Krips, and the orchestra responded with all the beauty, dignity, and solemnity that the composition evokes.

We left Hiroshima and traveled by bus and express train to Nagoya, Nagano, and Chiba, playing a concert in each city. In between Nagano and Chiba we had a free day, one of two planned for us on the trip. This was especially enjoyable, as we spent it in Karuizawa, a lovely mountain resort. Karuizawa is a sleepy little town amidst natural beauty, and it was an inspiration by those in charge to give us a rest there before we went on to Tokyo, where we would receive our most knowing and critical reviews.

Even though we had prepared our five programs before we left San Francisco, rehearsing them again in Osaka and playing most of them in between, we had two more rehearsals for our three Tokyo concerts. Krips was of the opinion that if two pills will help you, eight will do you four times as much good. Still, the headliner on Fried's review was "Symphony Falters in Tokyo," and Commanday's was "Tokyo Concert a Disappointment." We, in the orchestra, did not feel that the concerts had gone badly, but we may have been played out after the constant round of rehearsals and performances. Some time off might have been better than those additional rehearsals. The Tokyo concerts were not sold out, perhaps surprisingly, but we had to realize that there were six resident symphony orchestras in the city and a visiting one almost daily. Furthermore, our first concert was an all-Mozart one, which did not attract much curiosity from the knowledgeable audience.

There were seventeen pieces on the five programs we played in Japan. Of those, thirteen were German. Of the remaining four, one was American (Copland), one Japanese (Takemitsu), and two were Russian (Stravinsky and Tchaikovsky). The Germanic school was certainly Krips' forte, but the domination of this music over all others is open to question, especially in a foreign country. Mozart, Beethoven, and Brahms undoubtedly wrote the greatest symphonic music, but even with Krips' vast experience in conducting these works, the San Francisco Symphony was not so great an orchestra that it could show the Japanese, who have heard the best, the way it should be played. Would it not be better for an audience to hear an unusual and strong work representative of the orchestra's own country than to hear one more performance of a Beethoven symphony? Neither the "Quiet City" of Copland nor the "Requiem for Strings" of Takemitsu are long enough or strong enough compositions to truly represent their native countries; they were put into the programs as tokens, to show our audiences that we came from the United States and were performing in Japan. We should have brought more than that to justify our coming.

Nevertheless, the tour was a success in several ways. Removed from the provinciality of its native city, the orchestra could measure itself against other orchestras of the world. The musicians could hear how we sounded in different, more modern, and livelier halls. Our critics could listen to us in a different environment and get a better perspective on our virtues and faults. Plans for future tours could benefit from what we had learned on this one. Perhaps most important, we had a marvelous time. From that point on, the San Francisco Symphony members have had a greater affinity for Japan than for any other foreign country. We came home from the tour enthusiastic, tired and yet refreshed from our experience, ready to take on the remainder of the season in San Francisco.

The first event after our return from Japan was my appearance as soloist in the Roger Sessions Violin Concerto, in May 1968. I was fortunate to have as co-soloist on the program Andre Watts, a fine pianist and a special favorite in San Francisco, assuring me a large audience for all three performances. I had to admire the ambition of Krips, long considered an old-fashioned traditionalist, for scheduling the San Francisco premieres of two major contemporary works on the same program.

This was the only time I could remember that a soloist was required for every piece on the program. The Symphony no. 2 by Alfred Prinz, a contemporary Viennese composer, contained a short but important solo for the principal second violin, and Krips wanted me to play it. He also wanted me to lead the seconds in Mozart's "Eine Kleine Nachtmusik," as it is a chamber orchestra work, and he felt that the head of the section should be there. To my surprise, he even said he needed me for the Liszt Piano Concerto in A. I didn't argue. I was just grateful to be there as soloist.

A unique feature of the Sessions Concerto is that there are no violins in the orchestra. I believe Sessions felt that the solo violin should be the only high string sound to be heard, giving the soloist special prominence. The absence of violins made my fellow violinists very happy, for it meant they were excused from the entire Tuesday afternoon rehearsal and an hour of the Wednesday rehearsal. Some of them never heard the concerto and don't even remember that I played it, but the winds and percussions recall the work very well, because it was an extremely difficult one for the orchestra. Each wind player is himself a soloist, and there are some beautiful solo parts in the tutti sections.

The evening of the first performance was like every other concert I had played in the Opera House. I unpacked my violin where I always did backstage, as the artist's room was taken over by Andre Watts. I didn't really have a chance to warm up properly for my performance since I had to go on stage to play "Eine Kleine Nachtmusik." On the other hand, I didn't have time to get nervous either. I had just enough time after the Mozart to go offstage, tune up again, and come on for the Sessions. As was customary with modern works, I used the music during the performance, but in retrospect I feel I should have memorized it, because that would have required me to work harder and learn it better.

No matter. It was a great feeling standing up before the orchestra and playing this fine contemporary work. At each performance I felt I discovered new things about the piece, and I was absolutely exhilarated while playing it. They say that a professional athlete feels no pain during the excitement of a game, even though he may be playing with broken bones. While playing the Sessions I felt marvelous and could have gone on forever if need be.

The audience received the performance very cordially. The critics, who were looking forward to hearing the rare performance of a modern concerto, were flattering. Alexander Fried wrote:

The success of Roger Sessions' Violin Concerto came to some listeners as a surprise. Popular triumphs have not been his habit.

Its attractiveness last night grew out of the work itself and its performance, conducted by Josef Krips.

David Schneider, a violinist in the symphony, was its soloist. He did a beautiful, masterly job, so far as one can judge from first hearing. . . . Schneider's performance was secure, and full of melodic glow. His part was continuous, with little rest. At no point, in the difficult length of it, did Schneider falter or lose quality.

In retrospect, I am sorry to say, it was not a masterly performance, and in that respect I must differ with my friend, Alexander Fried. A work of this nature needs to be learned and then put away and then relearned before one can get a true perspective of it. I think this composition is a great one and should in the future be part of the standard concerto literature of the world's fine violinists. I harbor in a secret corner of my heart a desire to have the opportunity to play that work again, this time achieving a performance that could rightfully be called a "masterly reading."

Chapter 17

AUF WIEDERSEHEN, JOSEF KRIPS

It was not an easy task for Maestro Krips to adjust to the role imposed on him by the new contract. In Europe, even in Buffalo, he had free rein to do what he wanted—the traditional position of an Austrian emperor. But after the successful contract negotiations, orchestra members would no longer take so much abuse from the conductor. One morning when Krips was particularly piqued, he turned to the orchestra and screamed, "Peasants!" He was extremely conscious of the caste system, and at that moment we were the lowest. The orchestra committee went to see him in the intermission and said that not only would the musicians no longer tolerate that kind of invective, but he must apologize to us after the intermission. When we reassembled, Krips, in mock humility, bowed his head and said in a most abject manner, "I'm sorry." The next day when he was upset with something else the orchestra had done, he said, "I'm not allowed to say what I want to say, but nobody can stop me from thinking it."

The 1968–69 season gave the orchestra and the San Francisco public the privilege of meeting a number of outstanding guest conductors. One of the best was Rafael Kubelik. Son of the famous violin virtuoso, Jan Kubelik, Rafael was a violin soloist in his own right who finally chose conducting as his life work. The most interesting composition he directed with us was the six-tone-poem cycle of Bedrich Smetana, *Ma Vlast (My Country)*. Though *Ma Vlast* is not a masterpiece (the best piece

of the group is the well-known "Moldau"), under Kubelik's
direction it came to life and its hidden qualities could be heard.
That is a sign of a good conductor—to take a mediocre composition and make it sound better than even the composer could
expect. We enjoyed playing with Kubelik so much that we asked
when he would return to San Francisco. We were disappointed
to learn that he was booked for years. He has not yet returned
to conduct here.

The second week, Kubelik conducted a program of three
nonstandard B's—Britten, Bruch, and Brahms. This was San
Francisco's introduction of one of the two Israeli violinists who
made their debut in our city that year, Pinchas Zukerman. He
was to become a favorite of the audiences here and later conduct
the San Francisco Symphony Chamber Orchestra. The other
Israeli violinist was the sensational Itzhak Perlman. Perlman was
a fine violinist then, but his virtuosity and musicianship continued to grow so that many people believe he is now the greatest living violinist. His playing has become a standard by which
all other violinists are measured. No longer can great virtuosic
proficiencies excuse poor musicianship; no longer can slips in
intonation be condoned because of the difficulty of the composition. Perlman can do it all, so anything less than total control
of the instrument and understanding of the music is no longer
permissible. Added to Perlman's exquisite playing is his engaging personality. He often joins Zukerman in duo recitals, and
each brings out the best in the other as they play together,
making music with such joy.

Other conductors on the roster of guests that season were
Sixten Ehrling, conductor of the Detroit Symphony; Hans
Schmidt-Isserstedt, a Berliner who had become chief conductor
of the Stockholm Philharmonic Orchestra; Werner Torkanowsky; and the glamorous Antonio d'Almeida, the peripatetic
conductor born in Paris of a Portuguese father and American
mother, who had conducted all over the globe, his most important posts being in Stuttgart and Paris, where he worked with
the opera. Almeida's program with us was an interesting one

167

that included two works featuring our own musicians. The Ibert Concerto for Flute and Orchestra had Paul Renzi, our principal flutist, as soloist, and the Organ Symphony no. 3 of Saint-Saens featured Ludwig Altman. This last work had been one of Monteux's favorites, and playing it again after many years brought back fond memories of that time.

The highlight of the guest-conducting parade was Seiji Ozawa. This, his second appearance with us, showed the growth he had already made in his conducting technique. Ozawa had been a sensation wherever he conducted, both for his musical achievements and for his unorthodox and sometimes heretical behavior. He was known to have a free, modern style much different from the staid, orthodox one of men such as Monteux, Walter, and Krips, who personified the traditional conductor's way of life. In contrast to these very European conductors, Ozawa wanted to be more American than any American. He even played baseball with the New York Philharmonic team while he was assistant conductor there.

Ozawa's first program that year consisted of Haydn's Symphony no. 75, the Saint-Saens Piano Concerto no. 5, and the Mussorgsky *Pictures at an Exhibition*. Ozawa's accompaniment to the Saint-Saens concerto revealed a remarkable aspect of this conductor. The soloist was Jeanne-Marie Darre, a French pianist who, though she had been concertizing for forty-five years, was just then making her San Francisco debut. The usual pattern for working with guest artists was to have the main rehearsal on Tuesday afternoon and a run-through on Wednesday morning, the day of the first evening concert. We were all sure by the way Ozawa conducted on Tuesday that not only did he not know the work, he may never have heard it before. His conducting was inept, and he seemed to have a very difficult time following the soloist. In the Wednesday rehearsal, however, we were astounded to find that he had learned the concerto so well overnight that he barely looked at the music. Ozawa gave the appearance of being a carefree lightweight, but when it came to sheer concentrated work, I don't know anyone, anywhere, who could hold a candle to him.

The next week Ozawa introduced a Japanese composition featuring two native instruments. "November Steps no. 1," by Toru Takemitsu, which has since become a classic, featured Kinshu Tsubuta on the biwa, a four-stringed lutelike instrument played with a wood plectrum. Katsuya Yokoyama played the shakuhachi, a breathy, bamboo wind instrument, whose name suggests the sound it produces. Takemitsu combined the Western disciplines of Varese, Webern, and Cage with the color and sounds of these ancient instruments, giving his music a remarkably strong effect on the audience.

At this time, there were rumors almost every week of another major eastern orchestra for which Ozawa was to become chief conductor—New York, Chicago, Philadelphia, Boston— he was being groomed for this one or that one and would take over whenever the present conductor stepped down. So far, after being Bernstein's assistant in New York, he had become the music director of the Ravinia Festival and the Toronto Symphony, and the most sought-after guest conductor in the world. So it was quite a surprise to the music world, and to us as well, when it was announced that Seiji Ozawa would become permanent conductor and music director of the San Francisco Symphony Orchestra for the 1970–71 season, when Maestro Krips would retire.

We later learned that this news came as a surprise even to Josef Krips. Such are the politics of international music management that the whole deal was worked out without help from Krips. The critic Robert Commanday, while visiting Krips in Vienna, told him about what was to occur. Later, after being officially told about the change, Krips had the unhappy task of announcing his successor to the press. He did this graciously, as if it were he who had chosen Ozawa.

When interviewed after this surprising development was disclosed, Ozawa was queried about why he had chosen the San Francisco Symphony rather than one of the major eastern symphonies as his first United States orchestra. He answered modestly and succinctly, "They asked me."

We in the orchestra looked forward to the change. Though

Krips had done much to raise the level of the orchestra's playing and its esteem in the world's eyes, he had also left a great many nerves raw, and we felt we'd had enough of him. By the time he left, he would have conducted seven seasons, which seemed the limit a conductor could go without making himself too dull and familiar to attract audiences. Already ticket sales were beginning to falter. Ormandy's long stay in Philadelphia and Szell's in Cleveland were freakish phenomena not soon to be repeated in modern times (Stokowski and Koussevitzky had had long tenures earlier in the century).

As these developments were taking place, other changes were brewing in the orchestra. In the 1968–69 season, Krips had to select a new associate concertmaster. Our contract stipulated that any position in the orchestra could be filled for one season on an emergency basis without a formal audition, and Krips engaged Stuart Canin in this way. I had played quartets with Stuart the previous year at Laszlo Varga's house, and he'd impressed me then with his fine violin playing as well as his

Stuart Canin, concertmaster from 1970 to 1980, was also a fine chamber music player and soloist.

170

musicianship. He had just completed a stint as concertmaster of the Philadelphia Chamber Orchestra. Stuart was beginning to travel the precarious road of a solo career, but life was easier with a weekly check to fall back upon. Sitting in the second seat, first violin, he seemed a charming man, soft-spoken and pleasant to be with. My seat was just a foot or two from his, and everything I heard from his violin was polished and pure. His style was quite different from that of Jacob Krachmalnick, whose hearty and robust playing had a more "masculine" quality about it. Stuart did not much admire Jake's playing and openly expressed surprise at what he thought was faulty technique. I couldn't say that together they made an ideal stand.

In fact, Jacob Krachmalnick had become a burden to Krips in his final years with our orchestra. My own little squabbles with Jake were minor compared to what was happening with many other people. His contempt for most of his colleagues was obvious, and their reaction, not surprisingly, was hostile

Through a lot of arm-twisting and maneuvering, Krips was able to keep Stuart on as associate concertmaster for a second year. We were amused to hear that Stuart had purchased a home in a prestigious San Francisco neighborhood at the same time that Jake had rented a new apartment: it was clear who would stay and who would go. One of Ozawa's first acts when he took over was to release Krachmalnick and hire Canin as concertmaster. He went through the formality of listening to Stuart play for him, but it was a foregone conclusion that when the 1970–71 season opened with Ozawa as conductor, Canin would be sitting in the concertmaster's chair.

The 1969–70 season was Krips' last as our general director. We observed the Beethoven bicentennial by performing most of his orchestral works—an ideal way for Krips to leave the orchestra. Beethoven was one of his gods, and through his compositions Krips could best epitomize what he felt about music. In the orchestra, there was an air of anticipation about the excitement Ozawa would undoubtedly bring and a desire to get through the old and stodgy as soon and as painlessly as possible.

In the last printed program of the season, Philip Boone, association president, gave a well thought out and learned tribute to Krips' achievements with the orchestra. As part of this glowing review, he wrote:

> The highlights of Maestro Krips' years as conductor and music director of our orchestra are too many to enumerate in detail, but the following achievements cannot go without mention. During his tenure he has personally conducted 215 different works, of which 91 were works from the 20th century.

He then specified a number of world premieres, including two symphonies each of Imbrie and Mechem, an Emanuel Leplin symphony, a Nin-Culmell work, and two works of Roger Nixon —all Bay Area composers. He went on to mention other compositions Krips had brought to San Francisco audiences, commenting that:

> The richness and variety of this musical fare is a tribute in itself to the scope of the Maestro's artistic accomplishments in San Francisco during the past seven years.
>
> In saluting Maestro Josef Krips as he concludes his tenure as conductor and artistic director of the San Francisco Symphony Orchestra, we take great pride and pleasure from the knowledge that he now assumes the post of Conductor Emeritus.

There was, as always, another side to the coin. Two things that Maestro Krips had not done in San Francisco weren't mentioned either by Boone or by the newspaper writers. Though Krips had a long history of recording, he had done none with us. He thought the orchestra had never quite reached the degree of proficiency necessary for making recordings—"just one more change of personnel," and it could have been done. But since that never happened, he was never ready to record. Many works he conducted with us would have made memorable recordings, but all this has been lost.

It would have been a great privilege for the public to have

had Krips conduct the San Francisco Opera. From his earliest beginnings in music, he was associated with opera, and we might have seen an entirely different side of Krips if he could have conducted opera here.

We musicians were aware of Krips' achievement in taking the orchestra from the chaos in which he found it to its present musically disciplined state. It would only take a conductor with the imagination of Ozawa to raise us to the level of greatness we were destined to achieve.

Seiji Ozawa, conductor of the San Francisco Symphony from 1970 to 1977.

Chapter 18

SWINGING WITH SEIJI

The arrival of Seiji Ozawa as music director and conductor of the San Francisco Symphony created more excitement than San Francisco cultural circles had experienced in decades. Advance season subscriptions were at a new high, and everyone awaited the charismatic hero who would, at last, pull the symphony up to the level of the great eastern orchestras. Our executive director, Joseph Scafidi, even arranged to get OZAWA license plates for his Cadillac. This was the first time the orchestra was completely identified with one individual, and people who'd heretofore had no interest in symphony concerts were talking about the wonders of our new conductor.

The musicians were glad to get away from the stiff, arbitrary style of Krips and looked forward to the quick lightness and modern spirit of Ozawa. Almost immediately, he was on a first-name basis with each member of the orchestra, and even without his telling us to, we all called him Seiji. His long hair was seemingly unkempt, and, even in his attire, Ozawa gave the impression of complete relaxation; to rehearsals he wore a shirt, frayed, faded jeans, and sandals or loafers. With this costume, he used to carry a leather bag with his personal effects. We regaled each other with tales of his going to Tahoe or Reno to gamble and ski. We thought we had a real swinger this time; it was going to be fun and games from here on.

On the evening of a performance, the contrast between Ozawa and Krips was even more pronounced. Krips would arrive at the hall at least an hour before the concert. His clothes were brought to him from a wardrobe closet near his room, and he would start to get them ready for his appearance. He'd brush his suit thoroughly, select a shirt and tie, and then carefully buff his patent leather shoes. Everything was done slowly and methodically as a kind of ritual, a way of getting mentally and physically ready for the performance.

Ozawa's routine was quite the opposite. He had very unorthodox working hours. After rehearsal, he may have gone directly to sleep, as he had spent the entire previous night studying scores. He'd awaken no earlier than a half hour before the concert, slip into his casual clothes, and arrive at the Opera House no sooner than 8:28 for an 8:30 concert. He'd walk through the backstage area to his room, followed by various members of his entourage. During this casual ramble, he would greet everyone with a big smile and a "hello," as if he had nothing important ahead of him. He'd change into his concert clothes and in two minutes was transformed into a conventional symphony conductor—well, not entirely conventional. Though he wore a full-dress coat and trousers, with black shoes and socks, in place of shirt and vest or cumberbund he wore a black turtleneck and beads. For afternoon concerts, instead of his grey-striped trousers and Oxford grey jacket, he donned black trousers, the same type of shirt and beads he wore at night, and a coolie-type jacket.

This studied casualness was just a facade. In his conducting, Ozawa was rigorously intense. He exuded energy when he conducted, and there was not an inkling of flabbiness or indecisiveness about his beat. I remember when he was first a guest conductor with us: he brought down his baton on the first chord of the overture with a beat so clean and definite that the music could be heard just by watching it. The whole stage seemed to explode with sound. The audience is not in the best place to enjoy the music when they are behind a conductor such as Ozawa, because one misses so much expression by not seeing his face and the beautiful way it reflects the music.

The third week of his first season as general director Ozawa was scheduled to conduct but didn't. He was suffering from a flare-up of a recurrent neck injury, aggravated in September 1969 when he played baseball with members of the New York Philharmonic. He had conducted the second week of the season against his doctor's advice, because there was no one to take his place and "the show must go on." But this week his assistant, Niklaus Wyss, returned from a conducting engagement in Europe and took over for him in an all-Beethoven program. The next concert Ozawa conducted here was in January 1971. A neck brace was a most uncomfortable addition to his costume, but nothing could prevent his all-out effort to work.

Niklaus Wyss was the first assistant conductor we'd had in the orchestra for many years. Ozawa felt it necessary to have an assistant because of his busy schedule and fragile physical condition. It was his right to decide on whom he wanted in that post, but he solicited the advice of some members of the orchestra—first because he wanted to show that the orchestra had a voice in all music-making matters, and second because he had a difficult time making decisions. Ozawa knew Wyss and what he could do, and no one would have questioned Ozawa's decision to hire him. But Ozawa's inability or unwillingness to decide on his own in the matter of hiring was to be a pattern during his time with us. Nevertheless, in spite of the considerable time and money spent on auditions, the young Swiss conductor who had been Ozawa's assistant in Toronto came to conduct a rehearsal and was hired. Considering the short notice he had, Wyss gave an outstanding performance at his sudden debut with us. He was to conduct another subscription week in addition to the Youth Concerts.

Another unofficial resident conductor who would take a greater part in the San Francisco Symphony was George Cleve. Though he had no title with the orchestra, he attended most rehearsals, listening and preparing himself to take the podium when neither Ozawa nor Wyss was available. Cleve, a student of Monteux's, had shown a great deal of talent, and Ozawa was

177

fond of him and admired his conducting ability. He later became conductor of the San Jose Symphony, an orchestra that was to make an important cultural contribution to that growing community.

At the same time that Niklaus Wyss was announced as assistant conductor, Charles Darden, a 23-year-old black man, was appointed "apprentice" in conducting. This new position was created for Darden, who had shown great talent at the audition yet was not ready to assume the assistant conductor post. Unfortunately, Darden had no specific duties with the orchestra. Rather, he was an advanced student poised to step up to a conducting position when he was considered sufficiently schooled. He left after a very short time to study in New York and Europe and has never returned.

Though the management expressed a strong desire to have blacks as part of the orchestra, it had always been a difficult problem. As chairman of the orchestra committee in the forties, I tried to recruit blacks to audition for the orchestra, but many hindrances barred their entrance into our ranks. Most of them did not prepare sufficiently for the job and couldn't fill a position. Others were reluctant to leave good commercial jobs for more work and less pay. I approached Dennis de Coteau, a well-qualified violist, about applying for a seat in the viola section. He said he would have liked to years earlier, but blacks could not then be members of our union and, therefore, could not even try out for the symphony. Now that things had changed, he was a tenured teacher in the San Francisco school system and didn't want to give that up for the tenuous position and low salary the symphony offered. Dennis later became a conductor and a successful director of the Oakland Youth Symphony, the Hayward State University Symphony, and the San Francisco Ballet, and he has guest-conducted internationally.

We were happy when Charles Burrell, a black bass viol player, joined the orchestra. He felt uncomfortable here, however, and eventually returned to his native Salt Lake City. The atmosphere surrounding a person whose color, race, or sex is different than that of everyone else is very sensitive. No matter how friendly his or her colleagues, any supposed slight can be so magnified that the person feels unable to remain in the situation.

Up to that time, Burrell and Darden had been the only black persons even remotely involved with the orchestra. It is almost impossible to have an affirmative action program in symphony orchestras, unless that program starts at the grammar school level. To become a violinist capable of joining a professional symphony orchestra, one must start at no later than nine years of age, and for a child to begin music study at that age, he must get much encouragement and supervision at home In all my years of teaching, precious few black children have come across my path.

The first season of Ozawa's tenure had an interesting sidelight. After seven years of Krips' tyranny, we hoped to not see him again for a long while. So we were shocked when we found ourselves with not one but two Kripses. Not only was Josef invited for a week as conductor emeritus of the orchestra, but his brother Henry took over our annual New Year's program, "A Night in Old Vienna." Henry was the lighthearted half of the team. During this extremely informal concert, he would turn to the audience and say, "Have no fear, Henry is here." Realizing that we would have a pair of Kripses conducting us reminded us of the "Sorcerer's Apprentice," when the unhappy lad, in trying to stop the broom from bringing any more water, breaks it in two, whereupon both pieces of the broom begin to fetch water. Josef's program was typical of what we would expect from him—the *Don Juan* of Strauss, Brahms' Second Symphony, and the premiere of Prinz's Fourth Symphony.

When Stuart Canin moved over to the concertmaster's chair, the position of associate concertmaster was open. Many violinists, both in and out of the orchestra, auditioned for this job. I asked Joe Scafidi, executive director of the orchestra, if it would redound against me if I either tried out and failed or didn't try out at all, making the conductor think I was afraid to

179

pit myself against other musicians. Scafidi assured me that whatever decision I made would do me no harm, so I decided to audition. Among the auditioners from the orchestra was Robert Menga, a recent entrant to our first violin section. Menga had a fabulous violin technique but a mercurial temperament. When this new opportunity arose, he naturally tried out and certainly thought he should get the job.

My audition did not go well, and I was eliminated early. The final choice was between Menga and Peter Schaffer. Peter had held positions of some importance with many symphony orchestras and universities, both as violinist and conductor, among them the post of associate concertmaster with Canin in the Philadelphia Chamber Orchestra. Schaffer was selected both for his playing and for his pleasant personality. When Menga heard the results, he became irate and said that he was "done in" by Canin, who didn't like him and didn't want to sit next to him. This may have been true, but it was also true that Schaffer would have won in any case. Although Menga was the more flamboyant performer, in all-around musicianship and refined violinism, Schaffer was far ahead of him.

The results of this audition caused Menga to be miserable in the orchestra from then on, and he showed it. One morning after playing in a private recital, he came two hours late to rehearsal, and his pay was docked for this infraction. Menga completely lost his self-control, went upstairs to the office of Executive Director Joseph Scafidi, screamed at him, and ended up kicking him. Menga was immediately dismissed. He subsequently became concertmaster of the Honolulu Symphony, a position he held for one season, and then performed as concertmaster of many other orchestras. This violinist, almost a genius, is one of many people I have encountered whose tremendous talent was not matched by a personality that could handle it. The unhappy result was that he never achieved the success he should have had. Perhaps the training of such a virtuoso discourages the development of a well-rounded personality. His concentration must be so devoted to perfecting the technical aspects of music that his emotional side is ofttimes neglected.

In addition to his unique and intense conducting Ozawa brought to San Francisco unusual soloists and music of the twentieth century. One soloist who would appear with us often was pianist Yuji Takahashi. In his first concert, Takahashi played Takemitsu's *Asterism* and Scriabin's *Prometheus;* later in the season he appeared again, playing a work out of the ordinary for him, Bach's Concerto in D Minor for clavier and orchestra. Another unusual Ozawa presentation was the Corky Siegel Blues Band, who played with us "Three Pieces for Blues Band and Symphony" by William Russo—certainly a dramatic departure from the Beethoven, Brahms, and Mahler syndrome of Krips. There on stage at the ornate and sedate Opera House was the funkiest, most laid-back group of performers that the city's symphony-going public had ever laid eyes (or ears) on. Corky Siegel played the harmonica with immense and peculiar virtuosity. The music was just what its name implied, a combination of the square symphony sound with the wild "blues band" sound. The piece would get us back into the recording business,

Composer William Russo (left) and blues musician Corky Siegel (right) played and recorded with the San Francisco Symphony in 1973. Ozawa was known for bringing unusual programs to the Opera House.

181

as we were to immortalize this work for Deutsche Grammophon. In fact, one movement of the piece became a successful "single," high on the charts.

Another highly entertaining and exotic group that visited in our 1971–72 season was the Gagaku Orchestra from Japan. The Gagaku is an orchestra of native Japanese instruments that is an official adjunct to the Imperial Court of Japan. Traditionally, they play only in the Imperial Palace in Tokyo, and it was a rare experience, and a mark of recognition to Ozawa, for the Japanese government to allow the Gagaku out of the palace and out of the country. This group consisted of ten musicians who brought with them such ancient Japanese instruments as the sho, fue, hichiriki, koto, biwa, katsuko, taiko, and shoko. They performed Sogu no. 2 for Gagaku and orchestra. The composer, Ishii, was a Western-trained musician who wrote in the style of Webern and Boulez. In this instance, he combined the sounds of the ancient instruments and Western sounds to create equal but separate impressions of both cultures. We in the orchestra were fascinated by the sight and sound of the Gagaku. The music was extremely cacophonous at first hearing, and only after a few performances, when we were able to fathom some of the distinctive elements, did the music make sense to us.

The year 1971–72 was a momentous one for Ozawa. It was announced that he had accepted the post of music director of the Boston Symphony. The report first came to us in February from *Newsweek* magazine, which intimated that Ozawa would leave San Francisco in 1973. When this news came out, Ozawa was in Philadelphia as guest conductor of that orchestra. He canceled a rehearsal there to clarify his situation in San Francisco to the musicians. As part of a speech to us, he said:

> I am glad to come here because I wanted to talk to you firsthand. Also I want to avoid misunderstanding between you and me. I know you will understand me if I say one important thing. We started work together only last year, and we have a few more weeks this year. We have a long way to go with this work. I have

a great belief and hope about this work we can do here. I am not going to change my job from one place to another. This is not my thought at all.

He went on to talk about all the traveling he had done around North America, sometimes twenty-two weeks a year— and he did not like hotel life. Furthermore, since his wife had recently given birth to a baby girl, he wanted to concentrate his work. He continued:

> When the Boston offer first came, my reaction was to think they wanted a conductor there all the time in Boston. I thought nega-tively about it because I didn't want to leave San Francisco. Then they said they were willing to accept me with my San Fran-cisco commitment. This put me in a difficult position with much confusion in my head. I started to think about it and study if there is a possibility to do these two jobs. I thought at first it was a crazy thing.

He spoke about the changing role of a music director in recent history: that he didn't have to be present twenty-two to twenty-five weeks; about first-class orchestras having a variety of conductors; that it was good for musicians to get different interpretations of the same work. Much rationalization! He explained further:

> A music director gives character to an orchestra, but an orches-tra does not need its Maestro all the time. I am doing fourteen to fifteen weeks this year. I think we can get character in this much time, and I think the audience will agree. . . . It will become easier, as I have decided only to work two orchestras in America —San Francisco and Boston. In a few years I will arrange this so I don't have to stay in hotels.

Ozawa was a great man with words, and his reassurances sounded sincere and convincing. A few musicians asked him questions, which he answered easily and to their satisfaction, most dealing with which orchestra he would favor when important decisions had to be made. I asked about our recording future, and his answer was again quick and clear—each orchestra was signed up with a different company, and as many recordings would be done with one orchestra as the other. If only it had worked out that way.

There was every reason to believe that Ozawa would get an important eastern orchestra, and Boston was one of the most prestigious. It would be interesting to see if the older Boston audience would be ready for his Beatle haircut and turtleneck shirts. But surely the time was ripe for a young jet set conductor to attract the new youthful audience that was becoming aware of classical music. Ozawa, at thirty-six, seemed just the right choice.

Meanwhile, the 1971–72 season brought us some interesting guest conductors. Kazuyoshi Akiyama was Japanese and a graduate of the same school as Ozawa, but his style was quite different. His manner was more studied and quiet, and he drew a deep, sensuous sound from the orchestra that had seldom been heard before. He was to be conductor of the Vancouver Symphony for its next season, and our musicians felt that Canada might have one of the "big ones."

The other exciting person who came to us that year was Istvan Kertesz. Heuwell Tircuit wrote in the *Chronicle:*

> It is always a pleasure to see a man happy in his work, and guest conductor Istvan Kertesz was obviously that Wednesday evening in the Opera House. His San Francisco Symphony debut offered not only a polished, stirring concert, but one whale of a good time for audience, orchestra and conductor alike.

This was one time I agreed wholeheartedly with a critic. I think we all thoroughly enjoyed Kertesz, his personality, and his conducting.

In writing about the Haydn Symphony no. 67 in F that Kertesz conducted, Tircuit said:

The trio of the Minuet is a folk study for concertmaster on deliberately untuned violins. Some of the second violins—six in this case—tune their G strings down to an F, helping add a raw edge to the sound for a hurdy-gurdy—a charming effect from Haydn, the Berlioz of the 18th century. When the orchestra arrived at this place, Kertesz simply stopped conducting, leaving concertmaster Stuart Canin to lead the merry little band of six hurdy-gurdiers as chamber music. And they did it very well indeed.

Kertesz was so delighted that just before going into the full orchestra repeat, he pulled a coin out of his pocket (a quarter from the sound of it), reached over, and slid it down the music stand of David Schneider, leader of the seconds—right in the middle of the piece, the way you'd drop a coin in an open music case in Union Square. It was probably the first time a symphony musician has been paid during the performance (Schneider broke up, nearly fell off his chair).

Some people in the audience believe that this honorarium I received is the high point in my career.

Kertesz had everything necessary to become the great conductor we would enjoy making music with, and we considered him the ideal replacement for Ozawa. To our sorrow, a short time after his last performance with us, he lost his life by drowning in the Mediterranean—a great loss to those who knew him and to the music-loving public.

There were three other guest conductors of note that year. One was Gabriel Chmura, a twenty-six-year-old Israeli who had won the Von Karajan conductor's competition over a field of eighty-two candidates. But there is a vast difference between conducting in competition and the day-to-day preparation of a symphony orchestra for a concert, and, unfortunately, Chmura was a disappointment to all of us.

Our second distinguished guest was the preeminent black conductor Dean Dixon. He was the first and oldest of several blacks who have made their mark on the symphonic music field. He had formed a chamber orchestra in New York, in 1938, and had engagements with the NBC, New York, Philadelphia, and Boston symphony orchestras. But Dixon's real success came in Europe, where he was artistic and music director of Sweden's Goteburg Symphony Orchestra and then music director of the Hessischer Rundfunk Symphony Orchestra in Frankfurt, Germany. In the last few years, simultaneous with his post in Germany, he was music director of Australia's Sydney Symphony Orchestra. Though offered numerous guest appearances in the United States, it is significant that Dixon had to go abroad to get a permanent orchestra of his own. He was gone for twenty-one years, finally coming home when he was almost sixty years old.

Dixon's attitude toward conducting was pragmatic rather than romantic. Here is his extremely realistic description of a conductor:

> You have to love whichever piece you are doing right then, no matter what it is—without that, you can't get the adrenalin up. Energy, that's what conductors are made of, not temper. People think it [conducting] is an ego trip, something to thrill the conductor, but it cuts itself off right away. You are playing along, the ensemble is good, the players are knitting the music, and you are in the heat of it all, both letting and making it happen. Then comes the finale, and you have to begin to push for yourself, as well as the players. Go through that all evening and you are ready to collapse. The music is done, and you ask the orchestra to rise, shake the concertmaster's hand and bow—trying to remember if anyone in the orchestra who had a solo should stand. You walk in and out, worrying about the next work, or the next concert. What you really want to do is run out and lie down a bit.

Here was a professional with a down-to-earth attitude about his art, who still preserved his fervent love of it. The audience and orchestra were ecstatic about his performances. Unfortunately, he never returned to conduct in this city again.

As 1971–72 ended, a strange atmosphere pervaded the orchestra. While the excitement that Ozawa engendered gave us an optimistic view of our future, uncertainties about our individual destinies kept us from being completely carefree.

In September 1972, Heuwell Tircuit, in a long, leisurely interview with Seiji Ozawa in Japan, stated that Ozawa "has become the city's most popular anxiety. He ranks just behind the prospect for another earthquake, but not by much.' Ozawa was now leading three orchestras—Boston, Tokyo, and San Francisco—but most major conductors had a similar schedule. When Ozawa told us he would conduct only in Boston and San Francisco in America, it, of course, did not preclude his conducting in Europe and Asia. It might seem that to be the regular conductor of three, or even two, orchestras simultaneously, one must be a master juggler. But, in fact, aside from the great deal of flying one must do, it may be easier than being permanent conductor of only one. If he conducts each orchestra for three months, he has to learn only twelve weeks of repertoire, which he can then perform with all three orchestras. (Also the jet set conductor receives a full and generous year's salary from each orchestra.) Monteux had a much more difficult task; in his final years, he had to present the San Francisco audience twenty to twenty-two different programs every year.

Tircuit went on to ask, inevitably, if Ozawa was leaving or staying, then followed it with the next logical query: 'Is there life after Ozawa?"

Ozawa answered typically, "I'm tired denying that I plan to leave San Francisco. The more I deny it, the more they talk. . . . After I hang around six or seven years, the idea will simply die a natural death—I hope." He assured Tircuit that he loved the city and that, even if he were fired, he would come back to his house to study.

Then he talked about the orchestra. 'The players are like my family, and working together I feel we are making tremendous progress. Quickly, too. Oh, there are still things that must be done, some changes to make, but we are close to my hopes already." He was quite convincing about his real desire to stay in San Francisco, even saying that if he ever had to decide between Boston and San Francisco, he would choose San Francisco. "You should remember that I'm Japanese," he explained. "Crazy Oriental, right? I have my own system of values and priorities in life. If West Coasters are generally hung up on the East Coast, well, all right. But that's their problem. Don't transpose your hangups to me. I have my own."

Later, the discussion turned to the ambition he still had, and Ozawa commented, "Yes, I want to break Eugene Ormandy's record for longevity in one post." Tircuit gave the mathematical requirements for that—Ozawa in San Francisco through the year 2007 and in Boston to 2010.

That interview was a great reference source from which to judge what was actually going on at the time in the symphony and how closely the future would live up to Ozawa's predictions. My antennae were especially attuned to the phrase "the players are like my family." We were experiencing a period of turmoil in the orchestra, and, if we followed the analogy, certain musicians were being treated like poor relations. There had been several "voluntary" relinquishments of first-chair positions in the first years of Ozawa's tenure, accomplished through pressure from the maestro. He would call a musician into his room, tell him specifically what he had done wrong, and then make some cutting remark about his playing in general. He said to one, "If I played like you, I'd be ashamed to go home and face my family." Strong, indeed, is the person who can stand up to such blistering criticism. Roland Kohloff, our tympanist, was one man who gave up his position rather than endure Ozawa's relentless attacks. He then succeeded his teacher, being chosen as tympanist of the New York Philharmonic.

Elayne Jones, our new tympanist, was an exciting personality to add to the ranks. She was a black woman, the mother of three, divorced from a Jewish doctor—her personal statistics covered the whole gamut of experience. Professionally, she had been tympanist with the American Symphony Orchestra with Stokowski and had been a free-lance performer in New York, which embraced every facet of musical engagement imaginable.

The position of tympanist in a symphony orchestra is exceedingly important. It establishes the bass of the harmony and the rhythmic profile of most compositions. Therefore, in order to choose the winner of the tympani audition, Ozawa asked that the symphony's first-chair players join the audition committee to form a small orchestra with which the finalists would play. Ozawa conducted a few pieces in which the tympanist had a prominent part. Though the players who were not committee members had no official say in the outcome, we were asked for our opinions. On that day, a Friday, the final auditions started at 10:00 A.M. Eleven players had reached the finals, but as the day went on the field was narrowed to two, Elayne Jones and Anthony Orlando. This crucial decision was complicated by Ozawa's idealistic standards, and by 6:00 P.M., with a concert starting at 8:30, no decision had been reached. The two finalists were asked if they could stay overnight so they could play with the full orchestra at the morning rehearsal. Thus, the auditions dragged on to the third day. In the intermission, Ozawa ran around backstage asking everyone what he or she thought about the tympani finalists, especially Elayne. One could see that he wanted to hire her but needed reassurance from everybody else. At last, after getting the approval of enough musicians to make him comfortable, he made that momentous decision: he hired Elayne Jones.

Although she would not start until the next season, Jones was engaged at the end of the 1971–72 season for a recording session. We were doing Bernstein's *West Side Story*, and Ozawa was unhappy with the percussion section. So he hired Elayne to play percussion which, she admitted, was not her strong point —she had played tympani almost exclusively the previous few years. She did a competent job, however, and it was a good opportunity for a lot of us to get acquainted with her.

We had contract negotiations that year, and I was on the committee to look into the reseating (read demotion) clauses of the contract. Ozawa, of course, wanted our rather stringent provisions eased, so he could hurry the process of replacing first-chairmen. Before going to talk with Ozawa at his home, I received a call from Jerry Spain, president of the San Francisco Musicians' Union, telling me to be particularly careful about any concessions given Ozawa in this regard, because many first-

Seiji Ozawa and the San Francisco Orchestra with the lavish backdrop of the War Memorial Opera House stage.

190

chairmen were up for reseating—and I was one of them. This news was a shock to me, as my relations with Ozawa had been very cordial, and he hadn't indicated any dissatisfaction with my work. In fact, the season before he had given me a raise in salary. When I confronted Ozawa with this information, he was a master of cover-up, and by the time he'd finished answering, I had no idea what he'd said. Moreover, he was at both a psychological and a physical advantage during the meetings, as we all sat on cushions on the floor, Japanese style, which left me, at best, quite uncomfortable. By the end of these meetings, Ozawa had gained a little in his ability to demote, but if a musician carried out all his options, it would still be difficult for the conductor to reseat him. (There were seven steps a musician could take to forestall his demotion, any one of which could result in his keeping his seat.) I heard no more about my being reseated at that time.

There was such a fine feeling in the orchestra about Ozawa's friendliness and amiability that most of us soon forgot any acrimony caused by these negotiations. Besides, all were eagerly awaiting our coming tour.

Chapter 19

EUROPE IN '73

After our subscription season in 1973, on the fifth of May, the orchestra started on its first European tour. This was a way to break into the big leagues of symphony orchestras, and with Ozawa as our leader we had every chance of success. This would be my first European trip, too, and I was looking forward to it unashamedly.

We arrived in Paris a couple of days before our first concert, and I tried to embrace the entire city in my arms. I had a sentimental attachment to Paris because of my first great conductor, Monteux, because of French Impressionism, and French literature, but most of all I had in mind the scene of Paris from the opera *Louise*. In this musical drama of two ill-fated lovers, the sights and sounds of Paris are so interwoven into the plot that one questions whether Louise or the city is the real heroine of the opera. I had a nostalgic feeling for Paris without having been there, and it did not disappoint me. When Geri arrived the next day, I took her around to see everything I had seen, as if I had lived in Paris all my life.

The orchestra's first concert on the continent was at the famous Théâtre des Champs Elysées. It was "un succès fou," as Robert Commanday wrote: "The cheers, rhythmic clapping and stamping held Seiji Ozawa and his musicians on the platform for three encores and twenty-five minutes past the official end of the program until he led them offstage." It was the first time we encountered that rhythmic and steady applause denoting a request for an encore, but it was not the last. It became a regular event for Ozawa to personally pull Canin up and off the stage, and we'd all follow—otherwise, it seemed they would applaud all night. The consensus of those who knew our orchestra was that we never sounded better and seldom as good. We could hear, also, how much the hall had to do with the beauty of our music—the sound was more vibrant and we could hear each other better than at the Opera House.

That first program in Paris was telecast live to San Francisco in an unprecedented satellite hookup. It consisted of Gabrieli's *Canzon Dodecemi Toni*, the Fourth Piano Concerto of Beethoven with Andre Watts, and the Symphonie *Fantastique* of Berlioz. Watts was almost as much a sensation as Ozawa, who had the temerity to bring a Parisian composition (the Berlioz) from San Francisco to Paris with brilliant results and excellent acceptance. The review in *Le Monde* was a little less enthusiastic than the audience, but we were never as popular with the critics as with the public.

From Paris we went to Brussels, where we played an entirely different program but again were excitedly received. In the Brussels audience was our former conductor, Enrique Jordá, who was now heading the Antwerp Orchestra in Belgium. He happily greeted orchestra members who were still there after the rebuilding of Krips and Ozawa. A decade had passed since we had seen him, and it was pleasant to talk with Jordá for a few moments, forgetting the difficulties we had with his conducting and remembering what a fine gentleman he was.

In London we were joined by mezzo-soprano Janet Baker, one of the orchestra members' favorite singers. She sang "Les Nuits d'Ete" of Berlioz. Baker's voice was especially suited for this lyric suite, and she brought out the melancholy of the songs with haunting beauty. At the end of his review of this concert, Commanday wrote, "A pattern of success and approval for the orchestra on its tour is already beginning to become apparent." Edward Greenfield of the *Manchester Guardian* wrote, "It was the string section of the San Francisco Orchestra in this London appearance which most called attention to itself, but for once one felt the brilliance had been subordinated to warmth and responsiveness. Here was a European orchestra translated." After England we returned to France.

One highlight of the tour was our concert in the Cathedral of Chartres. Although the musicians admired the gorgeous architecture of the cathedral, we were puzzled by the reverberating acoustics. The Gabrieli calls for two orchestras; we played at both ends of the church, and the echo effect became part of the composition. As Commanday wrote:

> The tones of Gabrieli's *Canzon Dodecemi Toni* answered from north to south between the divided brass choir. The Gabrieli was not like a madrigal, as it had been in earlier concert hall performances, but was slow and had great festive dignity.

There were four concerts in Switzerland, whose fabled beauty we enjoyed, and whose cool, crisp climate invigorated us. We played in Zurich, Basel, Geneva, and Bern, and we were beginning to get tired. The Geneva concert was given when the city was very crowded. It seemed that everybody in the world wanted to be in Geneva in the latter half of May, so we could obtain no accommodations there. We were put up in a little French town, Divonne au Bain, right near the border. There was a casino in the town and quaint little stores. In one of these tiny emporiums, one musician spied a pair of patent leather shoes, the kind many of us wear for concerts. He purchased a pair and went out to spread the word, and there began a run on patent leather shoes such as the proprietress had never before experienced. In this little shop that carried all kinds of dry goods, I too found a pair that fit. Ten years later I was still wearing them. I believe I got my eight dollars' worth.

In Zurich, birthplace of our assistant conductor, Niklaus Wyss, the entire orchestra and spouses were treated to a dinner party by the Wyss family in a charming chalet. We appreciated this lovely gesture and the break it allowed us from our grueling schedule. After only one day off, we proceeded with one-night stands in Hanover, Berlin, Munich, and Frankfurt in Germany, and Linz in Austria.

The Munich concert was a solemn one, dedicated to the memory of Hans Schmidt-Isserstedt, who had suddenly died the day before. He was one of our favorite guest conductors and seemed to have a paternal feeling toward us. Just two days earlier, he had come to hear our Hanover concert.

Landing at Linz, we were delighted to see what seemed like the entire population at the airport to greet us. People were sitting on roofs of buildings and everywhere else, so they could see the plane arrive. "At last we are getting the recognition we deserve," we thought. "We are being welcomed by the famous musical city of Linz with enthusiasm." But when we debarked from the plane and waved at the awaiting populace, we received very little response. We soon found out that it was not us the good citizens of Linz came out to greet but the plane—the first 747 to land at their airport!

We were fortunate to have three days in Vienna, as the succession of one-night stands was beginning to wear on us. We had been engaged for only two concerts, so we had time to explore this fabled city and to rest. All Vienna had a musical atmosphere, and we kept seeing both students and adults carrying music cases. Felix Khuner, who had left Austria with the advent of Hitler, had bittersweet thoughts on returning to his native city. As our tour guide, he showed us all the important landmarks of his Vienna, the most noteworthy, of course being the house in which he was born. He couldn't resist going there and introducing himself to the present tenants.

Geri and I enjoyed the light music played by a small orchestra in the park near our hotel. In the intermission, an American violinist in the group told me about the job, and I was distressed to hear how backbreaking it was—they played seven days a week, five hours a day. He had no time to prepare himself for a more satisfying position.

It was in the Grinzig, a suburb of Vienna, that our conductor emeritus, Josef Krips, gave us a marvelous party celebrating the season of "new wine." There could have been no more genial host. Krips acted like an old world baron entertaining the nobility. (Like many other conductors, Krips was wonderful away from the podium. This is something we musicians have been told often by patrons of the arts, who know conductors only from social gatherings where these famous musical personalities are witty, charming, and intellectually stimulating. When we complain about problems with a conductor, they say, "You should see how pleasant he is socially." Unfortunately, our association with these conductors is not social but professional, and in those circumstances we often see them at their worst. That night it was a pleasure to enjoy Krips at his best.)

From Vienna we went to Florence, the only Italian city in which we played. We had two performances there and plenty of time to explore that art-filled city. Unfortunately, after Florence, we had to come to a parting of the ways. The orchestra went on to the Soviet Union, while some of our companions, including Geri, returned home. The government of the USSR had been very slow about issuing visas for the "dependents," and by the time they came we were already in Europe and it was too late to make new plans.

Walking into our old world Leningrad hotel, I encountered Ozawa, who said, succinctly, "The beer here is terrible." It was true. From a food and drink standpoint, we had a hard time in Russia, but otherwise our experience there was one of the most memorable of the tour. We gave four concerts in each of three cities—Leningrad, Vilnius, and Moscow. We had time to see the many unusual sights and treasures, and expert guides to show us the highlights of these cities and answer questions.

Our concerts in the Soviet Union were uniformly successful. We were the first American orchestra to appear in Russia in eight years, and the public responded ecstatically. The music critic for the Leningrad evening paper, *Vecherniy Leningrad*, wrote:

The vivid impression made by the San Francisco Symphony derives to a great extent from the individuality of its director, the highly gifted conductor, Seiji Ozawa. The musical phrases grow out of the movement of his hands, which is unusually delicate, accurate and which recalls the gestures of a dancer or a player of the Japanese Kabuki Theatre. . . . The performance characteristic of Ozawa is a fusion of the conductor with the music he performs. He neither imposes nor dictates to the orchestra, rather inviting the musicians to join him in a joyfully musical experiment.

The Russian public, which easily takes to heroes, found one in Ozawa. After each concert hundreds would be awaiting him for an autograph, a wave, or just a smile. Many of us wore Ozawa buttons, and we received many Russian pins, medals, and so on in exchange for them.

One of my private missions when touring Russia was to visit the synagogues. In both Leningrad and Vilnius I went to the synagogue on Saturday morning, took part in the services, and then inconspicuously left religious articles I had brought. In Leningrad the large, impressive synagogue was not being used for the services; since only a few men attended, they used a small chapel in back of the main building. I conversed with one man there in broken Yiddish and Hebrew, and he asked if I'd like to see the large synagogue after services. When I accepted, he cautioned me to silence. I couldn't understand what this secrecy was about, but when the services were over and he brought me to the main building, he again put his finger to his lips in the universal symbol of silence. He introduced me to the shamus (beadle) and then left. I engaged this shamus in conversation, again in broken Yiddish and Hebrew, he asking me about the kind of congregation I belonged to, and I trying to tell him about Israel and its achievements, in order to dispel some of the terrible rumors about that country circulated in Russia. When I left, my friend from the service was waiting outside. His first words to me were that the shamus was "a bad man"—a government "plant" who spied on his fellow Jews. From what I was able to later ascertain, this was not unusual.

We had one night off in Leningrad, and we were offered tickets for either the Russian Circus or the Leningrad Opera.

197

Most of the musicians including Ozawa opted for the circus, for it was known to be one of the most spectacular in the world—and besides, it was good to get away from music for a night. But about a dozen of us decided that we would prefer the opera. When I learned that the opera that night was Tchaikovsky's *Queen of Spades*, there was no doubt in my mind. It is one of my sentimental favorites, with the hauntingly morbid libretto so wonderfully expressed by Tchaikovsky's music. And the added ingredient of hearing an opera in the city in which the story takes place made it even more exciting. We were given good seats near the front of the orchestra section, so we could see and hear the orchestra well. The musicians were very fine, but, unhappily, their instruments ranged from mediocre to horrible.

The quality of instruments is crucially important to an orchestra. Wind instruments in poor condition can wreak havoc with the ensemble's intonation and sound. Getting good reeds for clarinets, oboes, and bassoons is a constant problem, even in the United States where players have access to the best. In the USSR, where consumer products are generally at a premium, it may not be part of the "grand plan" to manufacture reeds or violin strings, and imports are virtually impossible. Many of our string players brought along extra sets of strings to give to their Russian colleagues. (Good instruments are difficult to find anywhere, even if the musician has enough money, and they are extremely expensive. A good French violin costs $15,000 or more, and a fine Italian instrument would go from $25,000 up to $500,000 for a Stradivarius or a Guarnerius. Buying an instrument is almost as difficult as buying a house. The difference in sound between an orchestra that has good instruments and one that has poor instruments is tremendous, which is why many orchestras have a pool of fine instruments—usually strings—especially for the principal players.)

The Leningrad Opera singers were adequate, though not comparable to the artists we were used to in the San Francisco Opera. Nevertheless, I thoroughly enjoyed the evening, and, despite the praises I heard about the circus, I didn't regret my choice.

Compared to Leningrad, where people always seemed grey and noncommunicative, Vilnius (formerly Vilna of Lithuania) had a more pleasant aspect, perhaps because the populace stubbornly held on to some of its own ethnic customs and mores. There were many statues of the Communist head of that little country, but the people ignored these and, to the best of their ability, tried to live the way they had before being taken over by the USSR. Vilna had been the center of Jewish learning in the eighteenth and nineteenth centuries, but, under the combination of the Russian and German armies, almost the entire Jewish population had been destroyed. A small group had, fortunately, been exiled to Siberia before the coming of the German armies. A very few Jews still remained in Vilnius and I visited their synagogue, too. What struck me most upon seeing these houses of worship was the lack of young people; almost no one was under sixty years old. Most of the modern generation had been taught to despise religion, and only the miracle of Israel revived the religious fervor that was at one time an integral part of being a Russian Jew. There was also the fear of government reprisal, either overt or subtle, against those who practiced any religion in Russia, especially the Jewish religion.

Moscow was the climax of our entire tour. A glorious metropolis and world capital, it had much to offer the tourist. Our hotel was right off Red Square, and there was no end to what we could discover in that series of buildings. Unfortunately, we witnessed numerous examples of the fear and suspicion that seem so pervasive in this totalitarian country.

One of the great moments of my musical career took place in Moscow. When it was announced that the Soviet Union would be part of our tour, Ozawa insisted that the great cellist Mstislav Rostropovich play one concert in Moscow with us. At the time, Rostropovich was in disfavor with the Soviet government because of his friendship and support of Solzhenitsyn. He had not been allowed to play concerts in Russia for many years, nor had he been permitted to leave the country. This concert with the San Francisco Symphony was to bring him out of ostracism.

Rostropovich had showed a great deal of warmth toward our orchestra from the first time he had played with us, and when we rehearsed in Moscow he was like one of us, even helping us in our rendition of the Soviet national anthem. In the performance of the Dvorak Concerto that evening, there was a perfect fusion of the minds and souls of Ozawa and Rostropovich. The cellist played like a god—the beauty of tone and conception cannot be described—and in every nuance Ozawa was as if living in the skin of Rostropovich. For those forty minutes they were blood brothers. Even the hardened musicians were seen with tears running down their faces, so emotional, so beautiful, so remarkable was that performance. The audience, too, was caught up in the electricity of the occasion and responded with wild applause and huzzahs. I was standing next to Ozawa when Rostropovich was taking a bow, and he said to me, "He is something, isn't he?" I said, "You're something, too, maestro!" For indeed, of all the great accompaniments he had conducted for us, this was the greatest. The evening ended with Ozawa carrying Rostropovich's cello on stage for him to play a "Saraband" of Bach for an encore.

Mstislav Rostropovich, Russian cellist, was a frequent guest soloist with the San Francisco Symphony. In 1977, he became conductor of the National Symphony in Washington, D.C.

After this emotional high, I was soon brought down by a figurative "cold shower." At the tour's last concert in Moscow, I was asked to come backstage to see Ozawa in the intermission. When I arrived in his room, he was stripped to the waist and lying flat on his back on the floor. He looked quite lifeless (he had been having back trouble and had just had a massage). When he saw me, he jumped to his feet and quietly began telling me all the wrong things I had been doing and the ways I had been failing as principal second violin. Although I had been warned months ago by Jerry Spain, the union president, that my position was in jeopardy, I had put it in the back of my mind —so I was shocked. Ozawa had never told me any of this before. And since this was the last concert of the season, I could do nothing to demonstrate improvement, as I would not see him again until the beginning of our next season in November. My trip home, as well as the forthcoming summer, was spoiled.

My flight from Russia was miserable. Besides the chastisement from Ozawa, I had gotten sick from the terrible food we were served in the USSR. Ozawa's message and the possible consequences would not be a pleasant thing to bring home to Geri. I kept going over in my mind all the faults Ozawa found in my playing and wondering if my professional life would now be in shambles. My personal stock market had crashed, and I had to figure out how to pick myself up again and regain my self-respect.

Chapter 20

TOIL AND TROUBLE

At last the San Francisco Symphony had come of age. With our records and our European tour, we had established a reputation that put us up with the world's great orchestras. At the head of this "world-class" orchestra was one of the world's most renowned conductors, and he had vowed time and again to remain indefinitely with this symphony. It seemed that all the pain was behind us and only joy would remain. But that would violate the basic philosophy of conductors: what may be good can be better, and what is better can be best. And how is this achieved? By changing what can be changed and moving what can't be changed. Though Ozawa was an exceptional conductor, he was like all the others in this regard. And so began a season of upheaval.

From Ozawa's point of view, the first order of business was to take care of David Schneider. Since his criticism of me at that last Moscow concert, I had worked to overcome the faults he had pointed out, but it was to no avail. Early in 1974, I was told that Ozawa wanted to see me after rehearsal. I knew that this was the first step toward my reseating. If I proceeded according to the contract clause that protected those in my position, there would be seven steps to go through before the move could be completed. But bravely and foolishly, I decided I could fight it my own way, without the help of the committee or anyone else.

I had been practicing the Carl Nielsen Violin Concerto off and on for several months. The Nielsen was a twentieth-century work the symphony had not yet played, and I'd heard that Ozawa wanted to do it. It was difficult, but I knew that, given time, I could learn it and play it well. When I was notified of my official meeting with Ozawa, I told him I would like to play for him. He said, "All right! You mentioned before that you wanted to play for me. Why don't we set it up for tomorrow after the rehearsal?" Although I was not yet prepared to play the Nielsen, I agreed. In twenty-four hours, miracles could occur. I talked to my pianist, Reina Schivo, and arranged a rehearsal. She discouraged me from playing it. My wife begged me not to do it, insisting that no matter how well I played it would make no difference, since Ozawa obviously didn't want me in that first stand. Jerry Spain sent word that under no circumstance should I play for Ozawa at this time. But I would not be dissuaded.

After rehearsal the next day, a stand was set up for me on stage, the piano was moved in, and I handed the orchestra score to Ozawa, who sat in the middle of the hall with Joe Scafidi. A miracle did not occur. On the contrary, even the facility I had acquired in playing the Nielsen was marred by my nervousness. My stupid stubbornness was my undoing, and I learned another lesson about heeding the advice of cooler heads than mine.

Ozawa was not at all shy about pointing out my errors. He pounced on each one to emphasize my obvious incompetence. At the end of his long tirade about my inferior playing, he said, "This is a very difficult concerto. Why did you want to play it for me?" I couldn't give him the answer I wanted to give—that I had hoped to perform it with the symphony. That would have been ridiculous after what had just transpired. I knew that I could play the work well, but the psychological strain of the situation left me at a loss.

Negotiations began then about where I would go after leaving my post as principal second violin. Ozawa and Scafidi suggested I could be "promoted" to the last seat, first violin, as the musician sitting there, Francesco Mazzi, was retiring. I disagreed and suggested that since Ferdinand Claudio would retire a year later, they could wait until then and give me his position of outside seat, fourth stand, in the first violin section. Ozawa was not pleased with my idea. First of all, he didn't want to wait another whole season to replace me; secondly, he would have liked some younger person to get that choice place, one who would win the post by competition. He suggested that I could still try out for Ferdinand's spot when it became available. On the surface, this idea seemed completely fair. However, I never showed myself to best advantage in auditions. Furthermore, the auditions were not conducted anonymously behind a screen, as were auditions to get into the orchestra; so if Ozawa didn't want me in that stand and didn't like my playing now, why would he like it any better then? We left the matter up in the air. I had three days' time to decide whether I would fight the reseating.

On the third day, I had an appointment with Ozawa, Joe Scafidi, and Tom Heimberg, the union steward. We again discussed the possibility of my getting Ferdinand's position when he left. Again Ozawa said that he didn't want to wait a year, and he did want auditions for that post; and further, he didn't know if the orchestra members would approve of my moving there. The last point was an interesting one. If I moved to any open seat in the second violin section, it would be considered a demotion and I would be allowed by contract to have it. But since I was going to the first violin section, even though it was neither a "name" seat nor as much pay, it was still desirable, and it was unclear in the contract whether I could be appointed to it.

To Ozawa's first point I answered that an experienced musician for that position would most likely be holding a similar post in another orchestra, and it would take a year for him to free himself to assume the one in San Francisco. Secondly, I frankly told him that I was lousy at auditions, but since I had played in the first violin section for twenty-five years, ten of them on the second stand, I was undoubtedly capable of holding down that position. On the third point—that the members might not approve—I suggested that we let the union and orchestra decide, as long as Ozawa approved. For once my arguments prevailed. Tom Heimberg told me afterward that he had never seen anyone turn Ozawa around so persuasively and in such a logical manner. The members voted to allow me the seat in the first violin section, with a few more than the required two-thirds favorable votes; so my case was finished, with a few loose ends to be cleared up later on.

My reseating was the first one made by Ozawa in his giant revamping of the orchestra that season. He informed four other members by letter that they were subject to reseating—Rolf Persinger, principal viola; Robert Sayre, principal cello; Mary Hughson Claudio, inside first stand cello; and Donald Reinberg, principal trumpet. This wholesale reseating shook up the orchestra rather strongly. Both Persinger and Sayre had been brought in by Maestro Krips just a few years previously, to bolster the orchestra and raise its standards. Yesterday's heroes were today's rejects. Under Krips they were featured soloists every year. Now they were to be shoved to the rear and forgotten. Mary Claudio had won her seat in an open audition under Krips and was considered one of the stronger players in the section. Donald Reinberg had always been held in highest regard. Now both had to go through the humiliation of fighting for their own jobs.

Unlike me, they decided to fight the reseating in the manner suggested by the contract. One step in this procedure was that Ozawa had to give them help and advice, so they could improve to the point where they could keep their positions. In the final wrap-up of my situation, I asked Scafidi to have Ozawa give me the same opportunity to possibly change his mind. This was an absolutely futile exercise. If he corrected me on something one week, and I came back the next week and asked him if it was better, he would say "yes, but" and then tell me what was wrong now. It was like trying to stop the damage of a leaky roof with a pan. With the other four players, he started the procedure too late in the season, so he had to abandon his plans for reseating them until the next season.

Still another personnel problem arose during the 1973–74

season, which proved to be the most controversial issue that had ever befallen the San Francisco Symphony. Two probationary members were denied tenure in the orchestra, which was tantamount to being fired at the end of the season. The contract clause that dealt with gaining permanent status stipulated that either the orchestra, through its committee, or the conductor could deny tenure during a probationary member's first two years in the orchestra. The purpose of this clause was to assure the presence of only the best musicians in the group; for once in, it was virtually impossible to lose one's job. The previous year, one of our probationary members, principal trombonist Miles Anderson, was denied tenure by Maestro Ozawa, although he was approved by the orchestra committee. Some musicians were unhappy about Ozawa's decision, but it was understood that he had acted correctly according to the contract. There could be no argument, and there was none.

Now, after polling the orchestra, the orchestra committee had voted that neither Ryohei Nakagawa, principal bassoonist, nor Elayne Jones, tympanist, would achieve tenure. This caused immediate problems. Nakagawa was a personal friend of Ozawa, and it was the conductor's gentle persuasion of the audition committee that had assured Nakagawa's successful entry into the orchestra. Now, after almost two seasons, the committee had voted that the bassoonist wasn't good enough. Ozawa was furious about Nakagawa's case, more so, it seems, than about Jones'. But in the latter situation, the association realized it had a hot potato on its hands. Elayne Jones was one of the orchestra's most visible members. The tympani player is the only standing musician among a sea of sitting figures. And on top of that, Elayne was a black woman. Throughout the two seasons she had been in the orchestra, the audience had automatically looked at her and admired her. She had captured the fancy of many as a kind of folk heroine of the symphony. To deny her tenure, and to have that decision come from the orchestra, was foolhardy.

By the terms of the contract, there were no specified criteria to determine a probationary member's worthiness; no reasons had to be given for denying continued participation in the orchestra. But because of the controversial nature of both of these cases—each individual coming from a minority group, Nakagawa's special relationship with the conductor, and Jones' popular personality—explanations were asked for. They were given: Nakagawa's tone and ensemble playing were not good enough to hold the position of principal bassoonist, and Jones' intonation and rhythm were found wanting.

The Symphony Association's response to this committee action was immediate and rigorous. Joe Scafidi called for a meeting of the entire orchestra after our evening concert. He and Ozawa asked the musicians to overturn their committee's decision and retain Nakagawa and Jones. This request was contractually illegal, and Jerry Spain of the Musicians' Union was prepared to file a grievance with the National Labor Relations Board (NLRB). The orchestra upheld its committee. For a brief period, the other six probationary members, who had already received committee approval, feared that Ozawa would withhold his approval as reprisal for the action against the other two, but their tenure went through.

Nakagawa, though naturally unhappy about his fate, took it stoically and said he would attempt to get back into the orchestra at the next audition. Jones, on the other hand, felt terribly betrayed. Ozawa had not seemed displeased with her playing, nor had her colleagues given her the impression that she was not doing well. The fact is, it is very hard for an orchestra member to criticize a colleague. Because such comments may be misconstrued, most musicians will refrain from criticizing their fellows. The feeling is that it is up to the conductor to correct a musician's shortcomings. Moreover, one of Elayne's problems was intonation, which is considered so sensitive and personal a concern that it is particularly difficult to discuss. (An old musical adage goes, "Never argue with anyone about religion or intonation.")

When she recovered from the shock, Elayne lashed out at her adversaries, claiming they were racist and sexist. Since there were more women in ours than in any other major orchestra, sexism would be hard to prove. The accusation of racism, however, had to be answered. In the symphony's entire history there had been only one other black member, and it seemed we would lose the only one we now had. Elayne began marshaling forces for her case. She had strong support from the newspapers: the critics had always regarded her playing in a favorable light; a couple of them were personal friends of hers; and, above all, here was a cause célèbre to focus serious attention on an otherwise rather dull column. No matter how little readers may know about music, they take sides on a musical issue if the question of prejudice is brought into the picture.

Inflammatory language was used to arouse the anger of the public, and it worked. Commanday wrote:

> The decisions against Elayne Jones and Ryohei Nakagawa were preposterous, scandalous. In intonation, tone, and rhythm, the tympani playing of Miss Jones had been one of the symphony's strongest elements, giving it an accurate rhythmic structure, with a decisiveness that lent security to particularly crucial performances by guest and opera conductors.

His colleague, Heuwell Tircuit, said:

> In my considered estimation she [Jones] is one of the finest tympani players in the U.S., comparable only to the players with the Cleveland Orchestra and L.A. Philharmonic. The Europeans have no one in her class that I have heard. The many recordings on which she has performed prove it.

Against such authoritative statements, who could believe the judgment of seven mere musicians (none of whom were principals, the critics were quick to point out)? Letters began piling in from a public up in arms about the injustice being done. Music teachers had their students send in petitions demanding the reinstatement of Jones and Nakagawa. Acquaintances who had never been to a symphony concert asked me what kind of outfit I belonged to that would allow such prejudice to prevail.

Amidst all this turmoil, Elayne Jones' attorney Allan Brodtsky, brought suit against the committee, the union, and the association, charging racial and sexual prejudice. Depositions were taken from the committee members (who were now certain to be jumped on by the critics whenever they played a solo in concert). The trial went on and on but Jones finally lost her case. This did not stop her, however. She filed another suit requesting a reevaluation by a new committee. In order for the air to be completely cleared of any wrongdoing by the association and orchestra, both Jones and Nakagawa were allowed to continue in the orchestra for an unprecedented third probationary year.

During this whole period of time, abuse was heaped upon the orchestra and its committee from every quarter. It took years to recover from the damage done the symphony's reputation. Contrary to published reports, Ozawa had never voted on the tenure of the two controversial players, as the committee's vote had made his own unnecessary. He could have alleviated the situation if he had been more forthright in his comments, but he was so equivocal about his position that each side claimed he had said different things. When the second suit arose, the federal mediator required that both the second committee and Ozawa vote simultaneously. Both Ozawa and the committee voted her down, and, at the end of the 1974–75 season, Elayne Jones left the San Francisco Symphony. She is, however, still playing with the San Francisco Opera Orchestra.

The Jones problem was personally difficult for many musicians in the orchestra, including me. I was very much in favor of her becoming a member of the orchestra; I had always been a strong advocate for minority participation. Moreover, as she had an engaging and lively personality, I willingly overlooked inconsistencies in her audition playing. A couple of percussionists pointed out some errors at the time of her audition, but I for one didn't want to hear about them. I had made up my mind and didn't want logic to interfere with my opinion. It was reverse prejudice, and I'm afraid many other musicians felt the same

way. During the season, however, I admittedly was often bothered by her intonation and the fact that when her instruments
were out of tune she did not notice and correct the problem. It
was not consistently bad, but when it was, it was obvious. It was
also difficult to coordinate rhythms with her. I couldn't understand the wholehearted endorsement of her playing by the
critics.

No one had ever said that Jones was a poor tympani player;
the question was whether she was good enough to become a
permanent member of the orchestra. The honest opinion of the
orchestra committee members was that she was not. I do not
blame Elayne for fighting for her professional life, but I do
blame the critics for exacerbating the situation, the Symphony
Association for not being strong enough to stand by its contract
with the musicians, and Ozawa for not having the courage to
speak out clearly and strongly for what he believed.

Chapter 21

OZAWA AND A PARADE OF CONDUCTORS

The 1973–74 season featured many guest conductors. Ozawa was scheduled to conduct fourteen weeks of the season, but because of ill health he could do only eleven and a half. Monteux had come to us at almost "senior citizen" age (past sixty) and had rarely missed a rehearsal, let alone a concert, in his seventeen years with the symphony. His physical exercise consisted of waving his arms while conducting and walking to and from the vehicle that took him where he was going. Young and athletic Ozawa liked to ski, play baseball, and do anything that demonstrated his muscular prowess and physical agility. Yet he was either ill or overtired a major portion of the time he was here.

Ironically, youth had been glorified in the orchestra from the time Ozawa took over. At one time to be young was to be inexperienced, and maestros were wary of inexperience. But from the time of Ozawa's ascension to the San Francisco Symphony podium, the clarion call was "Get them here young and hot—I'll teach them what they have to know about orchestra playing." I cannot dispute the fact that young musicians now entering the orchestra are, on the average, better instrumental technicians than in previous years. But other qualities are necessary for good orchestral playing—flexibility, awareness of nuances, and a feel for a piece in one's bones, sinews, heart, and mind that comes only from playing works hundreds of times; in other words, experience. There are, naturally, exceptions— young musicians who instinctively know the way a piece should sound and can play it right immediately. And there are old duffers who never seem to get it. I think the philosophy that young is good and old is worn out has seen its day, and the pendulum will swing the other way.

There were other reasons besides Ozawa's illness for the plethora of guest conductors in our 1973–74 season: Josef Krips, our conductor emeritus, was forced to cancel his three weeks because of illness, and Hans Schmidt-Isserstedt had died while we were in Europe in 1973. Since schedules are set for all artists and conductors at least a year in advance, it is difficult to make last-minute replacements. Two of Krips' scheduled weeks were taken by Hans Vonk, a Dutch conductor who was disciplined and well schooled but not overly exciting. The other week was filled in by the American conductor John Mauceri, whose program included three unusual compositions—the Frank Martin Piano Concerto no. 2, with Paul Badura-Skoda as soloist, and Ives' *Three Places in New England* and *He Is There*. It is rare for guest conductors to play novelties, as it is "safer" to conduct the standard repertoire.

The first of the guests making his debut with our orchestra was Michael Tilson Thomas. At twenty-seven years of age and already the director of the Buffalo Philharmonic, principal guest conductor of the Boston Symphony, and director of the New York Philharmonic's Young People's Concerts, he was as much a child prodigy of the baton as Yehudi Menuhin was on the violin at the age of six. Conducting Mahler's Ninth Symphony, Thomas was sensational. He has since been a guest conductor with us many times, with varied degrees of success.

Another Dutch conductor to make his first appearance with our orchestra was Edo de Waart, who had come from Rotterdam, where, as general director for several seasons, he had built that orchestra up to challenge the Concertgebouw as Holland's most prestigious symphony. De Waart's program contained no surprises, but his conducting and personality made a very favorable impression on both the public and the orchestra. Though de Waart was a young, vigorous man, there was solidity and classicism about his musical approach that made the management sit up and take notice. After observing de Waart for only one week, the Symphony Association engaged him as principal guest conductor of the San Francisco Symphony, starting in the 1975–76 season. Principal guest conductor was a relatively new position created for the modern orchestra. Musical directors were at their main posts so little each season that, to avoid a steady parade of conductors and lend some stability to the orchestra, one guest conductor was engaged for a number of weeks in a row. This allowed him to reach a certain rapport with the musicians and create a repertoire of his own. In his first year as principal guest conductor, de Waart was to be with us six weeks.

Coming back for his third consecutive season was our other favorite Japanese conductor, Kazuyoshi Akiyama, who presented a repertoire replete with novelties. Sergiu Comissiona, a charming Romanian, had a delightful sense of humor, unlike most conductors. In his interview upon arriving in San Francisco, he showed that he knew what a hero figure Ozawa had become by pondering out loud, "I wonder if I should change my name to Seiji Comissiona?" He was currently the conductor of the Baltimore Symphony but had spent many years in Israel as conductor of the Haifa Symphony and Israel Chamber Orchestra. Toward the end of his week, I spoke with him about Israel, and he seemed so friendly and kind that I also told him of the difficulties I was having with Ozawa about my position in the orchestra. He acted surprised and made me the ego-boosting offer of coming to Baltimore in the same capacity I had in San Francisco. I had no intention of accepting and I'm sure he knew I wouldn't, but it did lift my spirits.

The first change in the conducting roster because of Ozawa's indisposition was made in the first week of April, when an entire program of Stravinsky's music was scheduled. Niklaus Wyss,

assistant conductor of the orchestra and acting director of the
Symphony Chorus, had prepared *The Wedding*, a complicated
work for symphony, chorus, and vocal and piano soloists.
Ozawa conducted the first half of the program—Concerto for
String Orchestra and Concerto for Piano and Wind Instruments—and Wyss conducted *The Wedding*, which took up the
second half. Wyss was a well-schooled conductor and Ozawa
depended on him a great deal, not only for help during emer-
gencies, as in this case, but also for general advice in musical
matters.

One composition Ozawa was in physical, mental, and spiritual shape for was the piece he prepared for our Easter program
—Bach's *St. Matthew's Passion*. This was the kind of work
Ozawa could do justice to—a double orchestra, a large chorus,
soloists, and gloriously solemnic music. He loved to have large
forces at his command and always did a marvelous job when an
opportunity like this arose. He was the general, directing the
armies of nations against evil.

But less than a month later, Ozawa was again hospitalized
with back and neck problems. The symphony was fortunate to
get the services of Kenneth Schermerhorn, director of the Mil-
waukee Symphony, to conduct the first week he was out. The
program was one magnificent work, the *Tragic* Symphony, the
Sixth of Gustav Mahler. The performance was elaborately
praised by the critics. Amazingly, this mammoth, deep, and
soul-searching work was rehearsed, absorbed, and presented by
the orchestra to the San Francisco public in a matter of four
days. With a great work, an inspired conductor and a professional orchestra can perform miracles when the winds are right.

Another replacement had to be found for Ozawa's second
week of illness, and, fortunately, George Cleve, conductor of
the San Jose Symphony, was available to conduct the series of
concerts. In the last week of the season, Ozawa was well enough
to conduct *Gurrelieder*, a full-length work by Schoenberg. Another giant composition—another Seiji Ozawa triumph. Despite
his physical problems, he was always up to the big works.

214

Ozawa reached the height of his popularity in San Francisco during the 1974–75 season—an atmosphere of cultism surrounded him. This was the first strong name identification with the symphony. Monteux, although beloved by many, was a hero only to the true music lover; the proverbial man in the street never felt his drawing power. Jordá, with his little body and dashing movements, might have developed into a charismatic personality if he had proved himself a better conductor. And Krips, though a fine conductor, was not the type of personality to enchant the world. But Ozawa had it all—a great conductor, an exciting personality, enough eccentricities to intrigue all who heard about him—he was the Elvis Presley of the symphony aficionado.

The critics joined the general audiences in acclaiming his interpretations. In writing about his conducting of Mozart's *Prague* Symphony, Commanday said, "The qualities for which he had been so often admired were there, the beautiful phrasing, the liquid continuity and nuancing of melody. This time, most importantly, the music was stirring." Speaking just as glowingly of Ozawa's *Eroica*, he evoked the spirit of Krips, who had died just two months before. He ended his review by writing:

> But of all, the "Funeral March" remained in the memory, a moving performance. I couldn't help but think of Josef Krips, for although he would, of course, have done it in other ways the spirit of Ozawa's Beethoven and Mozart was authentic. And Ozawa's feeling as a human was genuine and made most convincing contact.

It was not ever thus. In the past, critics had often called Ozawa's performances shallow, saying that he was more interested in spectacular effects than in revealing the essence of the music.

Ozawa made the critics happy in other respects. He conducted enough modern music and unusual oldies to please the most jaded concertgoer. On the same program with the *Prague* and the *Eroica*, he presented the first San Francisco performance of an American work, George Crumb's *Echoes of Time, and the River*, which Commanday labeled "a mystifying, fascinating and spaced out composition." This was one production that required acting as well as playing from the musicians. There was marching and blowing air through instruments without musical sound, as well as mixing musical symbols of the past, present, and future. At the next program, Ozawa presented a novelty of the last generation, Ravel's *L'Enfant et les Sortileges*, with a libretto by the French writer Colette. It is an animated fairy tale, and Mary and Lee Blair, who were affiliated with Walt Disney Productions, did the illustrations. The intricate work required the services of the symphony, chorus, and vocal soloists, and Ozawa was in his element when conducting it.

Early in 1975, Ozawa presented a world premiere of a work by Hungarian-born composer Gyorgy Ligeti, *The San Francisco Polyphony*, which had been commissioned by patrons Dr. and Mrs. Ralph Dorfman as a gift for the symphony's anniversary. The composition was a follow-up of another work of Ligeti, *Melodien*, which we had performed with Ozawa in 1972. Of this earlier composition, Ligeti said:

> In this piece there are many simultaneous but divergent melodic patterns, and you can hear them, by listening to the piece, each melody separately, or all together, forming a complex structure and musical form. I heard three performances of this piece before 1972, but was not happy with any of them. I couldn't clearly hear the separate voices. Then in May 1972, Seiji Ozawa and the San Francisco Symphony performed the piece and this happened to be the first real performance of this music. Each orchestra player studied his individual part before the first rehearsal, and Ozawa rehearsed the piece perfectly, coordinating the separate melodies to an overall and harmonious unity of musical form.

The very next week, Ozawa presented another San Francisco premiere, a full program-length work by Olivier Messiaen called *Turangalila* Symphonie. This required the symphony, a piano soloist, and a soloist on a unique electronic instrument—

les ondes-martenet. A chronicler of twentieth-century music
called this composition:

> . . . a symphony, yes, but forget all average ideas of the form.
> *Turangalila* is an impassioned musical document whose ten
> movements cover almost an hour and a half of playing time. . . .
> It is the equivalent of Tristan and Isolde converted into orches-
> tral fantasies by way of Hindu-promulgated metrical plans.

Most contemporary works are lucky if they are performed half a
dozen times; in Tokyo in 1972, *Turangalila* was given its 100th
performance.

A composition that Ozawa presented later in the season
brought out yet a different style of modern music. Carman
Moore's *Gospel Fuse* was, as its name implies, a fusion of gospel
music with traditional symphonic material. Moore wrote of it:

> Although my formal composition training is based on the music
> of Boulez, Berio, Bartok, Stravinsky, Cage, and company and
> one part of my compositional language lies there, I feel it is time
> for my own serious music to get serious about musical forms and
> tendencies in my blood. Making aspects of the gospel church—
> where piano, drums, organ and tambourine make a Sunday
> orchestra, where singers and accompanists make up their own
> cadenzas, recitatives, and word illuminations on the spot, where
> the congregation contributes to both text and percussion with
> "amens," clapping and foot stamping, and where somebody usu-
> ally faints or goes into a trance when the music gets too intense
> —fuse with the 20th century classical tradition of daring and
> fresh statement in this work has been an important challenge for
> me.

(Moore's description brought to mind some emotional performances in which I and other members of the orchestra partici-
pated at the Third Baptist Church, with the glorious voice of
Henrietta Davis singing gospel songs.)

This whole season was played with the anticipation of our
second trip to Japan in June. We knew Ozawa's presence would

make the tour even more exciting than the first. Ozawa, too, looked forward to showing off "his" orchestra to the Japanese and showing us his view of the country. The handsome and well-illustrated brochure for the tour was printed in both English and Japanese. Ozawa's physiognomy was not neglected —in fact, there were thirty pictures of him in it. We were issued T-shirts with Ozawa's picture across the front and large buttons to wear with our street clothes that identified us as Ozawa's boys and girls.

Our programs were made up of music that Ozawa knew would be sure-fire hits with his audiences. Romantic and impressionistic works were featured in the Dvorak *New World* Symphony, the Tchaikovsky Symphony no. 6 *(Pathetique)*, and the complete concert version of Ravel's *Daphnis et Chloe*. Peter Serkin was piano soloist for the Brahms Second Symphony and Mozart Concerto no. 27 in B-flat. Our concertmaster soloed in the only modern major work, the Leonard Bernstein *Serenade*. The other American composition was Charles Ives' *Central Park in the Dark Some Forty Years Ago*. Clearly, all this was safe and sane music that would not shock the most unsophisticated music lover. The only unconventional aspects of the program were the concert dress of our leader and our featured soloist— Ozawa with his black turtleneck shirt and beads, and Serkin with a rather sloppy business suit, sandals, and a horrendously loud, four-in-hand tie that he had worn for a number of programs in San Francisco. In an act of kindness to the orchestra, to the audiences in Japan, and possibly even to Serkin, I bought him a quieter, slightly less unattractive tie as a departure present. He accepted it graciously, wore it once in Japan, and then went back to his old one.

This was a fun tour. We had arranged to play no more than four days in a row without a day off. Although we played in more cities than on our first Japanese tour, we had more leisure time to absorb some of the unique flavor of life there, from the exquisitely peaceful Buddhist temples to the gorgeous giant irises in bloom.

One of the most pleasurable aspects of the tour was the way the orchestra was feted at parties, as though there were a contest to see who could give the most lavish affair. The Japanese Philharmonic honored us with a lovely midnight supper; our association and Joe Scafidi each entertained us in marvelous fashion, but the party to end all parties was the one given by Seiji Ozawa at a charming cafe near our hotel after our last concert. He spared no expense to make this a gala that would not be forgotten. On entering the room, we were greeted by the sight of a whole city of sculptured food around the entire long table. There were native Japanese orchestras to play for us, as well as actors from the Kabuki Theater. There were sushi bars and succulent Kobe beef bars, and sake flowed like water. At this banquet, my old friends Mafalda Guaraldi and Ferdinand Claudio were honored, as they were retiring at the end of the season.

My own situation was much more relaxed than on the first tour, when I had to prepare to be a soloist as soon as we returned. April 10 had marked my fifty-seventh birthday. Though I would be demoted in the orchestra, I wouldn't be devastated, since I was to enter the first violin section. After resigning myself to the inevitable, I began to rationalize about the good that would result from moving. I would be under absolutely no pressure. While it held a bit of prestige, the fourth stand, outside seat, in the first violin section was out of the firing line of both the conductor and concertmaster. Further, I'd have the opportunity to play the luscious first violin parts. Second violin is important in the overall performance of symphonic works, but now I was going back to what violinists should be doing—playing gorgeous melodies. In other ways, my professional career and personal life were going very well. I was teaching a great deal and beginning to find satisfaction in the success of some of my students. I looked forward to returning to San Francisco after the tour. The Lord was in His heaven and all was right in the world.

Chapter 22

SAYONARA, SEIJI

"The other shoe was dropped," wrote Robert Commanday shortly before the opening of the 1975–76 season, when it was announced that Ozawa was leaving the San Francisco Symphony. Many people had predicted this would happen as soon as Ozawa accepted the Boston appointment; the surprise was not that he had chosen to leave but that the Symphony Association did not offer more concessions to keep him. It had been made clear that if Ozawa were to continue here, he would have to devote more time to our orchestra, not only in conducting but in administrative duties. Ozawa was not ready to do this. He hated all the backstage preparation necessary for concerts, repertoire planning for the entire season, obtaining guest soloists and conductors, date planning, hiring and firing. Ozawa's ideal was to come to the hall to rehearse and conduct concerts, then leave all the minor details to others. Being musical director of a modern symphony orchestra, however, doesn't allow that luxury. Ironically, in addition to conducting nine weeks in our 1976–77 season, Ozawa was to be our "musical advisor" for that season, just the thing he didn't want to do. (And as far as I can tell, he didn't do it.) After 1976–77, he was to conduct up to six weeks a season here when invited.

Seiji came to the orchestra to make his statement personally, just as he did after the Boston appointment. No longer could he profess his undying love for San Francisco and "his" orchestra; he had deserted us. But again, in his clever way, he made a case for himself. He reiterated the time problem and the association's need for a director who could do more administrative work. Additionally, he said he needed more leisure time. "I must spend more time in Europe, in Germany and Austria, so I can absorb the atmosphere of the region where the great composers, Mozart, Beethoven and Brahms, lived. My entire youth was spent in the Far East, which did not allow me to really understand the great masters." This was an argument we had not heard, and for Ozawa to make such a declaration at this time in his life seemed ridiculous. Ozawa did mention that he might do some recording with us in the future, but this has not occurred.

Once we became reconciled to losing Ozawa, the foremost thought in everyone's mind was about his successor. It seemed that the Symphony Association would search seriously and soberly. Alexander Fried quoted the criteria of Lawrence Metcalf, president of the association, for choosing a future conductor and director. (In brackets are Fried's editorial comments.)

> Impeccable musical judgment [which obviously would mean fine, inspiring musicality and musical breadth].
> Ability to function on the podium and with the orchestra [which would mean not only musical knowledge and skills but authority as administrator of problems and people].
> Acceptance by the symphony constituency [meaning the public, ticket buyers, collaborators, and contributors].
> Availability at proper times of the season [which would help keep the orchestra musically in hand and improve it].
> Willingness to take and hold the job [which would relate the salary, contract, and artistic freedom].

Fried also mentioned age and health as factors to take into consideration in choosing the right man.

It would have been ideal to find an available, famous conductor who embodied these qualities, but such a possibility seemed remote indeed. All the "greats" already held substantial positions, and San Francisco offered little to lure them away. In fact, after the Jones-Nakagawa fiasco made the orchestra appear difficult to deal with, it would have been a feat to get anyone of renown to come here. Thus, the association had two categories of candidates: once-famous conductors in their waning years, and younger men (or women) who showed much promise. In both there were dangers. An older man might not be able to bring any fresh spark or excitement to the music, whereas it would be a gamble to chance a young hopeful making it to the top. We had already lost this gamble once and certainly couldn't afford another disastrous period in our history.

Many names were bandied about, but Edo de Waart, who was to come next year as our first principal guest conductor, was the one most frequently mentioned. De Waart's name had come up as early as the summer before, when Robert Commanday had interviewed him in Santa Fe, where he was conducting the opera *Falstaff*. De Waart had said then that he was looking forward to his guest appearances with the San Francisco orchestra. Although he admitted to knowing very little about the orchestra situation in San Francisco, he was not disturbed by the idea of orchestra members participating in musical policies; he felt that involvement in day-to-day decisions led to greater motivation. De Waart was extremely devoted to the Rotterdam Orchestra, however, and said he didn't want to be a "Flying Dutchman." If he took on another orchestra, he would have to give up all guest-conducting, which he was reluctant to do. Commanday concluded his article by saying, "De Waart as Ozawa's successor here? His attitude, not to say his talent, makes it seem as though he is what is wanted here. The chances? Very slight, I'd say."

From February 18 to March 13, 1976, Edo de Waart had a four-week engagement with the symphony, which allowed him to show San Francisco audiences the wide range of his repertoire. From the dozen works he conducted, ranging from Haydn to Bartok, one could readily observe that he was a very capable conductor. Although there was no immediate surge of excitement when he conducted, there was a general feeling that here was a young man who had a good head on his shoulders, who knew tempi and styles, and who had control.

On the Thursday of de Waart's last week with the symphony, Lawrence Metcalf, association president, held a press conference to reveal what, in his words, was "the worst kept secret of the week": Edo de Waart had been engaged as the new maestro of the San Francisco Symphony, starting with the 1977–78 season. Metcalf expressed the wholehearted support of the board of governors. Ozawa, contacted in Europe where he was on tour, sent word of his approval, saying that he had a "very good feeling about Maestro de Waart."

At the press conference, Edo comported himself with grace and charm and demonstrated his level-headed grasp of the problems that lay ahead. He spoke about his devotion to the Rotterdam Orchestra, which he had no plans to give up. He told of his dislike of the hotel life, bad food, and jet lag, and said he was beginning to think of "settling down." To most of us, having two major posts thousands of miles apart hardly seemed like settling down. But de Waart was in such demand that if he didn't take another major post, he would spend over half the year guest-conducting—in the long run an unsatisfactory life.

De Waart spoke favorably of the forces that would be under his command: "the first-rate chorus and the capacities of the orchestra." (To me, that meant that, with a nucleus of the current musicians, he could eventually rebuild the orchestra to where it, too, could be first-rate.)

On the whole, de Waart gave the impression that he thought long and hard before accepting the post of director of the San Francisco Symphony. Once he committed himself to this position, he would be thoroughly involved in every facet of the job, not only as conductor but as an administrator and prime figure in all the future plans of the orchestra. He looked forward to long years of association with the San Francisco Symphony, and he would do all he could to make that association a successful one.

While the local music community was absorbed in the

selection of its new symphony director, the Symphony Association had been engaged in negotiations with the orchestra for a new contract. There were rumors of a strike, as there had been many times in the past. Once again, the sticking point was the question of orchestra participation in personnel and other decision-making policies. The association pointed to the harm caused to the symphony's reputation because of the Jones-Nakagawa episode. The members, on the other hand, alleged that conductors before Ozawa had made some faulty and costly personnel decisions. They further noted that the role of music directors had changed; like Ozawa, many of them now held two or more posts and, therefore, could not devote the necessary time and energy to administrative problems.

All issues were settled amicably, and there was no strike. Though left without complete authority to allow a new member tenure, the orchestra retained a strong voice in the decision. More strength was returned to the conductor. There was some unhappiness at the backward step in the democratization of orchestra policy, but there was also a sense of relief that such heavy responsibility would no longer fall on the musicians' shoulders.

In other ways, the 1975–76 season was a disaster for the association. A city strike closed the Opera House, and a week of canceled concerts resulted in a financial loss. The next week's concerts were held in Masonic Auditorium, a bad place to hear music, and scheduled on this program was Bloch's *America*, a pastiche of patriotic tunes woven into a fabric of pseudomodern harmonies that satisfied no one. It was an embarrassment to play and an annoyance to hear. In order to balance some of the losses, the association engaged pianist Rudolf Serkin for two concerts, which immediately sold out. Serkin became ill and the concerts had to be canceled—another financial disaster.

Public interest in the symphony was beginning to flag, and morale was low. We could only hope that de Waart would bring with him a resurgence of interest.

But for the 1976–77 season, we were in transition. There was no musical director of the San Francisco Symphony—Seiji

Ozawa was the musical advisor and Edo de Waart was the principal guest conductor. Any personnel changes in either this or the next season seemed unlikely, except for those carry-overs from Ozawa's years as music director. The last two string principals, Rolf Persinger, viola, and Robert Sayre cello, were moved. Rolf accepted a lesser position in the section, but Robert resigned. Also, the replacements for Elayne Jones and Ryohei Nakagawa joined the orchestra.

Barry Jekowsky, who had been acting tympanist for the 1975–76 season, won that post permanently in the auditions. It was important for him to do well so that, artistically at least, the furor about Elayne's nonrenewal could die down. The press would certainly pounce on any weakness in the performance of Jones' successor. Although the critics could not bring themselves to praise Jekowsky, they did the next best thing by not mentioning him at all.

Taking over as principal viola was Geraldine Lamboley. When she arrived from Pittsburgh, where she had been the assistant principal, the headline above her interview in the *Chronicle* was "The Symphony's Exuberant Addition," and a word more apt for Geraldine could not be found.

The two players who joined the orchestra the following season were also defectors from the Pittsburgh Symphony— Stephen Paulson, bassoon, and Michael Grebanier, cello.

Very early in de Waart's reign, it became clear that all was not well between Stuart Canin and him. Ozawa had leaned heavily on Canin when any string problems arose, and Stuart expected this to continue. But something was amiss. Either de Waart wanted to show that he, and he alone, was running the orchestra, or he was unhappy with Stuart's bowing, style, and interpretation. It was also obvious that de Waart was not particularly pleased with the all-important first violin section. The whole situation would bear watching.

We had a sad occurrence in the orchestra in the latter part of 1976. Mary Hughson Claudio, one of our most respected cellists and the wife of my former first violin partner, Silvio Claudio, was stricken with cancer and had to leave the orches-

225

tra. Unhappily, she was not to return; she died on July 7, 1977. Mary had entered the orchestra in the days of Monteux, when joining a symphony was more difficult for a woman than for a man. Starting at the very bottom, she gradually moved up in the cello section until she became assistant principal cellist under Krips. She had taken a leave of absence during the Jordá period, as she found his conducting intolerable. A student of English literature, Mary did quite a bit of writing; I was moved when Silvio showed me some of it after her death.

The emergence of women in orchestras, particularly in the forefront of the conducting ranks, was extremely slow in coming. To be sure, Antonia Brico had made a small reputation as a conductor over a quarter of a century earlier, but this did not result in a flood of other female candidates in the field. Eve Queler, who formed her own symphony, The Opera Orchestra of New York, to have the opportunity to conduct on a regular basis, was asked if she had encountered any discrimination in pursuing her career. "Yes," she answered, "but one learns to take ignoramuses in stride. Surprisingly, it is not always the men; a woman manager of a major orchestra once told me that Mozart and Haydn can be conducted by women, but that Brahms and Mahler are 'men's music.' "

Not until the mid-seventies did women seriously emerge as leaders of symphony orchestras. Sarah Caldwell made her debut with the Metropolitan Opera Orchestra in 1976 and caused a sensation as the first woman to enter that orchestra pit as conductor. She made a creditable showing of her musical and leadership abilities.

In recognition of the era of the liberated woman, and because she had already made quite a name for herself, Sarah Caldwell conducted the San Francisco Symphony in a subscription week. Soprano Phyllis Curtin was the soloist, and the women of the Symphony Chorus sang; so this was really an all-female show. It is unfair to judge a conductor by a week's performance, but the orchestra members were not overly impressed with Caldwell's conducting. She was competent and knew her scores, but she did not demonstrate impressive interpretive powers. Perhaps one day soon a woman will arise from the conducting ranks who can electrify the public as well as the musicians with her outstanding ability. That will be the beginning of a major breakthrough.

Shortly after Sarah Caldwell left town, Edo de Waart arrived. Though listed on the roster as principal guest conductor, he was heir apparent to the position of music director. He sounded in newspaper interviews like an affable, pleasant, but very practical man. "I'm not entering this job with a lot of promises," he said. "Time will tell how we are doing."

During this time, de Waart backed off a bit from the star ranks to which most conductors aspire. He asserted that providing good music for the community was a team effort of the orchestra and conductor. He downplayed the glamorous part of his job to concentrate on musical and artistic goals, which sometimes made him appear prosaic and pedestrian after the charismatic Ozawa. But, according to Edo, he was not working for instant success but for the orchestra's satisfying and long-lasting musical growth. In these interviews, de Waart returned time and again to the need of the city, the music-loving public, and, most of all, the symphony for a new facility in which to present concerts. One felt that his coming to San Francisco as the symphony's principal conductor was based on the promise that a Performing Arts Hall would be built.

Featured on de Waart's first program of this season was Beethoven's Ninth Symphony. This monumental work could be a virtual litmus test for a director's conducting ability and musical assets. Could he conduct Beethoven? Could he control the 100-piece symphony, the chorus, and the four soloists, keeping the right balances and conveying to the audience the various, enigmatic messages that Beethoven presented? Could he delve into the music beyond simply solving its logistics problems? For de Waart, most of the answers were positive. One could see that he enjoyed conducting Beethoven's compositions and gave them a very personal and vital interpretation. That he often buried his head in the score bothered many of the musicians, perhaps spoiled by Ozawa's phenomenal memory. But they soon realized that this was just a conducting quirk of a fine musician who really knew the score. In the following weeks, de Waart showed the wide range of his repertoire, presenting works of Haydn, Mozart, Bruckner, and an entire program of Stravinsky. After a hiatus of several weeks, he came back to bring us almost into the operatic world by conducting Verdi's *Requiem*. Again with large orchestra, chorus, and soloist, he demonstrated his ability to blend and balance the various elements and present to the audience a true picture of Verdi's dramatic version of the final Mass.

After playing with de Waart during this time, we could see, hear, and feel that he was a fine conductor. Would he develop into a great one? The symphony's immediate future was based on an affirmative answer to that question.

Edo de Waart, conductor of the San Francisco Symphony from 1977 to 1985.

Chapter 23

WELKOM, DE WAART

In December 1977, at the age of thirty-six, Edo de Waart became
the music director of the San Francisco Symphony. He arrived
with a mission: like all his predecessors, de Waart wanted the
orchestra to be the best that he and the players could make it.
He did not expect it to be the best in the world or even the
country, but he wanted it to reach the ultimate of its special
capabilities. He pleaded with the critics and the public for
patience. "Don't expect miracles," he said. "Miracles don't happen and I don't want anybody to expect me to be a miracle
worker. . . . Give us three years of work together before our new
hall is built. When the new hall is open, you will be able to hear
the results." He again stressed that a new hall would not only
improve the orchestra's sound (the Opera House was really built
for opera) but also give it a place to function all year long, without having to move out for the opera and ballet.

De Waart's request for patience from the critics was duly
noted and ignored. Their first criticism dealt with de Waart's
programming. Music critics have always complained that music
directors are too conservative in their choice of repertoire for a
subscription series. "More modern music," they cry. "More
unusual older music. Bay Area composers should be featured—
local soloists should be presented." Edo de Waart was caught in
a bind. His primary task was to get the orchestra into shape,
and to do that he had to build up the sound and ensemble that
comes only from doing old, familiar compositions. If new and

unfamiliar works make up the majority of the programs, most of the rehearsal time is spent on learning the pieces, and orchestral improvements fall by the wayside. Furthermore, he didn't want to incur the wrath of his new public by performing works that most of the audience didn't know and most likely wouldn't appreciate. So de Waart had to walk a tightrope between what the critics wanted and what he desired to do. The inevitable result was great satisfaction for the audiences and vitriolic articles from the critics.

The critics, however, had ample reason to take the stand they did. One of the primary duties of a symphony orchestra is to present new music and unusual music. So, in his opening interview, de Waart was closely questioned about his overly conservative repertoire. He bristled with indignation in his replies. This was just the first of many skirmishes de Waart would have with the press. At the beginning, however, de Waart received complimentary reviews. Of the Bruckner Seventh Symphony at his opening concert, Commanday wrote: "De Waart creates this scheme (architecture) like a builder concerned less with the intensities of the moment than the effect of the juxtapositions, reading out towards the illuminations of tonality contrasts." (Commanday does have a way with words.) He went on to say, "There was everything to admire in the sweep of the first movement—romantic themes, the restless tread and the richness of sound. . . . The Adagio grew and glowered magnificently, and after the climax, resolved in a most poignant tribute. De Waart thinks deeply in romantic music, without being an exploitive emotionalist." I quote so extensively from this review because these words should be savored. It was one of the few reviews received by de Waart at that time that did not have a negative undercurrent.

Early in the season, de Waart requested a conference with the orchestra's players' committee, explaining that he wanted to establish a working relationship where problems could be worked out before they became too hard to solve. He said that such an arrangement in Rotterdam had proved very beneficial.

He commented, "I've felt a curiously suspicious nature about the members of the orchestra from the moment I arrived here. This hostility and antagonism is demonstrated by the reaction of the orchestra to any proposal offered by the management—even one that might benefit the musicians." Committee members offered what has become the standard answer to these charges: after living through many long years of tyrannical conductors and management, our musicians have become so sensitive and defensive about anything proposed by the "other side" that it is difficult for them to be rational about it. De Waart hoped to change that atmosphere.

The committee wanted to know the conductor's plans in regard to personnel. De Waart didn't deny that he expected to make changes, but he assured the committee that no one would be forced to leave the orchestra without being provided for financially. Obviously, he was talking about older members too young to be on pension but, for him, too old to be of use. The committee received this information with mixed feelings. While it was good to hear that our new conductor was sensitive about the older musicians, it was unpleasant to realize that he planned drastic personnel changes. The maestro reiterated his request for frequent meetings with the orchestra committee, adding, "If you have any problems that I can help you with, my door is always open."

From the moment de Waart assumed his new post, he seemed obsessed with bringing youth into the orchestra. Although he denied any bias, his actions belied his words. The first instance that brought this problem into direct focus was the audition for assistant principal cello. When Mary Claudio died, David Kadarauch was temporarily appointed to her seat. When he later auditioned for the permanent position, most orchestra members assumed that, barring a phenomenal audition by somebody outside the orchestra, the seat would be David's, as he had performed well and had been complimented by de Waart. However, someone outside the orchestra did win the post—Peter Shelton, a very young cellist with practically no experience. David was disappointed, possibly a little shocked, and curious as to why he had lost. The maestro said that he had played very well, maybe as well as Peter, but that Peter was twenty-one and moldable, while he, David, was already thirty-one and set in his ways. As this statement circulated around the orchestra, it was distorted to the extent that musicians were saying that if you're over thirty, you're over the hill and can expect nothing good to come your way from de Waart. Much later on, I asked de Waart about this matter, and he said he had been partially misquoted and completely misunderstood. It was not David's age that worried de Waart but his lack of flexibility: if, at the age of thirty-one, it was almost impossible to move David in any direction, what would happen years later if he occupied a key position? (Nevertheless, the impression persists among some of the musicians that de Waart inordinately stresses youth for both replacement and advancement candidates. When an important principal position recently went up for grabs, rumor held that de Waart wanted a twenty-one-year-old with twenty years' orchestral experience.)

During 1978, the Symphony Association made a most significant move—it changed its executive director. Although Joseph Scafidi did not attain the top post until 1964, he had been part of the association for twenty-six years. Now management felt that the symphony had become big business, and they wanted a professional with a reputation for getting things done. From Saint Louis, where he had been executive director of that orchestra, they brought in Peter Pastreich. He was thirty-nine years old and had a great deal of experience.

In his first interview with the press, Pastreich said:

One of the reasons I'm here is the perception on the part of the board of San Francisco's isolation. The orchestra is not entirely in the mainstream. The Symphony Association wants a change in this area and they felt I was plugged in nationally. It's important, I think, to compare our audience with those of other orchestras in the same national market. Part of my job is to bring information of what's going on in the orchestral world and the arts world. . . . I don't believe there is competition for the arts dollar here, or anywhere, but an expandable money supply that can be reached by presenting quality. One of the things that attracted me to San Francisco is that it responds to quality.

Pastreich spoke of working with other arts organizations within the community. He also mentioned that in his first year he would have the task of negotiating a new contract with the musicians.

The orchestra was well aware that a formidable effort would be necessary to end up with a contract we could live with comfortably. We were apprehensive that Pastreich, who had a reputation of being a hard bargainer, would cause us to accept a poor contract or bring about a strike, which we didn't want. In the past, the Orchestra Players' Committee had also acted as the negotiating team from the orchestra, along with the president of the Musicians' Union. This year, because of the seriousness of our problems, we elected a separate Negotiating Committee

Peter Pastreich, executive director of the San Francisco Symphony since 1978. His dynamic approach to symphony management brought the orchestra into the mainstream of the music world.

(including me) to deal only with contract matters. We committee members expected a real fight with Peter Pastreich.

The bargaining was long and arduous. The association's
first offer was a giant backward step in our working conditions.
We had to fight our way back to status quo and then attempt to
make a few gains. The final contract was far from what we
wanted, but better than we feared we might have to accept.

The stage was set for the 1978–79 season to open with great
drama—a new conductor, new management, a new contract,
and a new hall on the horizon.

In February 1980, the symphony musicians were given a
tour of that new hall. It was in such a primitive state that those
of us with little architectural imagination could not picture what
the finished structure would look like. There would be huge
plastic reflectors to focus the music into the audience and banners that could be raised or lowered to absorb the sound. Theo-
retically, the banners were so flexible that their length could be
changed with each piece, so they would be in one position for
Mozart and another for Tchaikovsky. At the time of our visit,
none of these accoutrements were actually in place: we were told
about them as we gazed into a huge, empty cavern. The new
hall would have more open space than any other symphonic
hall and no backdrop to reflect the music, so these "novelties"
were necessary for a controlled musical sound. The backstage
area appeared very small to us compared to the huge area in the
Opera House, which was important for the opera to keep
singers, choruses, and scenery prepared for the next scene. We
were told that there would be locker rooms, practice rooms, and
a large lounge for the musicians on the lower level. We left the
minitour a little enlightened and considerably bewildered. We
couldn't imagine how in seven months this skeleton of a building would be a symphony hall, ready for a performing orchestra
and a listening audience.

In the spring of 1980, an affair was given by the San Francisco Chamber of Commerce in honor of Sam Stewart, the
motivating force behind the fund raising for the new hall, and

235

all of his helpers. At this occasion, Stewart announced that in trying to find "angels" to sponsor this magnificent edifice, he came across one person who was outstanding not only for generosity but for cooperation—Louise M. Davies. The widow of an extremely successful businessman, Davies had devoted her time and money to furthering San Francisco's cultural life. Stewart said that when he first approached her, she was extremely kind and forthcoming. As the project progressed and Stewart realized he would need additional funds, he came back to Louise Davies time and time again, and she was most responsive. The culmination of all her donations was in the neighborhood of $5 million; so it was no wonder that the building was to be named the Louise M. Davies Symphony Hall. In meeting Mrs. Davies on numerous occasions, I found her to be very gracious, a lady in the true sense of the word, extremely interested in the music and the musicians who were to be the life-giving factor of "her" hall.

With the new hall, the symphony and opera would be performing simultaneously, and the decision of whether to go with the opera or stay with the symphony was a matter of grave concern for many musicians. Although there had been many delays in construction of the new hall, the Symphony Association was determined to open the 1980–81 season on time. Therefore, this decision could no longer be postponed: if a musician decided for the symphony, he would earn more money; if he decided for the opera, he would have more free time, as the opera, with all its seasons during the year, is in operation only about six months. Also, there were musical matters to be considered. To most musicians, symphony playing is much more satisfying, although some enjoy the excitement and glamour of opera. Most finally opted for the symphony, but the decision was not always left in their hands.

During our contract negotiations in the summer of 1978, we had discussed one of Peter Pastreich's methods of getting rid of unwanted players—to pay them off. I called this the "Peter Principle, Number Two." In order to avoid the complicated pro-

236

The patroness: Louise M. Davies for whom Davies Hall is named. Mrs. Davies has been a symphony-goer, and subscriber, since 1934.

cedure necessary to separate a musician from his position, Pastreich circumvented the problem by getting together with the player and settling on a price. The musician was happy, Pastreich was happy, and de Waart had a clear conscience about putting a man out on the street. A special fund was set up by the association to take care of such incidents.

When the musicians had to decide which way they were going, de Waart thought he'd help them. There were several musicians that he definitely wanted to go with the opera. Because this would cause them a financial loss, he suggested that the association pay the difference until they reached retirement age in the symphony, at which time their pension would take over. One day I asked a colleague which way he was going, and he answered, "Symphony—definitely!" Just then he was called into de Waart's room. When he came out, he said he was going to join the opera.

At the beginning of our season in November, Robert Commanday wrote an article in the *Chronicle* deploring the fact that most musical artists center their performances on a small group of popular concertos. He felt that there were many very fine works, both old and new, that had been neglected for many years. Among these he mentioned the Goldmark Violin Concerto. This struck a responsive chord in me. I remembered having played this work with the WPA Orchestra in the early thirties.

I took the Goldmark out of the drawer and began practicing it. It didn't sound too bad, so I approached de Waart and asked if I could play for him. When he asked why, I answered that the 1980–81 season would mark the forty-fifth anniversary of my joining the orchestra, and I would like to commemorate it by playing a concerto with the orchestra. He heartily acquiesced, and I made a date to play the Goldmark for him. I had been rehearsing with a fine pianist, Karen Rosenak, and it was she who came with me to that audition. De Waart had never heard the Goldmark before and was pleasantly surprised at its rich lyricism. After my performance, de Waart said that he found no difficulty in my playing, but he was a little disturbed by having someone from the ranks play a concerto with the orchestra, because it would open the floodgates for requests for the same privilege. He was already behind in granting some of the first-chairmen solo appearances. He was still in favor of my doing the Goldmark, "but . . ."

Months later, I received notice that I would definitely play the Goldmark with the orchestra. I was overjoyed. Unfortunately, however, I would have only one performance. I had taken it for granted that, as in the usual subscription weeks, I would play the work four times. De Waart explained that he had chosen to do it but once primarily because of management's fear that my unknown quality as a soloist could not draw four audiences. He did say, though, that this would be a special concert—the first subscription concert after our national tour, which he would conduct at Davies Hall. Though I recalled that the Japanese tour of 1968 was partially spoiled for me because I had to practice the Sessions, I was certainly not going to quibble when this great opportunity was offered me. It was more important to use all my energy to perfect the Goldmark.

Early in 1980, it became evident that season tickets for the opening year at Davies Symphony Hall were selling like hotcakes. There was such a terrific demand for them that the sale of season tickets was halted so that some tickets could be sold for single concerts. Nancy Carter, operating director of the symphony, said that such a phenomenon occurs whenever a new hall is built. The danger period is in the third season, she added, when the novelty of the new hall has worn off; so a solid foundation must be built to entice renewals. All this prosperity created personal problems for me. Since I was to play the Goldmark only once, I was afraid that my relatives, friends, and acquaintances would not be able to get tickets; but I was able to arrange with management that anyone who wanted to come would be afforded some kind of seat for that concert.

As the 1980–81 season approached, I had the Goldmark to look forward to, Davies Symphony Hall was to be inaugurated, and the orchestra would be going on a United States tour for the first time since 1947. A most exciting year was about to begin.

Louise M. Davies Symphony Hall interior. (See Appendix N, page 311, for a

discussion of the hall's acoustics.)

Chapter 24

OUR NEW HOME

The opening of the 1980–81 season at Davies Symphony Hall marked the beginning of a new, glamorous period in the history of the San Francisco Symphony Orchestra. Before this, it was the San Francisco Opera Company that had cornered the market on "opening night fever." Now the symphony would vie with the opera in presenting all the excitement of high society.

Three concerts were to be performed in the inaugural week of September 13. The program for all three was identical— *Roman Carnival* Overture of Berlioz; a world premiere, *Happy Voices*, by Del Tredici, commissioned by the ubiquitous Louise M. Davies; Mendelssohn's Piano Concerto no. 1, featuring Rudolf Serkin; and Beethoven's Fifth Symphony. David Del Tredici started his career as a pianist and, at a very early age, was a soloist with the San Francisco Symphony. Born in the Bay Area, he has been closely associated with our orchestra, both as soloist and composer. Aside from the Del Tredici, this program could have been conducted by Monteux, illustrating the recurring theme, "Plus ça change, plus c'est la même chose."

Significantly, the first concert of inaugural week was not the glamorous opening night but rather a concert given for all the workers who had constructed our new home. Everyone was invited to this free, shakedown concert—from the architects and acousticians to the electricians and painters—who had taken part in making this building the jewel it was intended to be.

The second concert of the week was the Gala Inaugural, with ticket prices reflecting the importance of the evening. This was the first in a series of annual concerts used as fund raisers to open each season. The actual concert was just part of the occasion—an event done to perfection in every way. Promenades before and after the concert, and in the intermission, gave patrons an opportunity to explore various areas of the building —the long, sweeping stairway, the nooks and crannies of each floor, and the semicircle of floor-to-ceiling windows around the front that offered a panoramic view of the city. While making the rounds, the formally dressed audience partook of delectable and exotic viands and liquors set out on tables on all levels of the building. Vendors of fine foods vied with each other for the honor of offering their wares to this discerning public. Unusual floral arrangements decorated the tables, to distract attention from still unfinished sections of the hall. It was a gala worthy of its name and purpose!

The third concert, called the "All San Francisco Premiere," was given without charge to neighborhoods from the entire city, in order to bring the general public into Davies Hall. From its inception, the project to build this hall had been criticized by certain groups as an elitist endeavor benefiting only the comparatively rich. This concert was one of many ways of showing that the entire spectrum of the community could enjoy Davies Hall. Along with concerts such as this, there would be other community events, including a stepped-up children's concert format, that would work toward the democratization of the symphonic scene. As was later seen, the hall itself drew a much broader segment of society than the Opera House had. Because its architectural lines were beautifully clean, the hall did not have the feeling of luxury that surrounded the older building. It could be called elegantly simple. People could feel more comfortable in their everyday clothes in this hall, which was built just to hear good music. Looking out into the audience, we saw many old friends, but with them sat people who may never have gone to a concert in the forbidding Opera House. It was especially gratifying to see young people, from their late teens to early thirties, who had discovered symphonic music and loved it.

The acoustics of Davies Symphony Hall were of great concern to the public and critics alike. When we had just begun to rehearse there, Commanday phoned me, along with others of the orchestra, to inquire about our reactions to the acoustics. I was to hear this question innumerable times during the next couple of years. I told Commanday that I thought the acoustics were going to be fine; I heard many good things, but the balance was still uneven, and some aspects of the sound mechanisms would have to be changed. We had started using the hall before it was really completed. Everything was behind schedule, and rehearsals planned for June, to test and refine the acoustics, were being held a week before the first performance. Banners that could be raised or lowered at the touch of a button to alter the echo length had been frozen in one position by an electrical malfunction. The plastic, cylindrical reflectors hanging from the ceiling were too thin for their purpose and had warped. Nevertheless, the sound from the orchestra was still much livelier and brighter than at the Opera House, and it was certainly wrong to expect the ideal sound this early on. Considering all the construction delays, it was miracle enough that the hall had opened on time. Commanday knew all this and agreed that it was unnecessary for him to make a snap judgment about the building.

Predictably, however, in his review of that first concert, Commanday was not the least bit hesitant to say how horrendous the acoustics were in Davies Symphony Hall. His fellow critics, as if following his lead, dutifully reported the same thing. The audiences, however, did not object to the acoustics. They enjoyed Davies Symphony Hall and the music therein the first time they heard it, and they returned over and over with equal enthusiasm.

In all truth, it must be said that there is a constant endeavor to improve the hall's acoustics. The acousticians have come back again and again to add more reflectors, to work with the banners, or to place the musicians more forward or farther back on the stage. They are working toward an ideal sound, which has not yet been reached. Yet I am constantly greeted by friends and strangers who tell me how much they enjoy our concerts.

In this inaugural year, more new members joined the orchestra in one season than at any other time since I had been a member. This was caused by a number of factors, the most important of which was the separation of the opera and symphony orchestras—thirteen musicians went to the opera. Added to this were the members persuaded by management to take an early retirement, one member who took a leave because of serious illness, and one legitimate retiree. Furthermore, several opera players were on leaves of absence; so their positions could not be permanently filled until they decided which orchestra they would choose. Veteran concertgoers were amazed at the change in personnel. Twenty percent of the orchestra now consisted of new faces. Surprisingly, it worked quite well.

Many of these newcomers came in under a seldom used clause in the contract; they were designated one-year substitutes. This emergency contract provision allowed the conductor to fill a spot when there was no time for formal auditions. The audition process takes at least two months to advertise, and the audition itself requires the services of ten orchestra members and the conductor for two days. Realistically, auditions for only one instrument can take place in a week. As a result, when the season started, there were eleven full-time substitutes in the orchestra, chosen by de Waart with the help of an advisory group of musicians. To permanently fill all the vacancies would take at least two years, and listening to or playing for auditions became a way of life for the orchestra.

Concertmaster was by far the most important change in orchestra personnel. Despite the fine solo playing of Stuart Canin, de Waart found that he could not work with him comfortably. There was a negativism about Stuart's attitude that Edo could not abide. The friction between them at rehearsals was very evident, and we knew that it could not go on forever.

245

In order to make the transition as smooth and painless as possible, Stuart was offered the position of associate concertmaster, or a spot for him as co-concertmaster would be created. Along with the title, de Waart arranged that Canin would lose very little money, have regular solo appearances with the orchestra, and play a certain number of weeks as concertmaster. Stuart eventually rejected this offer. He left his options open, however, by asking for and receiving a leave of absence for one season.

Meanwhile, the search for his replacement went on. This was unusual—it was assumed that de Waart had the new concertmaster waiting in the wings. But that was not true at all. When interviewed about Stuart's demotion or firing, de Waart said some questionable things: "Stuart has a good tone for chamber music, but not for concertmaster of a major symphony. We want to develop the sound of the Berlin Philharmonic here, and it can't be done with Canin as concertmaster."

Raymond Kobler became concertmaster of the San Francisco Symphony in 1980.

It was thought at first that when such an important position opened up, qualified candidates would come out of the woodwork. But there were only a few. The final candidate was Raymond Kobler, assistant concertmaster of the Cleveland Orchestra, who had all the correct qualifications, though he did not have the large and magnificent tone that Edo was quoted as wanting. But it was absolutely necessary for de Waart to have someone with whom he could work and whom he could trust, and he felt this way about Kobler. So here he was. Not only were we opening the new hall—starting a whole new era of our history—we were about to tour the United States for the first time in thirty-three years. We had to have an orchestra that was stable, responsible, and well integrated to face the wolves of the press in New York and Washington, D.C. With the help of Kobler and the experienced substitutes he brought in at the beginning of the season, de Waart hoped to have a first-rate orchestra by the end of October, when we would go forth on our new venture.

Chapter 25

FROM CARNEGIE TO GOLDMARK

The Symphony Association's primary aim, as it had been since the time of Krips, was to bring the San Francisco Symphony up to the level of a world-class orchestra, that is, on a par with the big five—New York, Philadelphia, Chicago, Boston, and Cleveland. Besides raising the artistic ability of the ensemble, three steps had to be taken. The first, a hall built to present symphonic music, had already been accomplished. For the first time in the orchestra's existence, it was not a mere tenant in someone else's house. The second and third steps were to tour and to record, and in order to do the latter, we had to be successful in the former. Our first national tour since 1947 began before we had been in Davies Symphony Hall three months.

The first stop, October 20, 1980, was in Boulder, Colorado. This was an easy beginning to prepare us for the tour's eventual climax, which would be—as in 1947—Carnegie Hall. After playing two concerts in Boulder, we had a day off. Most of the musicians used that beautiful day to ascend the mountain not far from the center of town, explore the area, and generally commune with nature. It was a relaxing hiatus between the hectic opening of our new hall and the tension we would soon feel in playing the Big Apple.

For me, however, there was no cessation of activity. As on our Japanese tour, I wanted to use all available time to prepare for my solo appearance when I returned to San Francisco. During the last few months at home, I had been most fortunate to work on the Goldmark with pianist Claire Friedling. Now I had to try to perfect all the nuances in the piece on my own. This, undoubtedly, would be the highlight of my career, and I didn't want any "accident" to occur because of unpreparedness. I did take one period off from practicing, though. The Denver Symphony had been locked out because of a dispute over their contract. I was asked, along with a number of other San Francisco Symphony musicians, to show solidarity with them in their plight. We appeared in front of their concert hall to express our sympathy with their cause to the press, radio, and television. San Francisco Symphony members demonstrated their concern in more than words: at that news conference, the chairman of our players' committee, Walter Green, presented their committee chairman with a check for $1,000. The Denver musicians were appreciative of our gesture, and a few weeks later they resumed their season.

From Boulder we continued on to college campuses in Madison, Wisconsin, Champaign, Illinois, and Ann Arbor, Michigan. These concerts served a dual purpose—to give the orchestra one more run-through of the repertoire it would play in New York and to help defray the expenses of this costly adventure. Universities have money for such concerts, and these were the only ones where we were guaranteed a net income. Orchestra members have often questioned the advisability of playing for small and isolated audiences, as we did on these occasions; but management is convinced that we could not attempt a U.S. tour without these comparatively lucrative engagements.

We finally arrived in New York on the afternoon of October 26, checked into our hotel rooms, and prepared to see as much of the city as possible in the time left that day. Though the Barbizon-Plaza is a prestigious hotel with prices to match, our rooms reminded me of the train compartments on our first cross-country tour.

The morning of the second day was taken up with a re-hearsal—a revisit to that most famous of all concert halls, Carnegie. Walking into the crowded backstage area brought back memories of our illustrious tour of 1947. There were still thirteen members in the symphony who had taken part in that tour, and after rehearsal we had our picture taken against the backdrop of that legendary building. Our first night's concert at Carnegie Hall would consist of just two works, Beethoven's Fifth Symphony and his Violin Concerto, with Isaac Stern as soloist. This was part of the Isaac Stern festival year in honor of his sixtieth birthday, in which he was to play a variety of con-certos with many orchestras, guest solo recitals, and chamber music concerts with old world–renowned artists. I know of no other artist who was so feted. He was to continue this cele-bration all across the country, coming to San Francisco for two weeks of solo appearances just after my performance of the Goldmark. When de Waart prepared the schedule for the year, he said I should play in the spring so that my appearance wouldn't be too close to Isaac's. I agreed that I shouldn't embar-rass Isaac by the comparison.

That night was the performance we had been waiting for—the San Francisco Symphony's modern debut at Carnegie Hall. The musicians were in great shape, and I never saw de Waart more outgoing, free, and expressive in his conducting. The Fifth Symphony was conducted without the score, and (it seemed to me) de Waart gave it a very personal interpretation. We went to bed exhilarated with our triumph, eagerly awaiting the morning reviews from the New York critics.

To our dismay, the writers could find nothing good about the performance. Most talked about the dullness of interpre-tation and the ineptness of execution. One even went so far as to say, "If one must bring coals to Newcastle, they should at least be good coals." At rehearsal that morning, de Waart said he could not let this event go by without responding. He felt we had played very well and should not take these barbs too seri-ously. Critics do not necessarily reflect the feelings of the general public, who had shown in a very real fashion how much they enjoyed our music. He urged us to just go on playing as well as we could and ignore the critics—as he would. These were brave words, and if I could have believed he meant them, I would have been happy. But the expression on his face and the tone of his voice did not match his statements. A cloud of gloom hung over the orchestra during that rehearsal, and nothing that was said or done could clear the atmosphere.

The second night's concert included Mahler's Fifth Symphony, and de Waart was on happier ground. Mahler had always been one of his favorite composers and one with whom he could feel very comfortable. This received much better notices, but the damage had already been done. We had been labeled a mediocre orchestra led by a mediocre conductor, and anything we did well after that would seem a mere accident.

On one of the short plane rides between stops on this tour, I had sat next to Edo. He told me that the "main man" from Phillips Records was going to hear us in New York, and whether or not we got a record contract would depend on how we played there. After the poor reaction of the New York press, I was sure the record contract had gone down the tubes, especially when months went by after the tour and nothing was mentioned about records. But in this I was wrong.

During our five days in New York City, we played three rehearsals and three concerts at Carnegie Hall and one concert at Rutgers University. Despite all this time-consuming activity and my continuing effort to perfect the Goldmark, Ger and I managed to explore this fascinating city. After one more stop, Washington, D.C., we returned home. The Washington audience loved us, and by this time I'd given up on the critics. Our two-week tour ended happily.

The fateful day when I would play the Goldmark was fast approaching. Unlike the previous time I had been the featured soloist with the symphony, in 1968, I wasn't required to play the entire program on Saturday night. The Symphony Association and de Waart were even kind enough to relieve me of any other duties that week. That left me Monday through Saturday to rest up after the tour, practice, rehearse with Claire Friedling, and get myself into the right frame of mind for the performance. A couple of days before the rehearsal with the orchestra, Claire and I played the concerto for de Waart. Everything went well, and the mood was very light. The stage was all set for Saturday.

There are usually two separate run-throughs of a concerto with the orchestra, especially for one like this, which hadn't been performed with the orchestra in over half a century. However, because of an exceptional number of activities that week, there was only time for one rehearsal. This rehearsal, though, was almost completely devoted to my concerto. Helping to establish a proper acoustical balance was our assistant conductor, David Ramadanoff. At 10:20 A.M., I walked on stage to start the Goldmark.

In the audience were my wife, son, daughter, and accompanist. My daughter had just flown in from Dallas for the occasion. There was also a group of students of a student of mine—my grand-students—whom I had arranged to be invited. Seeing them recalled the time, fifty years earlier, when my friend Henry Shweid and I sent Alfred Hertz a penny post card to get permission to come to rehearsals. Most rehearsals are closed to the public. There is a series of paid dress rehearsals, but otherwise, it is rare for anyone not directly connected with the symphony to be allowed in the hall while we are working. On this occasion, however, the house was sold out; so this was the only way the students would have an opportunity to hear me.

The first half of the rehearsal was a detailed exploration of the work. I was completely at ease and did not use the music. I felt I knew the Goldmark so well that de Waart could stop and start anywhere, and I'd immediately find the spot. After the intermission, we decided to go through the entire piece without a stop. Ray Kobler, our new concertmaster, was amazed that I had the energy to play so intensely for so long. Warm feelings from my colleagues surrounded me, encouraging my efforts. It was as though they were reaching out to help me all they could. Edo, too, was very supportive, and I was happy to be there among all these fine musicians and friends.

In the afternoon, after some patch-up work on the concerto,

I rested and felt well prepared for the evening's fray. Unlike the week of the Sessions Concerto, I was afforded a soloist room in which there were two lovely floral arrangements, one from the Symphony Association, and one from Diane Leka, finance director of the symphony. All was beautiful! I warmed up in the privacy of my room, but I felt cooped up and wanted to be backstage among friends. So I walked out of the room and talked with the musicians who were not playing in the opening piece. The overture was over, and Edo and I walked on stage together. The applause that greeted me was really appreciated, because I knew my family and friends were there wishing me well, and however I played they would love it.

When we began, it was like a continuation of the morning's rehearsal. In the tutti sections, I looked around and picked out some of the people I knew in the audience. It was gratifying to see that one of my friends felt so comfortable there he had fallen asleep. Then the concerto was over. Everything had gone well—not great, but very well. There was a strong response from the audience, and I received two bouquets of flowers on stage.

After the concert, a grand party was given in my honor by Bianca and Warren Hirsch, our very dear friends. At that party were many of my colleagues, some close friends, others who had traveled long distances for this occasion, de Waart, Peter Pastreich, and all my immediate family. I was glad my mother could see the fruition of a project she had started fifty-seven years earlier. It was a pleasure introducing her to Edo, who had a hard time believing that a man of my advanced age could have a vibrant, working, thinking mother. He must have thought, "Well, maybe David isn't so old after all!"

For the next few days, I received some lovely letters and phone calls. One letter I particularly cherish came from Michael Steinberg, artistic adviser of the symphony, for whom I have great respect both as a musician and as a human being. He wrote, in part:

I had enormous pleasure from your playing—the unaffected musicality of it, the sweetness of the sound, and the grace with which you uncoiled all those garlands of decorations. A lovely performance.

Music is more than the sum total of notes, rhythms, and nuances. Michael's words showed that he saw past any imperfections in my performance to the essence of what I was trying to convey with the Goldmark.

Robert Commanday was flattering, too, in his review in the *Chronicle*. The headline epitomized his evaluation: "Schneider's Spiritual Identity in Concerto." I could ask nothing more than to be spiritually identified with this fine work and its composer. There was, however, one annoying aspect of the review—Commanday mentioned that I was retiring at the end of the season. It had not been my intention, nor Edo's, for me to leave the orchestra at such a "young" age. Actually, I had spoken to Edo of retiring after completing my fiftieth season, in 1986.

This concert was not a farewell to the Goldmark—a second performance took place about five months after the first, just after my sixty-third birthday. It was a joy to prepare for this, because I knew exactly what needed to be worked on. It went quite well. I was so relaxed that I even came in during an orchestra tutti, and it didn't throw me. The review in the *Examiner* gave Allen Ulrich an opportunity for a headline pun: "A Veteran Makes His Goldmark!!!"

Chapter 26

THE UNFINISHED SYMPHONY

I was interviewed recently on television in connection with the inauguration of the San Francisco Symphony Youth Orchestra. I was asked about the future prospects for symphony orchestras, and I answered with great optimism. I see a much better outlook now for the continuance of this art form than I did when I joined the orchestra, almost half a century ago. At that time, there were problems with mounting a symphony season of any kind, even a meager one. We had difficulty filling the Opera House twice a week for sixteen weeks. Our financial base was extremely narrow, and the whole symphonic scene was indeed elitist. Now we have a year-round orchestra. Each year we play a couple of hundred concerts, which are attended by patrons of all ages and from every stratum of society. The season's budget has risen from a little more than $250,000 in 1936 to over $13½ million in 1982–83. The orchestra has grown from 80 musicians to a 105. Every category of musical taste from baroque to contemporary, has been accommodated. That a Youth Symphony can be started with eighty to ninety fine musicians, playing classical masterpieces under the direction of a professional conductor, gives credence to my strong belief that there is symphonic music in our future.

Certain threads of continuity run through the whole history of the San Francisco Symphony. We are recording again, having come a long way from those recordings made with Monteux over the phone to Los Angeles. To quote from a symphony press release about our recent recordings:

The recordings will be digitally produced and are scheduled to be released both digitally and as a part of Phonogram's first releases on the new "compact" discs utilizing laser beam technique. A Control room, complete with amplifiers, speakers and recorders, will be set up in the Hana Zellerbach Green Room of Davies Symphony Hall, and a maximum capacity of twenty-four microphones will be hung in various locations throughout the auditorium—over fifty parcels of recording equipment from Holland, weighing a total of two and one-half tons, have arrived already.

Along with this technical equipment, Phillips Recording, for whom we are making the discs, sent Wilhelm Hellwig, perhaps the finest producer of recordings in the world, and technicians Onno Scholtze and Henk Kooistra to assist in the project. The symphony set aside a week almost exclusively for recording, a great difference from the after-concert routine of the thirties and forties. All this to make three records—Mahler's Fourth Symphony, with Margaret Price, soprano; an all-Respighi recording; and an all-French recording, with Elly Ameling and Janice Taylor.

The question that arises from all this technical superiority is, simply: Are the recordings better? From the musicians' standpoint, they are much easier to make. No longer do we have to hold our breath so that we won't have to do the whole recording over. The fidelity of the sound is infinitely better than it was. A reviewer in the *Oakland Tribune* said of de Waart's Mahler:

> The orchestra sounds great, and the digital recording is marvelous, with resonant low strings and horns, very clear upper strings, and present woodwinds. It augurs well for San Francisco's future as a recording orchestra.

But it is questionable whether finer music, or greater fidelity to the composer, comes from these recordings. Nothing better can come out of the recordings than what goes into them. Some of our Monteux discs are still being issued and are considered top-notch musical products, albeit dated.

I still believe that recordings are just frozen moments in the flow of music. No matter how sophisticated the equipment it is recorded on or listened to, recorded music cannot compare to a live performance. That is another reason I so strongly believe that symphony orchestras are here to stay. When the recording industry first came into existence, many thought that a few orchestras would put all other live music out of existence. The opposite is now true. Recordings have whetted the appetites of music lovers and lured them into the concert hall to hear the real thing.

The life of an orchestra musician has also improved over the years of my career. Starting with a contract that allowed musicians barely enough to live on, with no job security, fringe benefits, or pension, a player in one of the top orchestras can now live reasonably well, if not luxuriously. Therefore, the competition to become a member of these major orchestras is extremely keen, and the standards have become more and more exacting. The young people who now join our symphony are marvelously adept on their instruments, knowledgeable about music, and sophisticated about auditions. This last talent is an important one. An aspiring musician might take fifteen or twenty auditions before landing a job.

There is always an ongoing endeavor to improve the orchestra's working conditions. I have often been a part of contract negotiations during my career with the symphony, and both sides have come a great distance to achieve what we now have. The Symphony Association (which recently changed its name to "Symphony") has shown that their interests are not too far from ours; the difference lies mainly in how we think our services should be used. We musicians would like to keep some semblance of a normal family and social life. We realize that concerts must be given in the evenings, because this is when the general public is able to attend; but for a number of years, we have kept Sundays more or less sacred. In San Francisco, we were even able to achieve a five-day week, Sunday and Monday being free almost the entire year. Now, however, management

257

has discovered that Sunday matinee concerts are a lucrative source of income, and it is in such areas that we find ourselves at loggerheads. Compromises must be made on both sides of the table. Through our latest negotiations, I think we have reached a balance that can bring management adequate income and afford musicians enough free time to keep this orchestra on a high artistic level. The San Francisco Symphony has a broad base of sponsorship and, therefore, can look forward to a healthy financial future.

While the symphony's future is secure, there will be critical changes in the coming years. On May 5, 1983, Edo de Waart announced to the orchestra, and later to the press, that he was leaving his post with the San Francisco Symphony at the end of the 1984–85 season to assume the position of general director and principal conductor of the Netherlands Opera. He will be occupied with his new post for at least thirty weeks a year and said he could see no way to continue as conductor of the San Francisco Symphony. He explained that opera has become more and more alluring to him in recent years; and when the Netherlands Opera asked him to head their revitalization program, he requested the Board of Governors of the Symphony to release him from the last two years of his contract. Also involved in his decision, besides love of conducting opera, is the fact that he will be working under a government subsidy system which will take him away from the commercialization he deplores here. And he will be able to spend more time in his homeland.

De Waart has accomplished a great deal during his tenure here. The orchestra has made important strides in the quality and reputation of its music. Under de Waart's direction, a New and Unusual Music Series has been started. A San Francisco Symphony Youth Orchestra has been created and already has a fine reputation, as has its conductor, Jahja Ling. A recording contract with Philips has been signed and implemented, and the orchestra's first releases have had very favorable reviews: *California* magazine calls Mahler's Fourth Symphony "de Waart's finest recording so far, and convincing proof of the excellent estate to which he has brought his orchestra"; Richard Pontzious, *San Francisco Examiner* music critic, says the recording is "a mighty step toward achieving international status."

The San Francisco Symphony is now considered one of the top orchestras of the country and is on the verge of becoming a "great" orchestra. It has fine personnel, excellent morale, and good management; all that is required is a conductor with that spark of genius to bring it to the heights. Many conductors have been discussed by management and musicians; among those prominently mentioned are Kurt Masur, Wolfgang Sawallisch, Simon Rattle, Neeme Jarvi, Michael Tilson Thomas, and Leonard Slatkin. There may be a dark horse stomping his hoof offstage. The orchestra and the general public eagerly await the outcome of this search.

Meanwhile, we have two more seasons of music-making under de Waart's direction. Personally, I will sorely miss him. I have never felt so close to a conductor. De Waart has exceptional qualities and has shown more understanding of the orchestra's human problems than any other conductor. He was the first to try to tear down the barrier between conductor and musicians. After Edo, it would be difficult to adjust to a dictatorial director. Some of the musicians have already expressed concern over a choice that would threaten the fine morale we now have.

Looking far into the future, I see a symphonic picture ever changing and yet remaining the same at its core. My great great-grandchildren will go to concert halls to hear Mozart, Beethoven, Brahms, Mahler (and who knows what new names will be added?). As they sit in these halls, the emotional content of this magnificent music will bring messages from great distances in time and space, messages that cannot be conveyed in any other way. Watching young audiences react to the plight of a Cio-Cio-San, or seeing their first awakening to the beauties of Beethoven and Mahler, reinforces my belief that as long as man exists there shall be music—good music, live music. For an audience can feel

Kurt Masur, colorful German conductor, much admired by San Francisco audiences, critics, and musicians.

the personal and timely interpretation of music only through the intimate contact of live performances. When all the elements jell and good music is beautifully expressed, there is no greater joy in the world.

Appendix A

THE FIRST SEASON

FIRST SEASON, 1911–12, COMPARED WITH 1982–83 SEASON

	1911–12	1982–83
Total Concerts	13 (6 subscription, 5 pops, 1 pops concert in Oakland, 1 concert for benefit of the Symphony Library Fund)	156 (subscription, pops, Beethoven Festival, Mostly Mozart Festival, miscellaneous others)
Personnel	60; later in season, 62	105 orchestra members; 52 administrative
Budget	Approx. $30,000 (258 guarantors, minimum $100)	Over $13.5 million

PAGES FROM THE PREMIERE CONCERT PROGRAM
Courtesy of San Francisco Public Library Art and Music Department

MUSICAL ASSOCIATION OF SAN FRANCISCO

To The Public:

The "Musical Association of San Francisco" was organized in 1911 for the purpose of fostering the love of music in San Francisco and the surrounding counties by establishing a permanent orchestral body along the lines of those maintained in the larger cities of Europe and the East and to arrange annual series of concerts of educational value which would interest not only the cultivated music lovers but the young and the wage-earners as well and thereby inculcate a love for the very best in musical art in our citizens of all classes and stations. Convinced that the only way to create a love for good music is to give the public an opportunity to hear it, the undersigned conceived and brought into existence the "Musical Association of San Francisco" whose membership has now reached nearly three hundred but it is earnestly hoped that a membership of five hundred may be obtained which would insure a permanent orchestra owned and controlled solely by this Association.

Orchestral concerts of different character will be given under the auspices of the Association such as Symphony Concerts, Students' Concerts, Wage-Earners Concerts, etc., each with appropriate programs but always of real musical importance and value.

For the first season, the concerts will be given in the afternoons as the formation of the Association was so late that it was impossible to secure sufficient musicians for evening concerts, but plans are being laid for both afternoon and evening concerts next season.

All the objects and ambitions of the Association cannot be attained the first season but an earnest start will be made, with the view to having an orchestra equal to any in the country and achieving the highest results both from an artistic and educational standpoint, within a few years.

The announcement of the first series of Symphony concerts is herewith submitted for your kind consideration and your subscription for season tickets is earnestly solicited.

Enclosed you will find a subscription blank which kindly fill out and mail as directed.

Sincerely

THE BOARD OF GOVERNORS

Dr. A. Barkan	W. H. Crocker	William Minter
T. B. Berry	Frank Deering	J. D. Redding
E. D. Beylard	Alfred Esberg	John Rothschild
Antoine Borel	I. D. Grant	Louis Sloss
W. B. Bourn	Frank Griffin	Sigmund Stern
J. W. Byrne	E. S. Heller	Dr. Stanley Stillman
C. H. Crocker	John D. McKee	R. M. Tobin

For particulars relating to Membership address

Mr. John Rothschild, Secretary
Cor. Market and Spear Street

Will L. Greenbaum, Manager
Office 101 Post Street

FIRST SEASON

THE SAN FRANCISCO ORCHESTRA

SIXTY PLAYERS

HENRY HADLEY, CONDUCTOR

SIX SYMPHONY CONCERTS
AT
THE CORT THEATRE

FRIDAY AFTERNOONS AT THREE-FIFTEEN

DECEMBER 8	FEBRUARY 2
JANUARY 5	FEBRUARY 16
JANUARY 19	MARCH 8

THREE EMINENT SOLOISTS
EDWARD TAK, VIOLINIST   EFREM ZIMBALLIST, VIOLINIST
AND
VLADIMIR DE PACHMANN, PIANIST

PRICES	SEASON TICKETS	SINGLE TICKET
Box Seats	$15.00	$3.00
Loge Seats	12.00	2.50
Orchestra	10.00	2.00
Balcony, three rows	10.00	2.00
Balcony, four rows	7.50	1.50
Balcony, seven rows	5.00	1.00
Gallery, eight rows	5.00	1.00
Gallery, eight rows	4.50	.75

BOX OFFICE for Season Tickets only opens Friday, December 1st, at Sherman, Clay & Co. Box Office for Single Concerts opens Monday, December 4th, at both, Sherman, Clay & Co. and Kohler & Chase. Address mail orders, inquiries, etc., to Will L. Greenbaum, 101 Post Street, San Francisco, Cal., or care Sherman, Clay & Company. Mail orders MUST be accompanied by check or money order.

WILL. L. GREENBAUM, MANAGER
101 POST STREET, SAN FRANCISCO

Appendix A

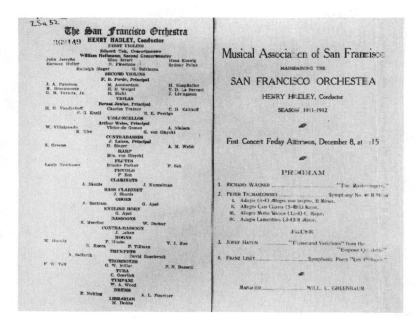

PRINCIPAL CONDUCTORS

1911–15	HENRY HADLEY		1936–52	PIERRE MONTEUX
1915–30	ALFRED HERTZ			Willem Van Den Burg, assistant conductor
1930–31	BASIL CAMERON ISSAY DOBROWEN			James Sample, assistant conductor — 1947
1931–32	ISSAY DOBROWEN BASIL CAMERON		1952–54	Guest conductors
1932–33	ISSAY DOBROWEN		1954–63	ENRIQUE JORDÁ Earl Bernard Murray, assistant conductor
1933–34	ISSAY DOBROWEN, regular conductor — 2 pairs of concerts ALFRED HERTZ — 2 pairs of concerts BERNARD MOLINARI —2 pairs of concerts		1963–70	JOSEF KRIPS
			1970–77	SEIJI OZAWA Niklaus Wyss and David Ramadanoff, assistant conductors
1934–35	No season		1977–	EDO DE WAART Jahja Ling, assistant conductor

CONCERTMASTERS

1911–12	Eduard Tak		1925–31	Mishel Piastro
1912–15	Adolph Rosenbecker		1931–32	Nathan Abas
1915–25	Louis Persinger (Rosenbecker becoming principal second violin and assistant conductor. In 1917, Persinger became assistant conductor.)		1932–57	Naoum Blinder
			1957–64	Frank Houser
			1964–70	Jacob Krachmalnik
			1970–80	Stuart Canin
			1980–	Raymond Kobler

MEMBERS OF THE SAN FRANCISCO SYMPHONY WHO PERFORMED AS YOUTH SOLOISTS WITH THE ORCHESTRA

Leonard Austria	Violinist
Michael Burr	Violin soloist, later switching to bass and becoming Principal Bass
Bernard Chevalier	Violinist
Darlene Gray	Violinist. Winner of Nevada contest to play solo with San Francisco Symphony and eventually Assistant Principal second violin
Mischa Myers	Violinist
George Nagata	Violinist
Donald Reinberg	Trumpet
Betty Rae Stanley	Violin
Robin Sutherland	Piano

Appendix E

SEATING ARRANGEMENTS: MONTEUX AND DE WAART

The principal difference between the seating arrangements of Monteux and de Waart is the disposition of the strings. Monteux still retained the late nineteenth-century arrangement of having the first and second violin sections on either side of the conductor. This classic setup worked well in music that featured a statement-answer effect from the two sections. There were definite disadvantages, however. The firsts and seconds could not achieve the ensemble they have now in the modern seating arrangement. The other disadvantage was that the second violins had their instruments (f-holes) facing the back of the stage, causing a muffled tone. (Monteux suggested a perfect, albeit drastic, solution to this problem: have all the second violins learn to play left-handed.) De Waart's seating arrangement offers a great deal of flexibility. It can be adjusted depending on the size of the orchestra for the composition played, or to accommodate a chorus, and it is sometimes varied for acoustical reasons.

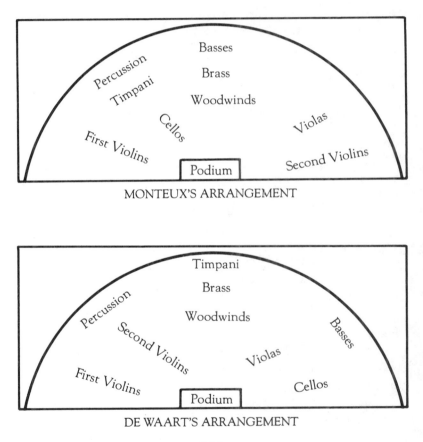

MONTEUX'S ARRANGEMENT

DE WAART'S ARRANGEMENT

Appendix F

HALLS

1911–18	Cort Theater	64 Ellis St.
1918–21	Curran Theater	445 Geary St.
1921–22	Tivoli Theater	74 Eddy St.
1922–31	Curran Theater	445 Geary St.
1931–32	Tivoli Theater	74 Eddy St.
1932–80	War Memorial Opera House (first concert November 11)	301 Van Ness Ave.
1980–	Louise M. Davies Symphony Hall (first concert September 13)	Grove St. at Van Ness Ave.

(Pop concerts have been held at Civic Auditorium, sometimes called Exposition Auditorium, and occasionally at Dreamland Auditorium.)

Appendix G

PRESIDENTS OF THE SAN FRANCISCO SYMPHONY ASSOCIATION

1910–12	T. B. Berry		1953–56	J. D. Zellerbach
1912–16	W. D. Bourn		1956–61	Kenneth Monteagle
1916–19	William Sproule		1961–63	J. D. Zellerbach
1919–27	John D. McKee		1963–72	Philip S. Boone
1927–33	J. B. Levison		1972–74	David N. Plant
1933–35	Richard Tobin		1974–80	Lawrence V. Metcalf
1935–36	Joseph S. Thompson		1980–	Brayton Wilbur Jr.
1936–53	Leonora Wood Armsby			

Appendix H

GUEST CONDUCTORS

A Selected List
(by date of first appearance with San Francisco Symphony)

1912   Paul Steindorff

1914   Atillio Parelli

1925   Georges Enesco
Henry Eichheim

1926   Howard Hanson
Louis Persinger
Earl Towner
Henry Hadley
(at the time conductor of
N.Y. Philharmonic)
Nikolai Sokoloff
Ossip Gabrilovitsch
Albert Coates
Rudolf Ganz
Jacques Gershkovitch
Alfred Hurtgen
Hans Leschke
Guilio Minetti
Gaetano Merola

1927   Ernst von Dohnanyi
Bruno Walter

1928   Mishel Piastro
Maurice Ravel

1929   Bernardino Molinari
Ottorino Respighi
Ernst Bloch

1930   Artur Rodzinski
Willem Van Hoogstraten
Antonia Brico
(first woman conductor)

1931   Walter Damrosch
Sir Hamilton Harty

Pierre Monteux
Alexander Smallens

1933   Ernest Schelling
(children's concerts,
1933–34)
Richard Lent
Fritz Reiner

1936   Otto Klemperer

1937   George Gershwin
Alexander Tansman
Igor Stravinsky
Willem Van Den Burg
(In 1937 Ballet Russe used
entire S.F. Symphony.
Conductors: Pierre Mon-
teux, Efrem Kurtz, and
Antal Dorati)

1940   Carlo Chavez

1941   Sir Thomas Beecham
John Barbirolli
Edwin McArthur
(Flagstad's accompanist)
Franz Allers
(with Ballet Russe)
Emanuel Leplin

1942   Charles O'Connell
Andre Kostelanetz
(with Lily Pons)

1945   Lorin Maazel
(2/23–24, one month
before his 15th birthday;
Rosamunde Overture of
Schubert and Italian

Symphony of Mendels-
sohn. His next appear-
ance was in 1971.)
Arnold Schoenberg
Victor Young
    (Hollywood conductor-
    composer conducted his
    own score to *For Whom
    the Bell Tolls.*)
William Steinberg
    (Conducted summer
    concert in 1945 and
    subscription concert in
    1948.)

1946   Leonard Bernstein

1947   James Sample

1949   Darius Milhaud
        Ernst Bacon
        Dimitri Mitropoulos

1950   Manuel Rosenthal

1951   Guido Cantelli
        William Denny
        Kurt Herbert Adler
            (Conducted youth con-
            certs 1950–53 and also
            Night in Old Vienna
            1978)
        Massima Freccia
        Charles Munch

1952   Enrique Jordá
        Erich Leinsdorf

1953   Alfred Wallenstein
        Victor De Sabata
        Karl Munchinger
        George Szell
        Ferenc Fricsay

1954   Georg Solti
        Fausto Cleva
        Carman Dragon

(Standard Broadcast)
Earl Murray
(1954–55 season — assis-
tant conductor)

1956   Edvard Von Beinum
        Sandor Salgo

1957   Thomas Schippers
        Igor Markevitch

1958   Virgil Thompson

1959   Werner Torkanowsky

1960   Johnny Green
        (Pops)
        Leon Kirchner

1961   Josef Krips
        Stanislaus Skrowaczewski
        Wendell Otey
            (Youth concerts)

1962   Seiji Ozawa
        Pablo Casals
        Jean-Louis LeRoux
        Walter Green
            (Youth concerts)
        David Scheinfeld
            (Youth concerts)
        Verne Sellin
            (Conducted youth con-
            certs for several years)

1963   Hans Schmidt-Isserstedt
        Howard Mitchell

1964   Paul Kletzki

1965   John Pritchard
        Paul Paray
        Georges Pretre

1966   Robert Craft
        Ulrich Meyer

1967   André Cluytens

1968	Donald Johanos		Christoph Eschenbach
	Lukus Foss		Kazimierz Kord
	Henry Lewis		Leonard Slatkin
1969	Peter Eros		Klaus Tennstedt
	Sixten Ehrling	1978	James Conlon
	Antonio De Almeida		David Zinman
	Rafael Kubelik		Andrew Davis
1970	Karel Ancerl		John Nelson
	Daniel Barenboim		Antonio Janigro
	Jean Martinon		Erich Kunzel
	Henry Mancini	1979	Bernard Klee
	Henry Krips		Walter Weller
1971	Okko Kamu		Nikolaus Harnoncourt
			Franz Brueggen
1972	Istvan Kertesz		Gerard Schwarz
	Dean Dixon		Raymond Leppard
	James Levine		Barry Tuckwell
	Rafael De Burgos	1980	Yevgeny Svetlanov
1973	Aldo Ceccato		Kurt Masur
	Kazuyoshi Akiyama		Walter Susskind
	Michael Tilson Thomas		Simon Rattle
1974	Sergui Commissiona		Bruce Ferden
	Kenneth Schermerhorn		Neemi Jarvi
	Edo de Waart		Jerzy Semkow
1975	Zdanek Macal		David Shallon
	Helen Quach	1981	Kiril Kondrashin
	Yuri Temirkanov		Eugene Ormandy
	Hans Vonk		Julius Rudel
	Alexander Schneider		Willi Boskovsky
	Jean-Pierre Rampal	1982	Varujan Kojian
	Jacques Delacotte		Christopher Hogwood
1976	Jorge Mester		Stephen Paulson
	Karl Richter		Oscar Shumsky
	Guido Ajmone-Marsan		David Agler
1977	Sarah Caldwell	1983	Mario Bernardi
	Antal Dorati		Joseph Silvers
	(Subscription season —		Myung-Whun Chung
	conducted ballet in 1937)		Garcia Navarro

SOLOISTS AND CHAMBER MUSIC ARTISTS WHO DEBUTED WITH THE SAN FRANCISCO SYMPHONY

David Abel	Violinist
Patricia Benkman	Pianist
Stephen Bishop (Later changed name to Stephen Bishop Kovacevich)	Pianist
Roy Bogas	Pianist
Lois Brandwynne	Pianist
Anshel Brusilov (Eventually concertmaster of Philadelphia Symphony and conductor of Dallas Symphony)	Violinist
David Del Tredici	Pianist and composer
Leon Fleisher	Pianist
Grisha Goluboff	Violinist
Janet Goodman (Later added Guggenheim to her name)	Pianist
Gita Karasik	Pianist
Samuel Lipman	Pianist
Yehudi Menuhin	Violinist
Patricia Michaelian	Pianist
Austin Reller	Violinist
Ruggiero Ricci	Violinist
Ruth Slenczynski (Subsequently Slenczynska)	Pianist
Miriam Solovieff	Violinist
Isaac Stern	Violinist

Appendix J

PROGRAMS CONDUCTED BY COMPOSERS

(Programs consist of composers' own works
except where otherwise noted)

January 21–23, 1927   ERNST VON DOHNANYI
Performed Beethoven's Piano Concerto No. IV in
G Major and conducted his own Symphony in
D Minor

February 3–5, 1928   MAURICE RAVEL
Le Tombeau de Couperin
Saraband and Dance (Debussy)
Rhapsodie Espagnole
Sheherazade
  Asia
  The Enchanted Flute
  The Indifferent One
    Lisa Roma, soprano
La Valse

January 11–12, 1929   OTTORINO RESPIGHI
Toccata for Piano and Orchestra
  (composer at keyboard)
Antique Dances for the Lute
Trittico Botticelliano
The Pines of Rome

January 22–23, 1937   ALEXANDER TANSMAN
Played his Concerto for Piano and Orchestra and
  conducted his "Aria" and "Alla Polacca"

March 23, 1937   IGOR STRAVINSKY
Conducted his *Symphony of Psalms* at the Civic
  Auditorium. (He conducted several other
  programs in subsequent years.)

June 15–16, 1937   GEORGE GERSHWIN
Played his Piano Concerto in F and conducted his
  Suite for Porgy and Bess

April 25, 1939   WILLIAM DENNY
            Concertino for Orchestra

March 29–30, 1940 CARLOS CHAVEZ
            Symphony C Major (Haydn)
            Symphony de Antique
            Symphony India
            La Mer (Debussy)
            Ballet Music from Three Cornered Hat (De Falla)

December 16, 1941 EMANUEL LEPLIN
            Prelude and Dance

February 8, 1945   ARNOLD SCHOENBERG
            Verklaerte Nacht (Ballet, Pillar of Fire)
            Conducted the San Francisco Symphony for the
             Ballet Theater

March 17–19, 1949 DARIUS MILHAUD
            First half, works by:
             Lalande
             Chabrier
             Satie
             Roussel
             Rameau
            Second half
             "Introduction et Marche Funebre"
             "Kentuckiana"
             "Symphony No. 3"

April 13, 1950   MANUEL ROSENTHAL
            "Jeanne D'Arc"

December 14–16, 1960 LEON KIRCHNER
            Piano Concerto
             Eugene Istomen, soloist

March 4, 1966   AARON COPLAND
            Holiday Overture (Carter)
            Symphony for Cello and Orchestra (Britten)
             Robert Sayre, soloist
            Pithoprakta (Xanakis)
            The Unanswered Question (Ives)
            Connotations for Orchestra

April 8–10, 1970   JEAN MARTINON
Overture to Beatrice et Benedict (Berlioz)
Symphony No. 4 (Les Altitudes)
Concerto No. 2 in G Minor for Piano and
  Orchestra (Saint-Saens)
  Philippe Entremont, soloist
Suite No. 2 from Daphnis et Chloe (Ravel)

Appendix K

UNUSUAL PROGRAMS

January 14, 1922	Ruth St. Denis Dance Program (Benefit for the Milk Fund of the Associated Charities) Rimsky-Korsakov — Scheherazade Massanet — Navarraise from Le Cid
March 11–12, 1938	Tilly Losch Dance Program
April 1–2, 1938	All-Shakespeare Program with Briane Aherne
April 13, 1940	Sustaining Program Peter and the Wolf with Basil Rathbone
December 2, 1941	Katherine Dunham Dancers (Gala 30th Birthday Party for Symphony) "Le Jazz Hot"
April 14, 1942	Larry Adler, harmonica soloist Berger Concerto for Harmonica and Orchestra Vivaldi-Adler Concerto Ravel's Bolero (with harmonica)
April 20, 1943	Gershwin Festival Including Paul Whiteman (once a viola player in San Francisco Symphony), Bing Crosby, Dinah Shore, San Francisco Symphony, and Famous Negro Chorus

March 3, 1957	Pension Fund Concert
	San Francisco Symphony
	Wally Rose Dixieland Band
	Burt Bales, ragtime pianist
	Earl "Fatha" Hines
	Bay City Jazz Band
	Joe Sullivan, pianist
	Kid Ory's Jazz Band
	Bob Scobey's Frisco Jazz Band
	(Rhapsody in Blue — Wally Rose, pianist
March 27, 1958	Marcel Marceau
	Conducted and mimed "The Ride of the Valkyries" of Wagner, and Dukas "Sorcerer's Apprentice"
March 2, 1959	Pension Fund Concert
	Jack Benny, violin
December 5, 1965	Pension Fund Concert
	Danny Kaye, conductor
January 4, 1967	Ronald Reagan's Inaugural Concert as Governor (Held in Sacramento) Conductors—Krips Henry Lewis and Harry Newstone. Soloists—Marilyn Horne, mezzo-soprano; Jack Benny, violinist

Appendix L

TOURS

1947 TRANSCONTINENTAL TOUR

March 16 to May 10
Pierre Monteux, conductor; James Sample, associate conductor
53 cities, 57 concerts

Tour Repertoire

Bach/Respighi	Passacaglia and Fugue in C Minor
Beethoven	Symphony No. 7 in A Major, Op. 92
	Egmont Overture
Belioz	Overture to Benvenuto Cellini
Brahms	Symphony No. 1 in C Minor, Op. 68
	Symphony No. 2 in D Major, Op. 73
	Academio Festival Overture
Debussy	Afternoon of a Faun
	Two Nocturnes — Clouds and Festivals
Denny	Praeludium (Bay Area composer)
Franck	Symphony in D Minor
Isadore Freed	Festival Overtone
Leplin	Comedy (Conducted by composer)
Mendelssohn	Concerto for Violin and Orchestra in E Minor
	Isaac Stern, soloist (no rehearsal)
Milhaud	La Bal Martinquais
	Suite Francais
Ravel	Albarado Del Gracioso
	Symphonic Fragments from Daphnis and Chloe
Saint-Saens	Concerto for Piano and Orchestra No. 2 in G Minor
	Lennard Pennario, soloist
Sheinfeld	Adagio and Allegro (Conducted by composer)
R. Strauss	Death and Transfiguration
	Don Juan
Tchaikovsky	Symphony No. 4 in F Minor, Op. 36
Wagner	Prelude and Love Death from Tristan and Isolde
	Good Friday Spell from Parsifal
	Prelude to Act Three of Lohengrin
	Overture to The Flying Dutchman

Appendix L

Concert Schedule

MARCH

Sun. 16	Visalia, Calif.; Montgomery, Aud.	2:30 P.M
Mon. 17	Ontario, Calif.; Chaffey Civic Aud.	8:15 P.M
Tues. 18	Pasadena, Calif.; Pasadena Civic Aud.	8:15 P.M
Wed. 19	San Diego, Calif.; Russ Aud.	8:15 P.M
Thurs. 20	Los Angeles, Calif.; Philharmonic Aud.	8:30 P.M
Fri. 21	Los Angeles, Calif.; Philharmonic Aud. (Mat.)	2:30 P.M
Sat. 22	Phoenix, Ariz.; Phoenix Union High School Aud.	8:30 P.M
Sun. 23	El Paso, Tex.; Liberty Hall	3:00 P.M
Mon. 24	San Antonio, Tex.; Municipal Aud.	8:20 P.M
Tues. 25	Denton, Tex.; Tex. State Coll. for Women Aud.	8:15 P.M
Wed. 26	Wichita Falls, Tex.; Wichita Falls Senior High Aud.	8:15 P.M
Thurs. 27	Fort Worth, Tex.; Will Rogers Aud.	8:15 P.M
Fri. 28	Galveston, Tex.; City Aud.	8:15 P.M
Sat. 29	Houston, Tex.; Music Hall	8:15 P.M
Sun. 30	Houston, Tex. Music Hall (Mat.)	
Mon. 31	Montgomery, Ala.; S. Lanier High School Aud. at Huntington College	8:15 P.M

APRIL

Tues. 1	Birmingham, Ala.; Municipal Aud.	8:30 P.M.
Wed. 2	Spartenburg, S.C.; Twitchell Aud. Converse Coll.	8:30 P.M.
Thurs. 3	Atlanta, Ga.; Atlanta Aud.	8:30 P.M.
Fri. 4	Norfolk, Va.; Norfolk Aud. Arena	8:15 P.M.
Sat. 5	Richmond, Va.; Mosque	8:30 P.M.
Sun. 6	Baltimore, Md.; Lyric Theatre	8:30 P.M.
Mon. 7	Washington, D.C.; Constitution Hall	8:30 P.M.
Tues. 8	Pittsburgh, Pa.; Syria Mosque	8:30 P.M.
Wed. 9	New Brunswick, N.J.; Rutgers University (Gym.)	8:30 P.M.
Thurs. 10	OPEN	
Fri. 11	New York City; Carnegie Hall	8:30 P.M.
Sat. 12	Worcester, Mass.; Memorial Aud.	8:00 P.M.
Sun. 13	Boston, Mass.; Symphony Hall (Mat.)	
Mon. 14	New London, Conn.; Palmer Auditorium, Connecticut College	8:30 P.M.
Tues. 15	Schenectady, N.Y.; Plaza Theatre	8:30 P.M.
Wed. 16	Ottawa, Can.; Ottawa Aud.	8:30 P.M.

Thurs. 17	Montreal, Can.; Sir Arthur Currie Memorial Gymnasium	8:30 P.M.
Fri. 18	Quebec, Can.; Capitol Theatre	8:30 P.M.
Sat. 19	Jamestown, N.Y.; High School Aud.	8:30 P.M.
Sun. 20	Buffalo, N.Y.; Kleinhans Music Hall	8:30 P.M.
Mon. 21	Columbus, Ohio; Memorial Hall	8:30 P.M.
Tues. 22	Newcastle, Pa.; Cathedral Aud.	8:30 P.M.
Wed. 23	Dayton, Ohio; National Cash Register Aud.	8:30 P.M.
Thurs. 24	Lima, Ohio; Warner Bros. Aud.	8:15 P.M.
Fri. 25	Chicago, Ill.; Orchestra Hall	8:15 P.M.
Sat. 26	St. Paul, Minn.; St. Paul Aud.	8:30 P.M.
Sun. 27	Madison, Wisc.; Wisc. Union Theatre (Mat.)	2:30 P.M.
Sun. 27	Madison, Wisc.; Wisc. Union Theatre (Eve.)	8:30 P.M.
Mon. 28	Milwaukee, Wisc.; Milwaukee Aud.	8:15 P.M.
Tues. 29	Davenport, Iowa; Orpheum	8:15 P.M.
Wed. 30	Burlington, Iowa; Memorial Aud.	8:15 P.M.

MAY

Thurs. 1	Ottumwa, Iowa; High School Aud.	8:15 P.M.
Fri. 2	Lincoln, Neb.; Coliseum, Univ. of Neb.	8:15 P.M.
Sat. 3	Denver, Colo.; Denver Aud.	8:20 P.M.
Sun. 4	Ogden, Utah; High School Aud. (Mat.)	
Mon. 5	Portland, Ore.; Portland Public Aud.	8:30 P.M.
Tues. 6	Seattle, Wash.; Moore Theatre	8:30 P.M.
Wed. 7	Vancouver, B.C.; Exhibition Aud.	8:30 P.M.
Thurs. 8	Bellingham, Wash.; Auditorium	8:15 P.M.
Fri. 9	Corvalis, Ore.; Men's Gym, Ore. State Coll.	8:15 P.M.
Sat. 10	Sacramento, Calif.; Memorial Aud.	8:30 P.M.

1968 JAPAN TOUR

April 9 to 26
Josef Krips, conductor
Guest artists: Jacob Krachmalnick, Rolf Persinger
7 cities, 12 concerts

Tour Repertoire:

Program One

Weber	Overture to "Euryanthe"
Haydn	Symphony No. 92 in G Major ("Oxford")

| Strauss | Don Juan, Opus 20 |
| Brahms | Symphony No. 1 in C Minor, Opus 68 |

Program Two

Wagner	Prelude and Love Death from "Tristan und Isolde"
Wagner	Siegfried Idyll
Bruckner	Symphony No. 7 in E Major

Program Three

Mozart	Symphony No. 35 in D Major, K. 385 ("Haffner")
	Sinfonia Concertante in E-flat Major for Violin, Viola and Orchestra, K. 364
	Symphony No. 41 in C Major, K. 551 ("Jupiter")

Program Four

Takemitsu	Requiem for Strings
Copland	Quiet City for Trumpet, English Horn and Strings
Stravinsky	Suite from "The Firebird"
Tchaikovsky	Symphony No. 5 in E Minor, Opus 64

Program Five

Beethoven	Leonore Overture No. 3, Opus 72a
	Symphony No. 4 in B-flat Major, Opus 60
	Symphony No. 3 in E-flat Major, Opus 55 ("Eroica")

1973 EUROPE/U.S.S.R. TOUR

May 15 to June 17
Seiji Ozawa, conductor; Niklaus Wyss, assistant conductor
Principal soloists: Andre Watts, Janet Baker, Jess Thomas
19 cities, 30 concerts

Tour Repertoire

J. C. Bach	Sinfonia No. 4
J. S. Bach	Cantata No. 189
	Jess Thomas, soloist
Bartok	Suite from "The Miraculous Mandarin"
Beethoven	Piano Concerto No. 4
	Andre Watts, soloist
	Symphony No. 4
Berlioz	Les Nuits d'Ete

Janet Baker, soloist
Roman Carnival Overture
Symphonie Fantastique
Bernstein   Serenade for Violin and Orchestra
Stuart Canin, soloist
Brahms   Symphony No. 2
Cowell   Sinfonietta
Debussy   La Mer
Gabrieli   Canzon duodecimi toni
Ives   Symphony No. 4
Prokofieff   Suite from "Romeo and Juliet"
Rush   The Cloud Messenger
Schoenberg   Five Pieces for Orchestra
Tchaikovsky   Piano Concerto No. 1
Andre Watts, soloist
Symphony No. 4

1975 JAPAN TOUR

June 4 to 19
Seiji Ozawa, conductor; Niklaus Wyss, summer/fall resident conductor
Principal soloist: Peter Serkin
11 cities, 12 concerts

Tour Repertoire

Berlioz   "Le Carnaval romain"
Bernstein   Serenade
Brahms   Piano Concerto No. 2 in B-flat Major, Op. 83
Dvorak   Symphony No. 9 in E Minor, Op. 95 "From the New
World"
Ives   Central Park in the Dark Some 40 Years Ago
Mozart   Piano Concerto No. 27 in B-flat Major, K.595
Ravel   "Daphnis et Chloe"
Tchaikovsky   Symphony No. 6 in B Minor, Op. 74 "Pathetique"

1980 UNITED STATES TOUR

October 20 to November 2
Edo de Waart, conductor; David Ramadanoff, associate conductor

Guest artists: Michael Grebanier, Raymond Kobler, Geraldine Walther,
Isaac Stern
7 cities, 10 concerts

Tour Repertoire

Beethoven	Symphony No. 5 in C Minor, Opus 67
	Violin Concerto in D, Opus 61; Isaac Stern, violin
Berio	"Entrata"
Bloch	"Schelomo"; Michael Grebanier, cello
Del Tredici	"Happy Voices"
Mahler	Symphony No. 5
Mendelssohn	Symphony No. XII in G Minor
Mozart	Sinfonia Concertante in E-flat for Violin and Viola;
	Raymond Kobler, violin; Geraldine Walther, viola
Sibelius	Violin Concerto in D Minor, Opus 47
Stravinsky	"Le Sacre du printemps"

1983 UNITED STATES TOUR
October 27 to November 12
Edo de Waart, conductor
Guest artists: Heinz Holliger, Horacio Gutierrez
11 cities, 13 concerts

Tour Repertoire

Elgar	Symphony No. 1
Liadov	"Kikimora"
Mozart	"Eine Kleine Nachtmusik"
	Oboe Concerto
	Overture to "Marriage of Figaro"
Rachmaninoff	Symphonic Dances
Saint-Saens	Piano Concerto No. 4
Sessions	Symphony No. 6
Tchaikovsky	Symphony No. 6
Wagner	Prelude and Liebestod from "Tristan and Isolde"

Appendix M

SAN FRANCISCO SYMPHONY DISCOGRAPHY

Compiled by Victor Ledin, KQED-FM Music Director

RECORDINGS MADE BETWEEN 1925 AND 1930 UNDER THE BATON OF ALFRED HERTZ

Composer and Selection	Soloist[s]	Date	US and UK Releases
AUBER, Daniel-Francois-Esprit (1782–1871)			
Fra Diavolo, ou L'hotellerie de Terracine (1830)			
Overture, Parts 1 and 2		1925	RCA 78rpm 6506 (12")
			HMV 78rpm DB869 (12")
BEETHOVEN, Ludwig van (1770–1827)			
Leonore Overture No. 3, Opus 72a			
Parts 1 and 2		1930	RCA 78rpm 6906 (12")
Parts 3 and 4			RCA 78rpm 6907 (12")
BRAHMS, Johannes (1833–1897)			
Hungarian Dances			
No. 5 in F-sharp Minor and		1929	RCA 78rpm 1296 (10")
No. 6 in D-flat Major			HMV 78rpm E607 (10")

DELIBES, Leo (1836–1891)
Coppelia Ballet (1870)
Dance of the Automatons and Waltz

1926   RCA 78rpm 6586 (12")
(with Kreisler's "Caprice
Viennois")

HMV 78rpm D1272 (12")
(with Kreisler's "Caprice
Viennois")

Sylvia Ballet (1876)
Intermezzo, Valse Lente and Pizzicato

1927   RCA 78rpm 1166 (10")
HMV 78rpm DA804 (10")

GLAZUNOV, Alexander (1865–1936)
Valse de Concert, No. 1, Opus 47
Parts 1 and 2

1929   RCA 78rpm 6826 (12")
HMV 78rpm D1492 (12")

GOUNOD, Charles (1818–1893)
Convoi Funebre d'une Marionette
(Funeral March of a Marionette)

1928   HMV 78rpm D1286 (12")
(with Schubert's "Marche
Militaire")

RCA 78rpm 6639 (12")
(with Schubert's "Marche
Militaire")

KREISLER, Fritz (1875–1962)
Caprice Viennois, Opus 2

1926   RCA 78rpm 6586 (12")
(with Delibes' selections from
Coppelia Ballet)

Composer and Selection	Soloist[s]	Date	US and UK Releases
Liebesleid ("Old Viennese Song")		1929	HMV 78rpm D1272 (12") (with Delibes' selections from Coppelia Ballet)
LISZT, Franz (1811–1886) Symphonic Poem No. 3, "Les Preludes" (1856) Parts 1 and 2 Parts 3 and 4		1929	RCA 78rpm 6802 (12") (with Moszkowski and Luigini) RCA 78rpm 6863 (12") RCA 78rpm 6864 (12")
LUIGINI, Alexandre (1850–1906) Aubade		1929	RCA 78rpm 6802 (12") (with Kreisler's "Liebesleid" and Moszkowski)
MASSENET, Jules (1842–1912) Le Cid (1885), Ballet Music		1930	RCA 78rpm Album M-56 (3 – 12" discs) (1406, 1407, 1408)
Phedre (1901), Overture Parts 1 and 2		1927	RCA 78rpm 7154 (12")

MENDELSSOHN, Felix (1809–1847)
Midsummer Night's Dream, Incidental Music, Opus 21

1928 — RCA 78rpm Albums
M/AM-18 (4 – 12" discs)
M(6675 to 6678)
AM(6987 to 6990)

Midsummer Night's Dream, Incidental Music, Opus 21
Overture, Parts 1 and 2
Overture, Part 3 and Scherzo
Wedding March

1928 — HMV 78rpm D1626 (12")
HMV 78rpm D1627 (12")
HMV 78rpm D1568 (12")
(with Schubert's Entr'act)

MOSZKOWSKI, Moritz (1854–1925)
Serenade, Opus 15, No. 1

1929 — RCA 78rpm 6802 (12")
(with Kreisler's "Liebesleid" and Luigini)

RIMSKY-KORSAKOV, Nikolai (1844–1908)
Capriccio espagnol, Opus 34
(Spanish Caprice, 1887)
Parts 1 and 2
Parts 3 and 4

1927 — RCA 78rpm 6603 (12")
RCA 78rpm 1185 (10")

SCHUBERT, Franz Peter (1797–1828)
Marche Militaire in D Major, Opus 51, No. 1 (D.733)

1928 — HMV 78rpm D1286 (12")
(with Gounod's March)
RCA 78rpm 6639 (12")
(with Gounod's March)

285

Composer and Selection	Soloist[s]	Date	US and UK Releases
Rosamunde Ballet (D.797) Entr'act		1928	RCA 78rpm 6678 (12") (included in Album M-18, see Mendelssohn) HMV 78rpm D1568 (12") (with Mendelssohn's Wedding March) RCA 78rpm 6987 (12") (included in Album AM-18, see Mendelssohn)
WAGNER, Richard (1813–1883) Parsifal (1882) Prelude, Parts 1 and 2		1925	RCA 78rpm 6498 (12") HMV 78rpm DB884 (12")
Prelude, Part 3 and Good Friday Spell, Part 1		1925	RCA 78rpm 6499 (12") HMV 78rpm DB885 (12")
Good Friday Spell, Parts 2 and 3		1925	RCA 78rpm 6500 (12")
Tristan und Isolde (1865) Liebestod, Parts 1 and 2		1928	RCA 78rpm 1169 (10") HMV 78rpm E469 and DA837 (10")
Prelude, Parts 1 and 2		1927	RCA 78rpm 6585 (12")
WEBER, Carl Maria von (1786–1826) Der Freischutz (J.291, 1823) Overture, Parts 1 and 2		1926	RCA 78rpm 6705 (12")

286

RECORDINGS MADE BETWEEN 1941 AND 1960 UNDER THE BATON OF PIERRE MONTEUX

BACH, Johann Sebastian (1685–1750)
Christmas Oratorio (BMV248, 1734)
Sinfonia: Shepherds' Christmas Music

1949

RCA 78rpm Album DM-1340
(with Bach-Respighi)
RCA 45rpm Set WDM-1340
(with Bach-Respighi)
HMV 78rpm DB 21051 (side 4, with Bach-Respighi)

BACH, Johann Sebastian. Arranged by Ottorino Respighi (1879–1936)
Passacaglia and Fugue in C Minor (BWV582)

1949

RCA 78rpm Album DM-1340
(with Bach)
RCA 45rpm Set WDM-1340
(with Bach)
RCA 33rpm LM-149 (10")
(with Brahms' Song of Destiny)
RCA 33rpm LVT-1039
(with Beethoven's 8th Symphony & Berlioz's Overture)
RCA 33rpm LM-1799
(with Beethoven's 8th Symphony & Berlioz's Overture)

Composer and Selection	Soloist[s]	Date	US and UK Releases
BEETHOVEN, Ludwig van (1770–1827) Die Ruinen von Athen (Ruins of Athens) Incidental Music to the Play by Kotzebue, Opus 113 (1811) Overture			RCA (Italy) 33rpm A 12 RO158 HMV 78rpm DB21053-21054 (three sides, with Bach's Sinfonia)
Symphony No. 2 in D Major, Opus 36 (1802)		1949	RCA 45rpm 49-3691 (in Set WDM-1637 RCA (Italy) 45rpm B 72 R0011
		Apr. 19, 1949	RCA 78rpm Album DM-1325 RCA 45rpm Set WDM-1325 RCA 33rpm LM-1024 HMV 33rpm FALP 114 HMV (Italy) 33rpm QALP 114 RCA (France) 33rpm GM 43357 (with Beethoven's 8th Symphony)
Symphony No. 4 in B-flat Major, Opus 60 (1806)		1952	RCA 33rpm LM-1714 (with Schumann's 4th Symphony) RCA 45rpm Set WDM-1714

Symphony No. 8 in F Major, Opus 93 (1812)

RCA (Holland) 33rpm L 16393 (with Schumann's 4th Symphony)

Feb. 28, 1950

RCA 78rpm Album DM-1450
RCA 45rpm Set WDM-1450
RCA 33rpm LM-43 (10")
RCA 33rpm LVT-1039 (with Bach-Respighi and Berlioz Overture)
RCA 33rpm LM-1799 (with Bach-Respighi and Berlioz Overture)
RCA (France) 33rpm GM 43357 (with Beethoven's 2nd Symphony)

BERLIOZ, Hector (1803–1869)
Benvenuto Cellini (1848)
Overture, Opus 23

Apr. 6, 1952

RCA 45rpm Set ERD 5
RCA (Italy) 33rpm A 12 R0158 (with Bach-Respighi)
RCA 33rpm LVT-1039 (with Beethoven's 8th Symphony and Bach-Respighi)
RCA 33rpm LM-1799 (with Beethoven's 8th Symphony and Bach-Respighi)

Composer and Selection	Soloist[s]	Date	US and Foreign Releases
			RCA (France) 33rpm GM 43359 (with Berlioz's Symphonie Fantastique)
La Damnation de Faust, Opus 24 (1846) Rakoczy March (Hungarian March)		1951	RCA 33rpm CAMDEN CAL 385 (with Debussy-Ravel; Milhaud; and two works by d'Indy)
			HMV 45rpm 7 RF 278
			RCA 45rpm Set ERB 5 (with Overture)
			RCA 45rpm Set WDM-1618
			RCA (UK) CAMDEN CDN 1005 (with Debussy-Ravel; Milhaud; and two works by d'Indy)
Symphonie fantastique, Opus 14 (1830, rev. 1831)		1945	RCA 78rpm Album M/DM-994 M(11-9027 to 11-9032) DM(11-9033 to 11-9038)
			HMV 78rpm DB 6670 to DB 6675
			HMV 78rpm DB 9342 to DB 9347

	Performers	Date	Recordings
		Feb. 27, 1950	RCA 45rpm Set WDM-994 RCA 33rpm LM-1131 HMV 33rpm ALP 1137 HMV 33rpm FALP 118 HMV (Italy) 33rpm QALP 118 RCA (Italy) 33rpm A 12 R0092 RCA (France) 33rpm GM 43359 (with Berlioz Overture)
BRAHMS, Johannes (1833-1897)			
Rhapsody for Alto, Chorus, and Orchestra, Opus 53 (after Goethe's "Harzreise im Winter")	Marian Anderson, contralto San Francisco Municipal Men's Chorus	1945	RCA 78rpm Album M/DM-1111 M(11-9500 to 11-9501) DM (11-9502 to 11-9503) RCA 78rpm Album SP 13 (11-8983 to 11-8984)
Schicksalslied, Opus 54 ("Song of Destiny," 1871, words by Holderlin)	Stanford University Chorus (in English)	1949	RCA 33rpm LM-149 (10") (with Bach-Respighi) RCA 45rpm Set WDM 1637 (with Beethoven Overture) RCA (Italy) 45rpm B 72 R0011/2
Symphony No. 2 in D Major, Opus 73 (1878)		1945	RCA 78rpm Album M/DM-1065

Composer and Selection	Soloist[s]	Date	US and Foreign Releases
			M(11-9237 to 11-9240) DM(11-9241 to 11-9244) RCA 45rpm Set WDM-1065
		1951	RCA 33rpm LM-1173
BRUCH, Max (1838–1920) Concerto in G Minor, Opus 26	Yehudi Menuhin, violin	1945	RCA 78rpm Album M/DM-1023 M(11-8951 to 11-8953) DM(11-8954 to 11-8956)
CHABRIER, Alexis Emmanuel (1841–1894) Le Roi Malgré Lui (1887) Fête Polonaise from Act 2		1947	RCA 78rpm 12-0978 RCA 45rpm 49-0517
CHAUSSON, Ernest (1855–1899) Symphony in B-flat Major, Opus 20 (1890)		1950	RCA 33rpm LM-1181 HMV FALP 227 RCA (France & Holland) 33rpm A 630254 RCA (Italy) 33rpm A 12 R0021
DEBUSSY, Claude (1862–1918) Images for orchestra (1906–1912) Gigues and Rondes de printemps		1942	RCA 78rpm Album M/DM-954

Gigues; Ibéria and Rondes de printemps		M(11-8520 to 11-8521) DM(11-8522 to 11-8523) HMV (France) DB11139 HMV DB6182 and DB6183 RCA (Italy) 45 rpm B 72 R0019 RCA 45rpm Set WEPR 12 RCA 33rpm CAMDEN CAL 161
Rondes de printemps	1951	RCA 33rpm LM-1197 RCA 33rpm LVT-1036 HMV 33rpm FALP 174 RCA 45rpm Set WDM-1618
Gigues	1951	RCA 33rpm CAMDEN CAL 336
	1942	HMV (France) 78rpm DB 11139
DEBUSSY, Claude. Arranged by Maurice Ravel (1875–1937)		
Sarabande from "Pour le Piano" (1896–1901) (orchestrated in 1920)	1946	RCA 78rpm in Album 1143 (11-9685) (with Ravel's Valses nobles et sentimentales and Daphnis et Chloe, Suite No. 1)

Composer and Selection	Soloist[s]	Date	US and Foreign Releases
			RCA (England) 33rpm CAMDEN CDN 1005
			RCA 33rpm CAMDEN CAL 385
FRANCK, Cesar (1822–1890) Symphony in D Minor (1886–1888)		1941	RCA 78rpm Album M/DM-840 M(18246 to 18250) DM(18251 to 18255)
			HMV 78rpm 21442 to 21446
		1950	RCA 78rpm Album DM-1382
			RCA 45rpm Set WDM-1382
			RCA 33rpm LM-1065
			RCA 33rpm CAMDEN CAL 107
			RCA (Holland) 33rpm L 16171
			HMV (Germany) 33rpm WALP 1019
			HMV (Italy) 33rpm QALP 123
			HMV 33rpm FALP 123
			HMV (UK and Sweden) 33rpm ALP 1019

FRANCK, Cesar. Arranged by
  Charles O'Connell (1900–1962)
Pièce Héroïque from "Trois Pieces pour Grand
  Orgue" (1878)

1941

RCA 78rpm 18485
HMV 78rpm DB 6135
HMV (France) 78 rpm
  DB 11117
RCA 33rpm CAMDEN CAL
  215

GRUENBERG, Louis (1884–1964)
Concerto for violin and orchestra

Jascha Heifetz,
  violin

Dec.
1945

RCA 78rpm Album
  M/DM-1079
M(11-9333 to 11-9336)
DM(11-9337 to 11-9340)
RCA 33rpm LVT-1017
RCA 33rpm LCT-1160 (with a
  trio performance of the Sere-
  nade Opus 10 by Dohnanyi)
RCA (France & Holland)
  33rpm A-630291

IBERT, Jacques (1890–1962)
Escales (Ports of Call)
  No. 1: Palermo
  No. 2: Tunis-Nefta
  No. 3: Valencia

1946

RCA 78rpm Album
  DM-1173
DM(11-9909 to 11-9910)
RCA 78rpm Album DV-10
  (vinyl)

Composer and Selection	Soloist[s]	Date	US and Foreign Releases
d'INDY, Vincent (1851–1931) Fervaal, Opus 40 (1889–1895) Introduction to Act 1		1945	DV(18-0082 to 18-0083) RCA 78rpm Album M/DM-1113 (final side, with d'Indy's Istar Variations) RCA 33rpm CAMDEN CAL 385 (with Berlioz March; d'Indy's Istar Variations; Milhaud; and Debussy-Ravel) RCA (UK) CAMDEN CDN 1005 (with Berlioz March; d'Indy's Istar Variations; Milhaud; and Debussy-Ravel)
Istar, Symphonic Variations, Opus 42 (1896)		1945	RCA 78rpm Album M/DM-1113 M(11-9508 to 11-9509) DM(11-9510 to 11-9511) RCA 33rpm CAMDEN CAL 385 (with Berlioz March; d'Indy's Fervaal; Debussy-Ravel and Milhaud) RCA 78rpm Set SP-16 (11-9104/5)

Symphonie sur un chant montagnard francais (Symphonie Cevenole) for orchestra and piano, Opus 25 (1886) ("Symphony on a French Mountain Air")

Year	Performer	Recording
1941	Maxim Schapiro, piano	RCA (UK) 33rpm CAMDEN CDN 1005
		RCA 78rpm Album M/DM-913 M(11-8367 to 11-8369) DM(11-8233 to 11-8235)

Symphony No. 2 in B-flat Major, Opus 57 (1902–1903)

Year	Performer	Recording
1942		RCA 78rpm Album M/DM-943 M(11-8441 to 11-8445) DM(11-8446 to 11-8450) RCA 45rpm Set WCT-1125 RCA 33rpm LCT-1125

LALO, Edouard (1823–1892)
Le Roi d'Ys (1875–1887) Overture

Year	Performer	Recording
1942	Boris Blinder, cello	RCA 78rpm 11-8489

MAHLER, Gustav (1860–1911)
Kindertotenlieder (1902)

Year	Performer	Recording
1950	Marian Anderson, contralto	RCA 33rpm LM-1146 (with Brahms' Alto Rhapsody with the RCA Victor Symphony Orchestra conducted by Fritz Reiner)

Composer and Selection	Soloist[s]	Date	US and Foreign Releases
			RCA 45rpm Set WDM-1531 HMV (UK and Sweden) ALP 1138
MENDELSSOHN, Felix (1809–1847) Ruy Blas Overture in C Minor, Opus 95 (1839)		1947	RCA 78rpm 12-0657 RCA 45rpm 49-0883 HMV 78rpm DB 4323 HMV 45rpm 7 RF 123
MILHAUD, Darius (1892–1974) Protée, Symphonic Suite Overture; Prelude and Fugue; Pastorale; Nocturne; Finale		1945	RCA 78rpm Album M/DM-1027 M(11-8977 to 11-8979) DM(11-8980 to 11-8982) RCA 33rpm CAMDEN CAL 385 (with Berlioz March; two works by d'Indy; and Debussy-Ravel) RCA (UK) 33rpm CAMDEN CDN DN 1005

RAVEL, Maurice (1875–1937)
(see also Debussy)

Alborada del gracioso (No. 4 from "Miroirs"—1905)

| | 1947 | RCA 78rpm 12-1107 |
| | | RCA 45rpm 49-0916 |

Daphnis et Chloé, Ballet Suite No. 1
Nocturne; Interlude; and Danse Guerriere

San Francisco
Municipal Chorus

	1946	RCA 78rpm Album
		DM-1143 (with Ravel's Valses
		nobles et sentimentales and
		Debussy-Ravel)
		DM(11-9685 to 11-9688)
		RCA 33rpm CAMDEN CAL
		156

La Valse, poeme choreographique (1920)

	1941	RCA 78rpm Album
		M/DM-820
		M(18160 to 18161)
		DM(18162 to 18163)
		HMV 78rpm DB5964 and
		DB5965 (with Rimsky
		Korsakov Bridal Procession)
		RCA 33rpm CAMDEN CAL
		282
		HMV (Australia) 78rpm
		ED 316 and ED 317
		RCA 45rpm CAMDEN Set
		CAE 130

Composer and Selection	Soloist[s]	Date	US and Foreign Releases
Valses nobles et sentimentales (1911)		1946	RCA 78rpm Album DM-1143 (with Ravel's Daphnis et Chloe Suite and Debussy-Ravel) HMV 78rpm DB6676 and DB6677 RCA 33rpm CAMDEN CAL 156 RCA 33rpm CAMDEN CAE 216
RIMSKY-KORSAKOV, Nikolai (1844–1908) Le Coq d'Or (1906–1907) (The Golden Cockerel) Introduction		1945	RCA 78rpm Album DM-1252 (with Rimsky-Korsakov's Sadko) (record 12-0503B)
Bridal Procession, from Act 3		Apr. 21, 1941	HMV 78rpm DB 5965 HMV (Australia) 78rpm ED 317 RCA 78rpm Album M/DM-820 (final side, with Ravel's La Valse) HMV 78rpm DB5965 (with Ravel's La Valse)

RCA (France) 33rpm
GM 43361 (with Rimsky-Korsakov's Scheherazade)
RCA 33rpm CAMDEN CAL 215

Sadko (1894–1896)
Symphonic Poem, Opus 5

1945

RCA 78rpm Album DM-1252
(with Introduction to Le Coq d'Or)
DM(12-0503 to 12-0504)

Scheherazade, symphonic suite (1888), Opus 35

Mar. 3–4, 1942

Naoum Blinder, violin

RCA 78rpm Album
M/DM-920
M(11-8384 to 11-8388)
DM(11-8264 to 11-8268)
RCA 45rpm Set WDM-920
RCA 33rpm LM-1002
RCA 33rpm CAMDEN CAL 151

RCA (Italy) 33rpm A 12 R0077
RCA 45rpm Set ERC 2
RCA (UK) CAMDEN CDN 1009

RCA (France) 33rpm
GM 43361 (with Rimsky-Korsakov's Bridal Procession)

Composer and Selection	Soloist[s]	Date	US and Foreign Releases
Symphony No. 2, "Antar," Opus 9 (composed 1868; revised in 1876 and again in 1897)		1946	RCA 78rpm Album DM-1203 DM(12-0179 to 12-0181) HMV 78rpm DB 6918 to DB 6920
Tsar Saltan (1899–1900) Introduction to Act 1 ("Warrior's March")		1942	RCA 78rpm Album M/DM-920 (final side, with Scheherazade) RCA 45rpm Set WDM-920 (final side, with Scheherazade) HMV 45rpm 7 RF 278
SCHUMANN, Robert (1810–1856) Symphony No. 4 in D Minor, Opus 120 (1841, revised 1851)		1952	RCA 33rpm LM-1714 (with Beethoven's 4th Symphony) RCA (Holland) 33rpm L 16393 (with Beethoven's 4th Symphony) RCA 45rpm Set WDM-1714
SCRIABIN, Alexander (1872–1915) Poème d'extase, Opus 54 (1907–1908) (Poem of Ecstasy, in C Major)		1947	RCA 78rpm Album DM-1270 DM(12-0641 to 12-0642)

302

STRAUSS, Richard (1864–1949)
Tod und Verklarung, Opus 24
(Death and Transfiguration)

1960   RCA 33rpm VICS-1457
        (stereo) (with Wagner)

STRAVINSKY, Igor (1882–1971)
Le Sacre du Printemps (1913)
(The Rite of Spring)

1945   RCA 78rpm Album
            M/DM-1052
            M(11-9164 to 11-9167)
            DM(11-9168 to 11-9171)
        RCA 33rpm CAMDEN CAL
            110
        HMV 78rpm DB6804 to
            DB6807
        HMV 78rpm DB9409 to
            DB9412
        HMV (Switzerland) 78rpm
            DB 20027 to 20030

WAGNER, Richard (1813–1883)
Siegfried Idyll (1870)

1960   RCA 33rpm VIC-1102
        RCA 33rpm VICS-1102
            (stereo)
        RCA 33rpm VICS-1457
            (stereo) (with Strauss)

Composer and Selection	Soloist[s]	Date	US and Foreign Releases
RECORDINGS MADE BETWEEN 1952 AND 1953 UNDER THE BATON OF LEOPOLD STOKOWSKI			
GOULD, Morton (1913–)			
Dance Variations	Arthur Whittemore and Jack Lowe, duo-pianists	1953	RCA 33rpm LM-1858 (with Menotti's Sebastian Ballet Suite recorded with the NBC Symphony Orchestra)
MUSSORGSKY, Modest (1839–1881)			
Boris Godunov (1868–1872) Highlights (Rimsky-Korsakov version)	Nicola Rossi-Lemeni, bass	Dec. 8–10, 1952	RCA 33rpm LM-1764
	San Francisco Opera Chorus San Francisco Boys' Chorus		dell'Arte (UK) DA9002
RECORDINGS MADE BETWEEN 1957 AND 1962 UNDER THE BATON OF ENRIQUE JORDA			
CUSHING, Charles (1905–)			
Cereus, Poem for Orchestra (1960)		1962	CRI 33rpm 152

FALLA, Manuel de (1876–1946)

Nights in the Gardens of Spain (1909–1915) — Artur Rubinstein, piano — 1957 — RCA 33rpm LM-2181
RCA 33rpm LM-2430
RCA 33rpm LSC-2430 (stereo)

IMBRIE, Andrew W. (1921–)

Legend for orchestra (1959) — 1962 — CRI 33rpm 152

PROKOFIEV, Sergei (1891–1953)

Concerto No. 3 in C Major, Opus 26 (1917) — Gary Graffman, piano — 1957 — RCA 33rpm LM-2138 (with Prokofiev's Classical Symphony)
RCA 33rpm VIC-1105
RCA 33rpm VICS-1105 (stereo) (both with Prokofiev's Classical Symphony)

Symphony No. 1 in D Major, Opus 25 ("Classical Symphony") — 1957 — RCA 33rpm LM-2138 (with 3rd Piano Concerto by Prokofiev)
RCA 33rpm VIC-1105
RCA 33rpm VICS-1105 (stereo) (both with 3rd Piano Concerto by Prokofiev)

RACHMANINOFF, Sergei (1873–1943)

Concerto No. 2 in C Minor, Opus 18 — Alexander Brailowsky, piano — 1958 — RCA 33rpm LM-2259
RCA 33rpm VIC-1024

Composer and Selection	Soloist[s]	Date	US and Foreign Releases
			RCA 33rpm VICS-1024 (stereo)
			RCA 33rpm VICS-1673 (stereo)

SAN FRANCISCO SYMPHONY MEMBERS (SMALL CHAMBER ORCHESTRA) RECORDED IN 1952

Composer and Selection	Soloist[s]	Date	US and Foreign Releases
KOHS, Ellis B. (1916–)			
Chamber Concerto for viola and strings (1949)	Ferenc Molnar, viola	1952	Music-Library 33rpm 7004 (12")
			Music-Library 78rpm MLR-17-21 (2 –12" discs)

NOTE: Between 1963 and 1970 no recordings were made with the orchestra under the baton of Josef Krips.

RECORDINGS MADE BETWEEN 1972 AND 1976 UNDER THE BATON OF SEIJI OZAWA

Composer and Selection	Soloist[s]	Date	US and Foreign Releases
BEETHOVEN, Ludwig van (1770–1827)			
Symphony No. 3 in E-flat, Opus 55 (1804, "Eroica" Symphony)		May 18–19, 1975	Philips 33rpm 950002 (stereo)

BERLIOZ, Hector (1803–1869) Romeo et Juliette (1838–1839) Selections	June 22–24, 1972	Deutsche Grammophon DG2530308 (stereo, with Prokofiev and Tchaikovsky)
BERNSTEIN, Leonard (1918–) West Side Story (1960) Symphonic Dances	June 22–24, 1972	Deutsch Grammophon DG2530309 (stereo, with Russo Three Pieces)
DVORAK, Antonin (1841–1904) Carnival Overture, Opus 92 (1891)	May 18–19, 1975	Philips 950001 (stereo) (with Dvorak's New World Symphony)
Symphony No. 9 in E Minor, Opus 95 ("From the New World," 1893)	May 18–19, 1975	Philips 950001 (stereo) (with Dvorak's Carnival Overture)
GERSHWIN, George (1898–1937) An American in Paris (1928)	May 23, 1976	Deutsche Grammophon DG2530788 (stereo, with Russo's Street Music)
PROKOFIEV, Sergei (1891–1953) Romeo and Juliet, Ballet (1935), Opus 64	June 22–24, 1972	Deutsche Grammophon DG2530308 (stereo, with Berlioz and Tchaikovsky)

Composer	Soloist[s]	Date	US and Foreign Releases
RUSSO, William Joseph (1928–) Street Music		May 23, 1976	Deutsche Grammophon DG2530788 (stereo, with Gershwin)
Three Pieces for Blues Band and Orchestra	Siegel-Schwall Band	June 22–24, 1972	Deutsche Grammophon DG2530309 (stereo, with Bernstein)
TCHAIKOVSKY, Peter Ilyich (1840–1893) Romeo and Juliet, Fantasy Overture (1869, revised 1880)		June 22–24, 1972	Deutsche Grammophon DG2530308 (stereo, with Prokofiev and Berlioz)

RECORDINGS MADE STARTING IN 1981 UNDER THE BATON OF EDO DE WAART

Composer	Soloist[s]	Date	US and Foreign Releases
DEBUSSY, Claude (1862–1918) La Damoiselle elue (1887–1888)	Elly Ameling, soprano, and Janice Taylor, mezzo-soprano	Oct. 21, 1981	Philips 6514 199 (digital stereo, with Duparc and Ravel)

DUPARC, Henri (1848–1933)			
Chanson Triste (1868, words by Lahor) and L'Invitation au voyage (1870, words by Baudelaire)	Elly Ameling, soprano	Oct. 20–22, 1981	Philips 6514 199 (digital stereo, with Ravel and Debussy)
GRIEG, Edward (1843–1907)			
Music from Peer Gynt		Oct. 25, 28, 29 1982	Philips* (digital stereo)
MAHLER, Gustav (1860–1911)			
Symphony No. 4 in G Major (1900)	Margaret Price, soprano	Oct. 19–22, 1981	Philips 6514 201 (digital stereo) Philips 7337 210 (cassette)
RACHMANINOFF, Sergei (1873–1943)			
Concerto No. 1 in F-sharp Minor, Opus 1 (1891, revised 1917)	Zoltán Kocsis, piano	Oct. 25–26, 1982	Philips* (digital stereo, with Rachmaninoff's 4th Concerto)
Concerto No. 4 in G Minor, Opus 40 (1927)	Zoltán Kocsis, piano	Oct. 27, 1983	Philips* (digital stereo, with Rachmaninoff's 1st Concerto)
RAVEL, Maurice (1875–1937)			
Shéhérazade (1903, words by Klingsor) Asie; La Flute enchantée; L'Indifférent	Elly Ameling, soprano	Oct. 20, 1981	Philips 6514 199 (digital stereo, with Duparc and Debussy)

Composer and Selection	Soloist[s]	Date	US and Foreign Releases
RESPIGHI, Ottorino (1879–1936)			
The Birds (1927)		Oct. 19, 1981	Philips* (digital stereo, with Respighi's Pines and Fountains of Rome)
Fountains of Rome (1917)		Oct. 16, 1981	Philips* (digital stereo, with Respighi's Pines of Rome and The Birds)
Pines of Rome (1924)		Oct. 16, 17, 19 1981	Philips* (digital stereo, with Respighi's Fountains of Rome and The Birds)
WAGNER, Richard (1813–1883)			
Symphony in C Major (1832)		Oct. 23, 25, 1982	Philips* (digital stereo, with Wagner's Faust Overture)
Eine Faust Ouverture (1840, revised 1855)		Oct. 23, 1982	Philips* (digital stereo, with Wagner Symphony)

*Not yet released

Appendix N

ACOUSTICS OF LOUISE M. DAVIES SYMPHONY HALL

by Theodore J. Schultz,
Technical Director, Architectural Acoustics and Noise-Control,
Bolt Beranek and Newman Inc.

The design proposal for Louise M. Davies Symphony Hall, and for new halls in Toronto and Melbourne, was influenced by the acoustical and visual intimacy and the excellent sound in the best seats of Old Massey Hall in Toronto. This results in a shorter and wider plan, as compared with the "shoebox" shape of a number of other excellent halls, such as Boston Symphony Hall. In long halls, a large part of the audience is placed at a great distance from the performers, and those seated in side balconies have poor sightlines to the stage. With a wider, shorter hall, the audience is closer to the performers and each member of the audience can have a good sightline.

The plan also included a few rows of seats at the sides and back of the stage. In contrast to the "surround" halls in Berlin and Denver, where a large percentage of the audience normally sits behind the orchestra, Davies Symphony Hall is a "semi-surround," like Rotterdam's De Doelen and a number of older halls in Great Britain. People in the rows at each side of the stage and at the back will not hear exactly the same sound as people in the main part of the hall, but the sound in those seats is still excellent; moreover, some people prefer to be very close to the performance and to see it from a new angle. (During the early tuning rehearsals in Toronto, the conductor, Andrew Davis, declared that the seats around the stage might be the most popular seats in the hall!)

The seats at the back of the stage are bench type and can be set up either for audience or for the chorus in large-scale musical works; this relieves crowding on the stage, since an oversize orchestra is usually called for in those works. Additional chorus risers are provided and can be placed on stage as required to accommodate the large San Francisco Symphony Choir.

In 1984, a large concert organ, designed and built by Ruffatti of Padua, Italy, will be installed behind the orchestra, above the audience/chorus area. The organ can be used either as a solo instrument or with choir and/or orchestra.

Above the stage and chorus, at a height of about thirty feet, that is, at the same level as the stage lighting, is an array of thirty-one round acrylic sound-reflecting panels. These sound reflectors are the most critical element in the acoustical design of the hall, both for aiding on-stage communication and for establishing the balance and the clarity of sound in the audience areas. Most of the panels are seven feet in diameter, but the panels above the chorus are only six feet in diameter. Each panel is slightly convex downward. They have been adjusted to give optimum sound reflection within the orchestra and chorus, and to the audience.

The hall itself is protected from outside noise by heavy concrete construction in at least two layers (a "box within a box"). Double sets of doors, with sound locks between them, assure that no noise will intrude from the lobbies or from outside traffic. The air-conditioning system has also been designed to be literally inaudible.

The interior of the hall, in order to give excellent reflection of sound even at the lowest frequencies, is made of poured-in-place and precast concrete, about six inches thick. The walls are built up of precast sections, shaped to reflect sound in various directions to achieve a more uniform, diffuse sound distribution.

The entire concrete floor is carpeted. The seats are upholstered in fabric to substitute as much as possible for absent audience during rehearsals. This is done to stabilize the reverberation time (about 2.0 seconds at 500–1000 cycles per second) with or without full audience. The hall will be even more reverberant when the organ is used alone with an empty stage.

A long reverberation time is desirable for large romantic orchestral works and for most choral and organ music while a lower reverberation time is better for baroque and classical music, for small-scale modern works, and for popular entertainers. To achieve this variability, large velour "banners" can be lowered from slots in the ceiling; when in place they can reduce the reverberation time to as low as 1.5 seconds.

The acoustics for orchestral, choral, and organ concerts has governed all of the acoustical design decisions, but Davies Symphony Hall also serves well for many other uses, such as concerts with popular entertainers and speeches or lectures. A high-quality sound reinforcement system has been provided for such use and for narration in symphony concerts. The large central cluster of loudspeakers is stored above the ceiling when not in use; it is lowered to the level of the sound-reflecting panels for sound system operation. Supplemental loudspeakers in various locations (with suitable time delays) augment the central cluster, so as to cover the entire audience with uniform, high-quality amplified sound.

Davies Symphony Hall is one of a number of new concert halls that have provisions for acoustical tuning. Such provisions are desirable because it is increasingly difficult to predict the acoustical outcome as halls increase in size to hold the large audiences essential for economic viability.

The adjustable acoustical elements usually take the form of sound-reflecting panels above the stage, as described above. Their heights and angles are critical in determining the quality of sound in the hall, and "tuning" the hall is the process of choosing optimum settings to suit a wide range of musical material. This means working with the orchestra and maestro during special rehearsals dedicated to the hall tuning: we hear a passage of music, make some adjustments to the panels, then hear the same passage again in order to evaluate the change. The procedure is exacting and tedious because we must deal evenhandedly with the 3,000 seats in the hall as well as those for all the musicians on the stage and in the choir.

Because the configuration of the reflecting panels is so critical, there were troubles at the opening of Davies Symphony Hall. The panels, as originally delivered, were badly warped and the sound reflections could not be controlled when the hall was first tuned. The problem largely disappeared when a new set of perfectly shaped panels was installed. Actually, the acoustical tuning process usually extends over a number of years, as we gain more experience in listening to different kinds of music in the hall, and as the orchestra continues to adapt itself to the new acoustical surroundings.

INDEX

Abel, David, 124
Acoustics, 139, 235, 244–45, 311–14
Adler, Kurt Herbert, 50–51, 52
Age, as factor in orchestra membership, 138, 211–12, 232–33
Akiyama, Kazuyoshi, 184
Albert, Agnes, 78–79
Allen, Gracie, 56
Allers, Franz, 60
Altman, Ludwig, 168
Ameling, Elly, 256
Anda, Geza, 96
Anders, Detlev, 62
Anderson, Marian, 15, 16, 36, 71
Anderson, Miles, 206
Anker, Sigmund, 12
Armsby, Lenora Wood, 11, 92
Associate concertmaster, position of, 170–71, 179–80
Auditions: importance of to musicians, 257; process of, 245

Bacon, Ernst, 2
Badura-Skoda, Paul, 212
Bahrs, George, 156
Baker, Janet, 193
Barati Chamber Orchestra, 133
Barati, George, 61, 62, 63, 69, 76, 133
Barzin, Leon, 143–44
Baton, use of, 32
Bay Area composers' works performed, 63, 72, 172
Beecham, Sir Thomas, 42, 76–78, 122
Beel, Sigmund, 6
Beethoven bicentennial, 171
Beinum, Eduard van, 102
Benny, Jack, 112, 113
Bergsma, William, 72
Bernstein, Leonard, 57–58, 71, 124, 169

Bishop, Stephen, 72
Biskind, Joseph, 139
Blacks, employment of by major symphony orchestras, 65–66, 178–79, 185–86, 188–89, 207–10
Blinder, Naoum, 11, 15, 69, 73, 74, 78, 99, 104, 105
Boone, Philip, 139, 157, 161, 172
Boston Symphony, 1, 155–56, 182–84, 187, 188, 212, 248
Boulez, Pierre, 112–14, 182, 217
Brailowsky, Alexander, 108–9
Braun, Edgar, 133
Brico, Antonia, 226
Britt, Horace, 11, 68
Brodtsky, Allan, 209
Brusilow, Anshel, 71, 73
Bubb, Charles, 36
Burrell, Charles, 178–79
Bussotti, Carlo, 134, 135

Caldwell, Sarah, 226–27
California String Quartet, 61–63, 65, 68–69, 133, 154
Callahan, James, 120, 124
Cameron, Basil, 10, 11, 16
Canin, Stuart, 170–71, 179, 180, 185, 193, 225, 245–46
Cantelli, Guido, 71
Carnegie Hall concerts, 67–68, 250–51
Carroll, Don, 134
Carter, Nancy, 239
Casadesus, Robert, 71
Casals, Pablo, 116, 124–25
Casiglia, Arturo, 48–49
Chamber music, 61–63, 68–69, 73, 89, 90, 132, 133–34, 154, 170–71
Chartres Cathedral concert, 194
Chicago Symphony, 91, 248

Chmura, Gabriel, 185
Ciccolini, Aldo, 71
Civic Auditorium, 25, 55, 143
Classic Interlude concerts, 73–74
Claudio, Cesare, 53
Claudio, Ferdinand, 69, 99, 141, 146, 203, 204, 219
Claudio, Mary Hughson, 205, 225, 232
Claudio, Silvio, 225
Cleve, George, 177–78, 214
Cleveland Symphony Orchestra, 90, 125, 141, 170, 247, 248
Cliburn, Van, 111
Cohen, Deborah, 135
Comissiona, Sergiu, 213
Commanday, Robert, 160, 161, 162, 169, 192, 193, 194, 208, 215, 216, 220, 222, 231, 238, 244, 254
Composers' Forum, the, 62
Concertgebouw Orchestra (Amsterdam), 1, 102, 142, 212
Concertmasters of SFS, listed, 264. *See also* under individual names
Concerts of special interest, 56, 59, 67, 111–12, 113, 161, 193, 194, 243, 250–51. *See also* Unusual programs
Conducting, as profession, 29–33, 75–76, 100, 102–3, 115, 121, 156, 157, 170, 183, 186, 187, 196, 220
Conductors of the SFS, listed, 264, 268–70. *See also* under individual names
Contracts between Musicians' Union and Symphony Association, 39–42, 80, 117, 142, 147, 153, 155–59, 166, 170, 189–91, 202, 204, 205, 206–7, 224, 234–35, 236–37, 245, 257
Coolidge, Elizabeth Sprague, 69
Coppola, Anton, 49
Corky Siegel Blues Band, 181
Cort Theater, 8, 9
Cosmopolitan Opera Company, 49
Criticism, questions affecting, 123
Curtin, Phyllis, 226
Curtis Institute of Music, 3

Curzon, Clifford, 71

Darden, Charles, 178
Davies, Louise M., 236, 237, 242
Davies Symphony Hall. *See* Louise M. Davies Symphony Hall
Davis, Henrietta, 217
De Alessio, Camille, 12
De Coteau, Dennis, 178
Del Tredici, David, 97, 242
Denny, William, 72
Denver Symphony, 249
Depression, the, 10, 11, 39
Deutsche Grammophon, 182
De Waart, Edo: accepts directorship SFS, 223; accomplishments as conductor SFS, 258–59; attitude to musicians' age, 232–33; conducting technique of, 222–23, 227–28; contrasted with Ozawa, 227, 228; critics' response to, 230–31, 250–51, 256, 258–59; first appearance with SFS, 212–13; goals for SFS, 227, 230; personnel changes under, 232–33, 237–38, 245–47; pictured, 229; plans to leave SFS, 258; as principal guest conductor, 213, 225, 250, 252; programming of, 212–13, 222, 227, 228, 230–31, 242, 250; records with SFS, 255–56, 258–59, 308–10; relationship with orchestra members, 225, 231–33, 245–47, 251, 253, 254, 260; seating arrangement of, 266; tours with SFS, 250–51
Dicterow, Harold, 53, 60
Dixon, Dean, 185–86
Dobrowen, Issay, 10, 11
Dorfman, Herman, 120
Dorfman, Mr. and Mrs. Ralph, 216
Dorre, Jeanne-Marie, 168
Downes, Olin, 67

Earthquake of 1906, 6–7
Edmunds, Cicely, 69, 74
Ehrling, Sixten, 167
Electronic music, 112–15, 216–17
Elkus, Dr. Albert, 2, 12, 58

Encores, 106, 193
Erickson, Robert, 63, 113
European tour. *See* Tours

Fath, Philip, 98
Ferras, Christian, 119
Ferrier, Kathleen, 71
Fiedler, Arthur, 74, 115, 142–44
Firestone, Nathan, 7, 60
Fleisher, Leon, 72, 96
Floch, Hanns, 63
Francescatti, Zinc, 71
Frankenstein, Alfred, 84, 87, 95,
   121–23, 125, 126–27, 139
Franklin, Bruce, 134
Frantz, Rosalyn, 97
Freccia, Massimo, 84
Freed, Isidor, 72
Fricsay, Ferenc, 84, 91
Fried, Alexander, 102, 110, 117, 119,
   121–23, 125, 137, 160, 162, 164–65,
   221
Friedling, Claire, 249, 251

Gagaku Orchestra, 182
Gershwin, George, 15, 16–18, 24
Golden Jubilee season, 123–24
Goldmark Violin Concerto, 238,
   249, 250, 251–54
Goossens, Eugene, 59
Gould, Glenn, 96–97
Graffman, Gary, 96
Graitzer, Murray, 33–34
Grebanier, Michael, 225
Green, Walter, 98, 249
Greenfield, Edward, 193–94
Grover, John, 34
Guaraldi, Malfalda, 26, 45, 69, 219
Guest conductors, 15, 17, 57–59, 71,
   84–92, 97, 111, 115, 116, 120,
   124–26, 166–68, 179, 184–86,
   212–14; listed, 268–70

Hadley, Henry, K., 7, 8, 9
Haug, Julius, 26, 46
Heifetz, Jascha, 36–37, 57, 71, 112
Heimberg, Tom, 204, 205

Hellwig, Wilhelm, 256
Henrich-Bee. Symphony Orchestra,
   6
Henrich, Gustav, 5, 6
Hertz, Alfred, 9, 10, 58, 108, 120,
   252, 282–86
Hesse, Karl, 52
Hibschle, Frank, 140–41
Hiroshima memorial concert, 161
Hirsch, Bianca and Warren, 253
Holmes, Henry, 6
Houser, Frank, 53, 69, 99, 105, 106,
   120
Huberman Bronslaw, 80

Imbrie, Andrew, 63, 113–14, 172
Imperial Vienna Prater Orchestra, 6
Instruments, importance of quality,
   21, 198
Interpretation, elements of con-
   ductor's, 29–34
Israel Philharmonic, 80
Istomin, Eugene 96, 120

Japanese Philharmonic, 219
Japanese tours. *See* Tours
Jarvi, Neeme, 259
Jekowsky, Barry, 225
Jones, Elaine, 138–89, 206–10, 222,
   225
Jones, William Corbett, 134
Jordá, Enrique: appointed to succeed
   Monteux, 93; background of, 84;
   conducting technique of, 85, 100–2,
   110–11, 152; contract with SFS
   extended, 103, 110; contract with
   SFS terminated, 128; contrasted
   with Monteux, 84, 85, 95, 98; controversy surrounding performance
   of, 121–22, 126–27; critics' response
   to, 84, 92, 95, 102, 104, 110, 117–18,
   119, 121–23, 126–29; effect on SFS,
   126, 144; first season with SFS
   (1954–55), 95, musicians' attitude
   to, 85, 92, 93, 99–103, 110, 193, 225;
   opens season of discovery, 84; personnel changes under 98, 106;

pictured, 94; programming of, 95–96, 97–98, 115, 120, 122, 161; public response to, 84–85, 98, 102, 110, 117–18, 119, 215; records with SFS, 108–9, 304–6; in rehearsal, 100–1, 110, 149; reseating of orchestra members by, 98–99; during season of decision, 91

Kadarauch, David, 232–33
Kapell, William, 71
Karasik, Manfred, 2, 53
Karp, Philip, 66
Keilholz, Heinrich, 139
Kertesz, Istvan, 184–85
Khuner, Felix, 53–54, 61, 62, 65, 69, 89, 195
Kirchner, Leon, 120–21
Kirs, Rudolf, 7
Kirsten, Dorothy, 48
Klatzkin, Benjamin, 35–36
Kobler, Raymond, 246, 247, 252
Kogan, Leonid, 119
Kohloff, Roland, 98, 188
Kohs, Ellis, 72
Kooistra, Henk, 256
Kostelanetz, Andre, 68, 111
Koussevitzky, Serge, 80, 170
KPFA, 128
Krachmalnick, Jacob, 141–42, 144, 145–47, 150–51, 154, 171
Krips, Henry, 179
Krips, Josef: appointed conductor SFS, 129; conducting technique of, 137, 149–50, 151–52; as conductor emeritus, 179, 212; contrasted with Jordá, 149, 152; critics' reaction to, 137, 160–61, 164–65; debut with SFS, 120; early career of, 138; effect on SFS, 170, 172, 173; final season with SFS, 171; first season with SFS, 139–41; goals for SFS, 137; hosts members of SFS in Europe, 195–96; and Krachmalnick (concertmaster), 145, 171; on Mozart, 152; as opera conductor, 138; personnel changes under, 138–39, 141–42, 193, 205; pictured, 136;

programming of, 139, 144, 149, 154, 162–63, 172, 179, 181; public reaction to, 139, 144, 215; quoted, 137 reaction to musicians' contract, 166; as recording artist, 138, 172; in rehearsals, 149; relations with orchestra members, 139–42, 144, 149–50, 152–53, 155, 156, 166, 170, 226; retirement from SFS announced, 169; tours Japan with SFS, 159–63; tribute to, 172; world premieres conducted by, 172
Kubelik, Rafael, 166–67
Kurtz, Efrem, 68

Lambaley, Geraldine, 225
Laufer, Robin, 141
Leinsdorf, Erich, 88–89, 91
Leka, Diane, 253
Leningrad Opera, 197–98
Leplin, Emanuel, 72, 116, 172
Lewando, Ralph, 66
Lifschey, Marc, 146
Ligeti, Gyorgy, 216
Ling, Jahja, 258
Lipman, Samuel, 124
Little Symphony of San Francisco, 133
Live performance, validity of, 257, 259–61
Los Angeles, 17, 35, 48, 89
Louise M. Davies Symphony Hall: acoustics of, 235, 244–45, 311–14; de Waart's advocacy of, 227, 230; fund raising for, 235–36; importance to SFS, 248; inaugural week of, 242–43; inaugural week program, 242; interior pictured, 240–41; naming of, 236, 237; opening season of (1980–81), 239, 242–44, 245, 247; orchestra's first tour of, 235; public enthusiasm for, 239, 243–44; tuning of, 313–14
Lozano, Amy, 132

Mauceri, John, 212
Mautner, Ervin, 74, 112
Mazzi, Francesco, 203

Mazzonini, Brunetta, 50
Meachem, Charles, 148
Melikian, Zaven, 134
Menga, Robert, 180
Menuhin, Yalta, 71
Menuhin, Yehudi, 15, 36, 71, 106-8, 124, 212
Meriz, Emilio, 7
Merola, Gaetano, 47, 48, 49-50
Merrill, Jeremy, 120
Metcalf, Lawrence, 221, 223
Michaelian, Ernest, 53
Michelangeli, Arturo Benedetti, 71
Milhaud, Darius, 116, 131
Millar, Gregory, 133
Mills College, 131
Milstein, Nathan, 112
Mitropoulos, Dimitri, 71
Modern music, performance of, 62-63, 72, 120-21, 134-35, 154, 163-65, 172, 181, 215-17, 218, 230-31
Molnar, Ferenc, 60
Monteux, Doris, 25-26, 57, 73, 81
Monteux, Pierre: auditions string section, 19-20, 22, 23-24; authority of, 33-34; conducting technique of, 14, 18, 29-34, 36, 85; critics' response to, 66-67, 72; David Schneider auditions for, 1-5; early career of, 1; evaluation of, 79-82; farewell party for, 81, 82; final concert with SFS, 78; first season with SFS (1935-36), 12; health of, 211; Jewish background of, 57; knowledge of scores, 29-30; Madame Monteux's influence with, 25-26; musicians' attitude to, 42-43, 79-82; pictured, 28, 30, 55, 64, 81; programming of, 14, 56, 67, 72, 78, 79, 98, 120, 161, 168, 187, 242; public reaction to, 72, 85, 215; rebuilds SFS after Depression, 11-12; records with SFS, 34-38, 115, 255, 256, 287-303; reseating by, 22-25, 26-27, 60; retires from SFS, 78-80, 82; returns to SFS as guest conductor, 115, 120, 124; search for successor to, 83-93; seating arrangement of, 265-66; sponsorship of local musicians by, 71-72, 73; sponsors violin competition, 73-74; students of, 97, 177; tours with SFS, 63-64, 66-68; treatment of musicians by, 13, 14, 24-25, 41-43, 73, 80, 82
Moore, Carman, 217
Morgan, Virginia, 57
Morini, Alice, 119-20
Morini, Erica, 119
Moulin, Harry, 45
Mozart, Wolfgang Amadeus, music of, 22, 152
Mueller, Robert, 97
Munchinger, Karl, 89-90
Murray, Earl Bernard, 97
Musical Association of San Francisco, 11, 41, 42
Musicians' Union, 40, 83, 155, 191, 204, 207, 209. *See also* Contracts between MU and Symphony Association

Nagata, George, 97
Nakagawa, Ryohei, 206, 222, 225
National Labor Relations Board (NLRB), 207
New and Unusual Music Series, 258
New York, 67-68, 249-51
New York Ballet, 143
New York Philharmonic, 57, 67, 106-7, 155-56, 177, 212, 248
New York Times, 67
Nin-Culmell, Joaquin, 53, 172
Nixon, Roger, 63, 172

Oesterreicher, Walter, 1, 5, 7-9, 24
Olshausen, Detlev, 53, 61, 62
Onncv, Alphonse, 22, 46
Opera House. *See* War Memorial Opera House
Orlando, Anthony, 189
Ormandy, Eugene, 170, 188
Ozawa, Seiji: accepts directorship of Boston Symphony, 182-84; as administrator, 177, 189, 209, 220; announces decision to leave SFS,

220–21; appointed permanent conductor SFS, 169; attitude to
musicians' age, 211; capacity for
work of, 168; conducting technique
of, 168, 176, 181, 214; contrasted
with Krips, 175–76; critics' response
to, 193–94, 196–97, 215; European
tour with SFS (1973), 192–201; first
appearance with SFS, 124; on future
with SFS, 182–84, 187–88; as guest
conductor, 124, 168–69; illnesses of,
177, 211, 212, 213, 214; Japanese
tour with SFS (1974), 217–19;
lionized by Russian public, 196–97;
as musical advisor to SFS, 220, 225;
negotiates contract with orchestra
members, 189–91; personnel
changes under, 171, 180, 188–89,
205–10, 225; pictured, 174, 190;
programming of, 168, 169, 177,
181–82, 193, 213–14, 215–17, 218;
public response to, 175, 187,
192–93, 196–97, 214, 215; records
with SFS, 181–82, 184, 189, 255,
256, 306–8; relationship with
orchestra members, 177, 187, 188,
191, 201; reseating by, 188, 190–91,
202–5; on simultaneous posts for
conductors, 187; tenure controversy
under, 206–10; unorthodox
behavior of, 168, 176; unusual programming by, 181–82, 216; in
USSR, 196–201

Pachman, Vladimir De, 9
Pacific Opera Company, 49
Paris concert telecast, 193
Parlow, Kathleen, 13
Pastreich, Peter, 233–37, 253
Patterson, John, 7
Paulson, Stephen, 225
Pension fund, 70, 98, 112, 155, 158.
    See also working conditions of
    orchestra members
Pension fund concerts, 112, 113, 275
Perlman, Itzhak, 167
Persinger, Louis, 68

Persinger, Rolf, 151, 205, 225
Petty, Suzanne, 45
Petty, Winston, 45
Philadelphia Symphony, 156, 170,
    248
Philips Recording Co., 251, 256, 258
Piastro, Mishel, 2, 68
Pinza, Ezio, 47–48
Pontzious, Richard, 259
Popper, Hans, 113
Pops concerts by SFS, 111, 142, 143
Portland Symphony Orchestra, 74,
    76
Premieres of new works, 63, 72, 74,
    91, 119, 153–54, 163, 172, 179,
    215–16, 242
Prevost, Germain, 46
Price, Margaret, 256
Principal guest conductor, position
    established, 213
Pringsheim, Klaus, 160
Prinz, Alfred, 163

Queler, Eve, 226

Ramadanoff, David, 252
Rattle, Simon, 259
Rauhut, Otto, 12
RCA Victor Recording Co., 34–35,
    63, 109
Record contracts, 34, 251, 258
Recordings: list of, 282–310; making
    of, 34–38, 42–43, 108–9, 172,
    181–82, 184, 189, 221, 248, 255–57,
    258–59
Rehearsals, 100, 149
Reinberg, Donald, 205
Reller, Austin, 124
Renardy, Ossy, 71
Renzi, Paul, 120, 134, 168
Reseating of orchestra members,
    22–25, 98–99, 147–49, 155, 158,
    189–91, 202–5, 225
Rethberg, Elisabeth, 47
Ricci, Ruggiero, 71, 124
Rich, Alan, 128, 137
Riedel, Ernestine, 151

Rodzinski, Artur, 71
Rose, Leonard, 106
Rosenak, Karen, 135, 238
Rostropovich, Mstislav, 97, 199–200
Rotterdam Orchestra, 212, 222, 223
Rubenstein, Arthur, 71, 91, 96
Russo, William, 181

Salgo, Sandor, 97
Sample, James, 64, 68, 74–75
Sandburg, Carl, 111
San Francisco Art Commission, 41, 42
San Francisco Chamber of Commerce, 235
San Francisco Chamber Orchestra, 133
San Francisco Chronicle, 55, 64, 84, 107, 127, 160, 184, 225, 238, 254
San Francisco Conservatory of Music, 131, 134, 141
San Francisco Examiner, 102, 161, 254, 260
San Francisco Museum of Modern Art, 62
San Francisco Opera, 40, 46–48, 49–52, 142, 156, 158, 173, 236–38, 242, 245
San Francisco Philharmonic Society, 5
San Francisco State College (later. University), 131, 134, 153–54
San Francisco String Ensemble, 133–34
San Francisco Symphony: auditions for, 1–4, 138–39, 179–80, 189, 245; blacks in, 178–79, 188–89, 207–9; budget of, 40, 255, 262; charter members of, 8–9; concertmasters of, listed, 264. *See also* under individual names; concerts of special interest, 56, 59, 67, 111–12, 113, 161, 193, 243, 250–51; conductors of, listed, 264. *See also* under individual names; contracts of orchestra members, 39–42, 80, 117, 142, 147, 153, 155–59, 166, 170, 189–91, 202, 204,

205, 206–7, 224, 234–35, 236–37, 245, 257; controversy over extension of Jordá's contract, 121–22, 126–29; critics' reactions to, 66–67, 99, 123, 124, 160, 162, 164–65, 184–85, 205, 214, 250–51, 256, 258–59; during Depression, 11; discography of, 282–310; early programming of, 5–6, 123–24; European tour (1973), 192–201, 279–80; finances of, 11, 40–41, 69–70, 116–17, 119, 224, 255, 253, 262; first concert by, 9, 123–24, 262–63; founding of, 5–7; funding of, 11, 40–41, 97, 116–17, 158, 258; future of, 258–61; Golden Jubilee season (1961–62), 123–24; guest conductors of, 15, 17, 57–59, 71, 83–92, 97, 102, 111, 115, 116, 120–21, 124–28, 165–69, 179, 184–86, 211, 212–13, 214, 226–27, 259, 260, 268–70, 273–74; inaugural season of (1911–12), 9, 19–20, 124, 262; Japanese tours, (1953) 159–63, 273–79, (1974) 217–19, 230; Louise M. Davies Symphony Hall as home of, 235–36, 239–45; modern music in repertoire of, 72, 120–21, 163–65, 172, 181, 215–17, 218, 230–31; musicians' wages, 23, 39–40, 80, 117, 130, 156, 158; pension fund for members of, 70, 98, 112, 155, 158; pictured, 3, 30–31, 190, 240–41; recording contracts of, 34, 251, 258; recording of, 34–38, 42–43, 108–9, 172, 181–82, 134, 189, 221, 248, 255–57, 258–59, 282–310; reseating of orchestra members, 22–25, 98–99, 147–49, 155, 158, 189–91, 202–3, 225; season of decision (1953), 83, 91–93; season of discovery (1952), 83–91, 92; seating arrangements of orchestra, 23, 265–66; separation of opera and symphony orchestras, 237–38, 245; soloists with, 9, 15–19, 55, 59, 71, 91, 96–97, 99, 106–9, 111–12, 119–20, 124, 151, 154, 163–65, 167,

168, 181, 193, 199–200, 218, 226, 238–39, 242, 246, 249, 250, 251–54, 256, 265, 271; strike by musicians of, 156–58; tenure controversy in, 206–10, 222; transcontinental tour (1947), 63–70, 276–78; transitional season for (1975–76), 224–25; United States tours, (1980) 248–51, 280–81, (1983) 281; Unusual programs by, 55–56, 97–98, 181–82, 216, 274–75; in USSR, 196–201; working conditions of orchestra members, 39–43, 80, 98, 138, 155–59, 257–58; during World War II, 53–57; youth soloists with, 265
San Francisco Symphony Association, 34, 40, 98, 124, 139, 156, 158, 210, 213, 220, 221, 224, 233, 236, 248, 251, 253, 257, 267
San Francisco Symphony Youth Orchestra, 255, 258
San Jose Symphony, 178, 214
Sawallisch, Wolfgang, 259
Sayre, Robert, 151, 205, 225
Scafidi, Joseph, 175, 179, 203, 204, 205, 207, 219, 233
Scarpini, Pietro, 96
Schaffer, Peter, 180
Schell, Fritz, 6
Schermerhorn, Kenneth, 214
Schivo, Reina, 134, 203
Schmidt-Isserstedt, Hans, 195, 212
Schneider, Bart, 76, 252
Schneider, David: auditions for assistant concertmaster, 179–80; auditions for principal viola, 138–39; auditions for SFS, 1–4; birth of daughter to, 54–55; birth of son to, 76; in California String Quartet, 61–63; as chamber musician, 13, 61–63, 133–34, 154; considers conducting career, 74–75; critics' response to, 164–65, 253–54; education of, 12–13; joins SFS, 5; marriage of, 43–45; in Paris, 192; participates in contract negotiations,

189–91, 234–35; position in orchestra of, 22, 26–27, 59–60, 147–49, 202–5; as principal second violin, 149; probationary period with SFS, 5, 13–14; promoted to first violin section, 60; purchases violin, 21; recitals by, 134–35; reprimanded by Ozawa, 201; on role of performer, 114–15; in San Francisco Opera orchestra, 46–47, 51–52; as soloist on Goldmark Violin Concerto, 238–39, 248–49, 250, 251–54; as soloist on Sessions Violin Concerto, 153–54, 163–65; as soloist on Vivaldi Four Violin Concerto, 99; as teacher, 130–32, 135, 219, 252; teachers of, 12, 13, 22, 46; as violist, 46, 59–60, 138–39; visits Russian synagogues, 197–99; wartime schedule of, 54
Schneider, Geraldine (née Schultz), 43–45, 160, 192, 195, 196, 201, 251, 252
Schneider, Sandra Diane, 55, 252
Schoenberg, Arnold, 69
"Schoenberg circle," 17
Scholtze, Onno, 256
Score, importance of knowing, 29–30
"Season of decision," 83, 91, 92
"Season of discovery," 83, 84–91, 92
Seating arrangements of orchestra, 23, 265–66
Segovia, Andre, 105, 115–16
Serkin, Peter, 218
Serkin, Rudolf, 71, 112, 224, 242
Sessions, Roger, 153, 154; Violin Concerto of, 153–54, 163–65
Shapro, David, 53
Sheinfeld, David, 69, 72
Shelton, Peter, 232–33
Shweid, Henry, 9, 69, 99, 252
Siegel, Corky, 181
Simms, Ginny, 55
Slatkin, Leonard, 259
Slenczynska, Ruth, 72, 124
Soloists, role of, 106

Solti, Georg, 84, 91
Sotomayor, Antonio, 55, 64, 107
Spaeth, Sigmund, 44
Spain, Jerry, 190, 201, 203, 207
Spivakovsky, Tossy, 71, 89
Spring Opera, 49
Standard Oil broadcast, 11, 34, 45
Steinberg, Michael, 253-54
Steinberg, William, 68, 91-92
Steindorf, Paul, 6
Stern Grove, 49-50
Stern, Isaac, 15-16, 68, 71, 104, 106,
    124, 250
Stern, Sigmund, 50
Stevens, Risë, 59
Stewart, Sam, 235-36
Stokowski, Leopold, 85-88, 91, 115,
    170, 188, 304
Stotyama, Fuzo, 160
Stravinsky, Igor, 17, 71, 108
Strike by orchestra members, 156-58
Symphony Foundation, 97, 159
Szell, George, 90, 122, 125-27, 128,
    145, 150, 170

Takahashi, Yuji, 181
Takeda, Mark, 159
Tal, Josef, 112-13
Tansman, Alexander, 15, 18-19, 24
Taylor, Janice, 256
Taylor, Ross, 98, 120
Teaching, symphony musicians and,
    130-32, 135
Tenure dispute, 206-10, 222
Third Baptist Church, 217
Thomas, Michael Tilson, 212, 259
Tircuit, Heuwell, 184, 185, 187-88,
    208
Toscanini, Arturo, 68, 88, 115
Tourel, Jennie, 71
Tours: European (1973), under
    Ozawa, 192-201, 279-80; Japanese
    (1968), under Krips, 159-63,
    278-79; Japanese (1974), under
    Ozawa, 217-19, 280; list of, with
    repertoires, 276-81; transcontinen-

tal (1947), under Monteux, 63-70,
    276-78; United States (1980), under
    de Waart, 243-51, 280-81; United
    States (1983), under de Waart, 281
Tsubuta, Kinshu, 169
Turangalila Symphonie of Messiaen,
    216-17
Tympanist, role of, 90, 189

Ulrich, Allen, 254
United Nations conference concert,
    59
United States tours. *See* Tours
University of California, 2, 12, 62,
    131, 153
Unusual programs, 55-56, 97-98,
    181-82, 216, 274-75. *See also* Con-
    certs of special interest
Usigli, Gastone, 49, 72
USSR, 196-201

Van Dyke, Marcia, 68, 69
Varga, Laszlo, 153, 170
Veissi, Jascha, 12
Violin, as instrument: cost of, 198;
    difficulty of playing, 131; purchase
    of, 21; teaching of, 131-32, 179;
    tone of, 21
Vonk, Hans, 212

Walker, Dorothy, 84
Wallenstein, Alfred, 89
Walter, Bruno, 32, 57, 58-59, 71, 88,
    90, 91, 97, 168
War Memorial Opera House, 31, 80,
    139, 190, 193, 224, 230, 243
Watts, Andre, 154, 163, 164, 193
White, Albert, 46, 140, 1-1-42
Wickham, Harvey, 9
Wolski, William, 69, 120
Women in symphony orchestras, 9,
    226-27
Woolf, Kathlyn, 43
Working conditions of orchestra
    members, 39-43, 80, 93, 138,
    155-59, 257-58

World War II, 53–54, 59–60, 61
WPA Symphony, 2, 4, 5, 15, 238
Wyss, Niklaus, 177, 178, 194, 213–14

Yokoyama, Katsuja, 169

Youth soloists, listed, 265

Zellerbach, J. D., 92–93, 127–28, 139
Zimbalist, Efrem, 8, 9
Zukerman, Pinchas, 167